Logic, Argumentation & Reasoning

Interdisciplinary Perspectives from the Humanities and Social Sciences

Volume 8

Series editor
Shahid Rahman

Logic, Argumentation & Reasoning explores the links between Humanities and the Social Sciences, with theories including, decision and action theory as well as cognitive sciences, economy, sociology, law, logic, and philosophy of sciences. It's two main ambitions are to develop a theoretical framework that will encourage and enable interaction between disciplines as well as to federate the Humanities and Social Sciences around their main contributions to public life: using informed debate, lucid decision-making and action based on reflection.

The series welcomes research from the analytic and continental traditions, putting emphasis on four main focus areas:

- Argumentation models and studies
- Communication, language and techniques of argumentation
- Reception of arguments, persuasion and the impact of power
- Diachronic transformations of argumentative practices

The Series is developed in partnership with the Maison Européenne des Sciences de l'Homme et de la Société (MESHS) at Nord - Pas de Calais and the UMR-STL: 8163 (CNRS).

Proposals should include:

- A short synopsis of the work or the introduction chapter
- The proposed Table of Contents
- The CV of the lead author(s)
- If available: one sample chapter

We aim to make a first decision within 1 month of submission. In case of a positive first decision the work will be provisionally contracted: the final decision about publication will depend upon the result of the anonymous peer review of the complete manuscript. We aim to have the complete work peer-reviewed within 3 months of submission.

The series discourages the submission of manuscripts that contain reprints of previous published material and/or manuscripts that are below 150 pages / 85,000 words.

For inquiries and submission of proposals authors can contact the editor-in-chief Shahid Rahman via: shahid.rahman@univ-lille3.fr or managing editor, Laurent Keiff at laurent.keiff@gmail.com.

More information about this series at http://www.springer.com/series/11547

Can Başkent
Editor

Perspectives on Interrogative Models of Inquiry

Developments in Inquiry and Questions

Springer

Editor
Can Başkent
Department of Computer Science
University of Bath
Bath, UK

ISSN 2214-9120 ISSN 2214-9139 (electronic)
Logic, Argumentation & Reasoning
ISBN 978-3-319-38729-1 ISBN 978-3-319-20762-9 (eBook)
DOI 10.1007/978-3-319-20762-9

Springer Cham Heidelberg New York Dordrecht London

Softcover re-print of the Hardcover 1st edition 2016

Printed on acid-free paper

Springer International Publishing AG Switzerland is part of Springer Science+Business Media (www.springer.com)

Preface

Hintikka's theory of interrogative models of inquiry is the starting point of this volume. Interrogative models of inquiry (IMI, for short) present an interesting take on various epistemic issues including Socratic *elenchus*, learning theory, abductive reasoning, social choice theory, and nonclassical and modal logics. This relates IMI very closely to a variety of different fields, and this relation is perfectly well displayed by the articles in this volume.

It is important to note that Hintikka's contribution to logic and formal epistemology is usually clouded by his work on other fields, such as epistemic logic and game semantics. Perhaps for this reason, IMI does not seem to be very popular among researchers. One of the goals of producing this volume is to change this tendency by showing that IMI has influence on many different subfields in logic and formal philosophy.

This volume also demonstrates it very clearly that IMI in itself is a very rich theory. Helping in understanding its (current) depth and breadth, the volume includes both technical and logical articles as well as conceptual and analytical work.

In short, there are three main goals behind producing this volume: (i) showing that IMI heavily relates to a wide variety of fields in logic and philosophy, (ii) underlying the centrality of IMI in Hintikkan thought, and (iii) showing the breadth and depth of the field. I leave it to the reader to judge how much we managed to achieve our goals.

*

The volume opens with Hakli's article on inquiry and justification. Hakli's account argues as to how Hintikkan interrogative theory can unite inquiry and justification. The second paper, by Genot and Gulz, carries the debate over to learning theory. At first glance, the connection between the learning theory and IMI is clear, yet Genot and Gulz develop the connection further by resorting to various game theoretical elements. Then Angere, Olsson, and Genot take an interesting step and introduce formal epistemological and social choice theoretical issues to the discussion. They focus on jury sizes and use Bayesian methods to present an analytical solution. In my own article, I suggest that Hintikkan inquiry and Lakatosian method of proofs and refutations share some common themes, which interestingly include both of them being inconsistency-friendly. This paper relates IMI to nonclassical logic. Van Bendegem's article considers mathematical practice and its connection to problem solving which can be seen as a Hintikkan inquiry. Antonelli presents a formal application of defeasible logic to IMI and suggests two different approaches. Urbański and Wiśniewski's article reminds us of the Socratic roots of Hintikkan epistemology and in particular of IMI and presents an elaborated formal structure. Hamami's article relates IMI to a quite broad field of dynamic epistemic logic and presents an axiomatic system for dynamic logic of interrogative inquiry. Naibo, Petrolo, and Seiller discuss an important epicenter of Hintikkan epistemology and introduce a novel philosophical perspective from a computational angle.

*

The volume originated within the framework of a research project which was funded by the French National Research Agency (ANR, *Agence Nationale de la Recherche*). The project was conducted at IHPST (*Institut d'histoire et de philosophie des sciences et des techniques*) which is a research institute affiliated with CNRS and the University of Paris 1 Panthéon – Sorbonne. During its two-year lifespan, I was employed at the project for one year in 2012–2013. The project produced two international workshops and conferences, numerous monthly seminars, research visits, conference participations, and a variety of research articles. Once the project came to an end, there already has been established an international network of researchers who were heavily influenced by Hintikka's philosophy and willing to share their expertise. This volume can be considered as an output of this network.

For this project and the volume, I am grateful to many people. Gabriel Sandu, who first developed the idea behind this project, was helpful in every stage of the project; hosted me and Yacin in Helsinki, and even organized a lunch for us with Hintikka himself. My colleagues Francesca Poggiolesi, Yacin Hamami, and Henri Galinon were always there when I needed some help and assistance. I am also more than thankful to our anonymous reviewers who helped us immensely with their feedback and guidance.

My deepest special gratitude is for Marco Panza, the director of the project, who encouraged me immensely for producing this volume. The idea of making this book belongs to him. Without him, this volume would not have existed.

*

Finally, I hope that this volume will serve as a bridge between Hintikkan theory of interrogative inquiry and the researchers working on similar fields and show that there is still a lot left to be worked on.

Bath, UK Can Başkent

Contents

Inquiry and Justification 1
Raul Hakli

The Interrogative Model of Inquiry and Inquiry Learning 15
Emmanuel J. Genot and Agneta Gulz

Inquiry and Deliberation in Judicial Systems: The Problem of Jury Size 35
Staffan Angere, Erik J. Olsson, and Emmanuel J. Genot

Inquiry, Refutations and the Inconsistent 57
Can Başkent

The Heterogeneity of Mathematical Research 73
Jean Paul Van Bendegem

Interrogative Inquiry as Defeasible Reasoning 95
G. Aldo Antonelli

On Search for Law-Like Statements as Abductive Hypotheses by Socratic Transformations 111
Mariusz Urbański and Andrzej Wiśniewski

A Dynamic Logic of Interrogative Inquiry 129
Yacin Hamami

Verificationism and Classical Realizability 163
Alberto Naibo, Mattia Petrolo, and Thomas Seiller

Inquiry and Justification

Raul Hakli

Abstract Traditionally, inquiry and justification have been treated as two distinct phenomena that are largely independent of each other. Seeing both as interrogative processes can help to see how they are connected. Inquiry is seen as such in Hintikka's model of interrogative inquiry, and justification is seen as such in the dialectical account of justification. It is argued that processes of inquiry and justification are not independent of each other: On the one hand, successfully carrying out processes of inquiry may require engaging in processes of justification. On the other hand, processes of justification may require engaging in processes of inquiry. Production of scientific knowledge requires both types of processes.

Keywords Interrogative inquiry • Epistemic justification • Dialectical justification • Scientific knowledge

1 Introduction

This essay will study the connections between scientific inquiry and epistemic justification. Traditionally, justification and inquiry have been seen as two quite distinct phenomena that are largely independent of each other. Justification has been a central concern of analytical epistemology, in particular, for the analysis of knowledge which is usually taken to require justification. Inquiry, on the other hand, is often associated with discovery of knowledge and has been more of a concern of philosophy of science. To an extent, these two lines of research have been isolated from each other.

In philosophy of science there is a traditional distinction between contexts of discovery and contexts of justification, which not only indicates that inquiry and justification are separated from each other but also suggests that they should be

R. Hakli (✉)
Department of Culture and Society, Aarhus University, Jens Chr. Skous Vej 7, DK-8000 Aarhus C, Denmark
e-mail: raul.hakli@cas.au.dk

C. Başkent (ed.), *Perspectives on Interrogative Models of Inquiry*, Logic, Argumentation & Reasoning 8, DOI 10.1007/978-3-319-20762-9_1

kept so separated. It has been thought that coming up with theories or hypotheses is different from assessing the extent to which theories or hypotheses are supported by available evidence.

The focus of philosophy of science has been on activities that concern production of scientific knowledge whereas the focus of epistemology has been on analysis of knowledge and on evaluation of alleged instances of existing knowledge. Activities of knowledge production include steps of discovery, reasoning, and accepting hypotheses. Justification plays a role in them, but its focus is on evaluating steps of reasoning and assessing evidential relations between data and hypotheses. In mainstream epistemology, justification has been important because traditional analyses of knowledge have taken justification as a necessary criterion that beliefs must satisfy in order to count as knowledge. Attempts to spell out exactly when somebody's beliefs are justified has led to an abundance of theories of justification (see, e.g., Lammenranta 2004).

There have been attempts to shift focus of epistemology from justification of beliefs to questions of inquiry. Jaakko Hintikka (2007) criticises epistemologists' preoccupation with justification and claims that studying how to acquire new knowledge is more crucial for epistemology than studying how to secure old knowledge. Provocatively, he suggests an "epistemology without knowledge and belief", in which traditional studies focussed on analysis of concepts of belief and knowledge have been replaced by a logical study of information acquisition.

Related criticisms can be found in the writings of philosophers who have been influenced by pragmatism such as Isaac Levi (2012) and Christopher Hookway (2006). Levi (2012, 1) notes in an approval tone that pragmatists like Peirce and Dewey were not interested in justification of beliefs but justification of changes of beliefs, that is, justification of steps of inquiry. According to Hookway (2006), epistemology is committed to what he calls a "doxastic paradigm", in which the focus is on beliefs and their evaluation. The epistemologists' primary interest is in the state of belief of an agent, not in the process of reasoning that leads to it. He argues for "epistemology as theory of inquiry", in which the target for epistemic evaluation lies, not in the justificatory status of our beliefs, but in our ability to successfully carry out inquiries. Also Bernard Williams (1973) points out that our main interest with respect to knowledge is in finding sources of reliable information rather than in examining whether somebody really knows or merely believes something that we already know, which has been the central concern in epistemology. The suggestion for epistemology, then, is to replace the viewpoint of an examiner with that of an inquirer.

While acknowledging the importance of inquiry, this essay suggests that inquiry need not replace justification in epistemology, but complement it. The aim is to argue that there are deep interconnections between inquiry and justification, and neither of them can be fully studied in isolation. Firstly, as Hintikka (2007, 19–20) noted and as I will try to argue in more detail below, inquiry is important even in the context of justification. This is so because in order to settle whether one is justified in one's belief or judgement, one may sometimes have to acquire new knowledge. It is not always enough to simply reflect upon one's evidence or to evaluate the reliability of one's cognitive faculties. Sometimes, and this happens typically in scientific contexts, one has to come up with new experiments that can be used to confirm or disconfirm the content of the belief or the judgement.

Secondly, I would like to claim that inquiry is not independent of justification either. In order to engage in a successful process of inquiry, one needs to consider which assumptions and methodological principles are reasonable. In addition, in the course of inquiry there are several choice points that require assessment of different sources of information in order to select which of them to trust. These are questions that concern epistemic justification.

In order to defend these general claims, I will study two accounts or models of inquiry and justification, respectively. The model of inquiry I will focus on is Hintikka's Interrogative Model of Inquiry (IMI), which sees inquiry as a process of asking questions and drawing logical inferences from the answers received. I will give a brief description of the model in Sect. 2. In several places, Hintikka (2007, e.g., p. 3, 8, 22, 224) says that both inquiry and justification are accomplished by the same interrogative process. However, he does not state explicitly what is the nature of justification that the process is supposed to accomplish. What does the process of interrogative inquiry produce that justifies its results? There are several possibilities here because the nature of justification can be understood in several ways.

I will review some candidates in Sect. 3. My main thesis will be that the best way to understand Hintikka's claim is by taking justification to consist of being in a position to answer critical challenges. Such a view has been called the dialectical account of justification and it has been defended by several philosophers including David Annis (1978) and Michael Williams (2001). Even though this model of justification has not been developed to the same level of technical detail as the IMI, it could be called the Interrogative Model of Justification (IMJ). This is because according to the dialectical approach, justification, too, involves a process of asking questions and answering them. Seeing both inquiry and justification as inherently social processes that involve question-answering dialogues not only reveals analogies between them but it also shows that they are deeply interconnected. In particular, it shows how processes of justification may create a need for further inquiry. In Sect. 4, I will argue that processes of inquiry also create a need to engage in processes of justification. I will conclude by looking at the consequences of the presented views for the concept of scientific knowledge in Sect. 5.

2 Interrogative Model of Inquiry

The main idea in Hintikka's Interrogative Model of Inquiry is to reconstruct processes of knowledge acquisition as steps of logical reasoning extended with interrogative steps for obtaining new information. Such reasoning can be represented using tableau (or sequent calculus) systems in which the conclusion to be proved is on the right hand side and the initial assumptions on the left hand side. Using the rules of the system, complex formulas are broken into simpler parts, which may involve branching. The goal is to show that the conclusion follows by closing all the branches in the tableau: If a formula and its negation appear in the same branch, or if the same formula appears both on the left hand side and the right hand side, the branch closes.

Hintikka extends the basic model by interrogative steps that are used for bringing in new information by asking an oracle a question. A question can be asked once its presupposition has been established. For instance, if in a branch we have formula $A \vee B$ on the left hand side, we may consult an oracle and ask whether A is the case or B is the case. We then add the oracle's answer to the left hand side and continue the process. In the basic version of IMI, there is only one oracle and all of its answers are assumed to be correct and remain constant.

The basic version can be extended by allowing for uncertain answers or several oracles. Such extensions create the possibility of inconsistent answers. In cases of inconsistency, the inquirer must select which answers to accept. The answers that are not accepted at the current stage will still be represented in the tableaux, but they will be bracketed which means they will not be taken into account when applying rules, unless they are later unbracketed. A detailed exposition of the rules that define the deductive, interrogative and bracketing moves of the Interrogative Model is presented by Hintikka et al. (1999).

In addition to the above *definitory rules*, there are also *strategic rules* that tell the inquirer how to use the definitory rules in an effective way. The content of the strategic rules is left out of the model in order to keep it general: Different strategic rules can be used in different types of inquiries. In particular, which answers to bracket in order to keep the inquiry on secure grounds is an important strategic question, a question involving epistemic justification (Hintikka 2007, 20–21).

According to Hintikka (2007, 19), the various oracles can represent different sources of information, like nature (in the sense of providing results to experiments), human witnesses, research databases, the inquirer's own memory, or tacit knowledge. The reliability of a source can then be assessed by comparing the source's answers to the previous answers from the same source and the knowledge obtained from the other sources (Hintikka 2007, 214). Emmanuel Genot (2009) presents a bookkeeping method for keeping track of the answers given by different sources of information.

3 How Inquiry Produces Justification

Let us now consider how we should understand the nature of justification in light of Hintikka's idea that inquiry not only produces scientific discoveries, but also justification for these discoveries. The variety of existing theories of justification gives many possible options to select from. For instance, according to reliabilist approaches, one's beliefs are justified just in case they are produced by reliable processes. One might claim that processes of inquiry generally produce reliable results: Inquiry is a process that systematically eliminates epistemic alternatives, or possible worlds, in light of obtained information, and the remaining alternatives are then the ones that are not ruled out, so we are justified in thinking that the actual world must be among them.

However, this may not be the right way to think of justification at the level of generality of the interrogative model of inquiry. This is because reliability crucially depends on the strategic rules that we use during the inquiry. In particular, it depends on our theoretical assumptions and our policies to rely on certain sources of information. If the reliability of the process depends crucially on their reliability, then the process itself cannot guarantee reliability. It does not guarantee that the actual world is not among the worlds eliminated. (This is not to say that reliability cannot play an important role in comparing different methods of inquiry in which the strategic rules are fixed.)

I suggest instead that the general capacity of the process of interrogative inquiry to deliver justification lies in its capacity to provide reasons for the conclusions acquired. Even if such inquiry cannot guarantee reliability it can guarantee that there are reasons for the way the elimination was carried out. Assuming that the process of inquiry can be reconstructed by using the IMI, these reasons are, furthermore, represented in an explicit and communicable form. The interrogative model provides the inquirer immediate reasons for an accepted proposition in the form of the premisses from which the conclusion was derived or of information concerning the sources (together with the strategic judgement that these sources can be trusted). And if these reasons are not enough to convince someone who challenges the accepted proposition, one can trace the reasoning all the way back to the initial assumptions.

But there are still several theories of justification that take the existence of reasons as a necessary ingredient of justification, in particular, foundationalism, coherentism, and infinitism. Which one should we choose if we want to integrate justification and inquiry in the way that Hintikka seems to suggest?

According to foundationalism, an agent's belief is justified if and only if either the belief is a so-called basic belief (these are taken to be "given", "self-justified" or something similar) or the agent has other justified beliefs that serve as reasons for the belief. This model of justification would fit well with the IMI only with the additional assumption that the premisses from which the inquiry starts are basic beliefs. This is a substantial assumption, however, since the choice of premisses is a strategic choice left open by the model.

According to coherentism, an agent's belief is justified if and only if it is a part of a coherent network of beliefs which mutually support one another. While the process of inquiry certainly provides support from the premisses to the conclusions, the reverse direction is not guaranteed. In IMI, the direction of support follows the direction of reasoning which is from premisses to conclusions, as in foundationalism. Thus, inquiry does not seem to produce justified conclusions in the sense required by coherentists.

Finally, according to infinitism, a belief may be justified by an infinite chain of reasons, but this idea is very difficult to reconcile with the IMI because the model does not allow for reaching conclusions by infinite chains of reasoning. It thus seems that none of these theories fit very well with Hintikka's view that inquiry produces justification. Let us turn to an alternative theory that seems better suited for the purpose.

According to the dialectical account, in order for an agent's acceptance of a proposition to be justified, the agent must be able to respond to other agents' appropriate critical questions and challenges by providing reasons for the judgement. This is in stark contrast to standard individualistic theories like evidentialism and reliabilism that take justification to be a function of agent's evidence or of the reliability of the agent's cognitive processes. Similarly, foundationalism, coherentism and infinitism are individualistic theories because they only consider the agent's internal mental state. In the dialectical approach, the criteria for justification depend not only on the agent's internal states and her relation to external environment but on the social relationships between the agent and other agents, more specifically, on an interrogative process in which the agent answers questions posed by others. The agent not only needs to have reasons for her view, she must also be able to articulate those reasons and be prepared to defend them in response to criticism: Justification requires that one is in a position to justify one's views to others.

How far an agent has to go in providing reasons depends on the social context: Once the agent has given reasons for her view the challenger may ask for further reasons to accept these reasons. This may continue until the process reaches such beliefs that have a *default justification*. Such beliefs can be challenged further too, but only in so far as the challenges themselves are backed up by positive reasons to doubt the beliefs with default justification (Williams 2001). Which beliefs enjoy the default status and which rules govern appropriateness of challenges depend on the epistemic context in which the dialogue takes place. In science, the context is provided by the discipline: Certain disciplines (or research paradigms to use a Kuhnian term) are committed to certain methods and principles that are usually taken for granted when doing research. A researcher working within a discipline and presenting her results is assumed to be able to defend her specific assumptions and the ways she has conducted her experiments but she need not normally be prepared to defend the general assumptions that are shared in the community. These are only to be doubted if there is specific reason, for instance, in cases of puzzles and anomalies that may eventually reveal the inadequacy of the shared assumptions of the discipline. When accumulated, such problems may lead to the assumptions being revised or abandoned in favour of some other assumptions.

Note the parallelism with the Interrogative Model of Inquiry: There are definitory rules saying that if one accepts something, others are entitled to challenge it by asking for reasons and one will then have to be able to provide acceptable reasons or retract the claim, unless the proposition enjoys default status in which case it is the challenge that needs further support. In addition, there are strategic rules that specify which propositions enjoy default status and which challenges are appropriate. This is a very general model of justification that can be applied both in everyday conversations and in scientific debates in different disciplines. Similarly to the IMI, it leaves open the strategic rules, which here govern default status and criticism that one can present against a given view. These depend on the epistemic reason-giving practices of the relevant epistemic community. (As in the case of methods, all of this is consistent with the possibility that different epistemic practices could also be assessed in terms of their reliability.)

This parallelism is not the reason why this model of justification fits so well with the IMI, however. The reason is that this model of justification explains what it is in the interrogative process of inquiry that produces justification. As a result of the process, the inquirer has, in the form of a tableau or a proof tree, an explicit representation of the reasons that support the inquirer's conclusion: The premisses, the steps of inference, the various sources of information, and hopefully also the strategic rules guiding the inquiry. This information puts the inquirer in a very good position to defend her results against possible challenges. When a conclusion is challenged, the inquirer may give reasons for it by saying that the conclusion follows by application of such and such a rule from such and such propositions that she also accepts. Or she may say that the conclusion was as an answer to such and such a question by such and such an oracle that she, in accordance with her strategy of inquiry, takes to be a reliable source. These replies may again be challenged in which case the inquirer may have to review the chain of reasoning further, possibly all the way back to her initial assumptions. Assuming that she has relied on theoretical and methodological assumptions generally accepted in her epistemic community she will be able to provide reasons for her own results and point to the direction of the external sources in cases in which she has relied on testimony.

Of course, the possibility remains that the critic is not satisfied with some of the inquirer's assumptions. The critic can question some of the theoretical assumptions by pointing out to error possibilities that the inquirer has failed to take into account. The critic can also question some of the methodological assumptions, which may or may not be explicitly stated by the inquirer: They may be explicitly formulated strategic rules but in practice they may be merely habits and conventions that are tacitly or even unconsciously followed during the process of inquiry. Critical questioning can bring such implicit research heuristics into light and force them to be articulated into explicit strategic rules. (Of course, the model itself makes some assumptions like the use of classical logic. Also the selection of the language in which the inquiry is carried out is an assumption that could in principle be questioned.)

A situation in which an assumption is questioned creates a need to acquire new information, which can be modelled in the Interrogative Model of Inquiry by starting a new tableau with the questioned premiss as the conclusion to be proved. Since contested assumptions are rarely redundant, they usually cannot be proved from the remaining premisses alone without consulting oracles for additional information. Thus, the need to justify assumptions creates a requirement to come up with new experiments or sources of evidence. In order to successfully complete the process of justification, a new process of inquiry must be carried out first.

The part of questioning the inquirer's assumptions and strategies is not as such accounted for in the standard Interrogative Model of Inquiry. Even though the model allows the inquirer to ask the oracle further questions, the structure of the oracle's epistemic state is left outside of the model. An interesting extension then would be a multi-agent—or a multi-inquirer—version in which the agents sometimes take the role of an inquirer asking questions and sometimes the role of an oracle answering questions and justifying their results to other inquirers. This kind of a model with multiple inquirers with different disciplines with their own assumptions and strategic rules would provide a model of science as a social activity of epistemically interdependent inquirers.

4 How Inquiry Needs Justification

As we have seen, inquiry produces justification for its conclusions. Of course, this may not always be the purpose of inquiry. Sometimes inquiry may be used for pure discovery in which case the strategies of inquiry are different: The goal is not to maximise reliability of the results but perhaps their novelty (see Kiikeri 1999). Still, one purpose of inquiry is to produce scientific knowledge, which conceptually requires justification. Hence questions of justification are present in inquiry as well: Justification of the conclusions obtained in inquiry depends on the justificatory status of the assumptions and the reasoning steps of the inquiry.

Justification of assumptions is a problem, because the requirement to have secure grounds for knowledge quickly leads to scepticism. We have learned from Descartes' method of doubt that very little can be known without making any assumptions. Science would not get off the ground if we were supposed to prove the existence of the external world before being able to do empirical inquiry: In order to study the world, an inquirer must assume there is a world to be studied. A Cartesian sceptic pointing to the error possibility that scientists have overlooked, namely that there might not be external world, would not be taken seriously in science, because scientific justification is not foundationalist in nature. That there is an external world can be seen as a "hinge proposition" (Wittgenstein 1969) that is necessary to assume in order to be able to gain knowledge about the world. The dialectical account of justification provides a more accurate picture of the structure of justification in science because it contextualises the question of which assumptions can be taken for granted to the type of the inquiry in question. In certain contexts, for instance in some fields of research, certain assumptions are collectively accepted as legitimate in that field. The assumptions are not dogmatically believed but provisionally accepted. They enjoy the default status of justification in that field and can be relied on as long as there is no positive reason to doubt them. In other fields, however, they might need to be scrutinised. Even Cartesian sceptical hypotheses can receive serious consideration in philosophical studies.

The same kind of contextualism may apply to the justification of steps of inquiry as well: In different fields, different reasoning methods may apply. For example, in many empirical fields, there are standard statistical methods for data analysis that serve as reasons to accept the conclusions drawn by the scientists. These methods are typically not questioned in these fields but are justified by default. If somebody asks a question about the methods of data analysis, it suffices to give a reference to a standard statistics textbook. However, statisticians, mathematicians, philosophers, computer scientists and others interested in foundations of statistics may certainly question the validity of standard statistical methods and develop alternative ones. In contexts of inquiry focussing on methodology of statistics, the standard methods do not have the default status because it is precisely their justification that is under study. If sufficient reason to question the standard methods emerges from these debates, these reasons may be transferred to discussions in the empirical fields and legitimise questioning the use of the standard methods there as well, thereby overriding their default status.

Another salient point in which justification is needed in the context of the Interrogative Model of Inquiry is in the strategic choice of which oracles to trust: Whose answers to accept and whose to bracket? One possible answer is to consider the track record of the oracles' previous answers (Hintikka et al. 1999): In order to decide whether an oracle's answer should be accepted we should see how well its previous answers have been in line with what is known from other sources. However, there are problems with this suggestion. One obvious problem is that we may not have a complete track record of a particular oracle available. And even if we had one, it only tells about past history, not about the current case. Accepting the answer given by the oracle based on its previous successes brings in the usual difficulties involved in inductive inference. Moreover, there is a problem similar to the generality problem often discussed in the context of reliabilism that some instances of the oracle's previous answers may not be relevant for estimating its reliability in this particular case. Consider the case of scientific experts, for instance; the oracle may be reliable on certain subject matters but not on others.

In the context of IMI, there is a more fundamental problem of using track record data to estimate the reliability of a source. This concerns the feature of the model that all information that is not assumed prior to the process, comes from oracles: Thus there is no independent source of information that could be used to verify answers obtained from oracles, only other answers obtained from oracles. Therefore, a track record can only be made relative to other answers but there is no principled way of saying which answer should be taken as the correct answer against which to compare the other. If an answer by an oracle differs from its previous answers, how do we know whether the oracle has forgotten or learned, that is, whether it is now making an error or whether it has gained more knowledge and now gives more accurate information? Or if an answer of one oracle differs from an answer given by another oracle, how do we know which one to trust? We cannot say that we should trust the one that we have found to be more reliable because their reliability is exactly what we are trying to find out.

Of course, in case of conflicts, we may always ask yet another oracle. However, there is no guarantee that we will be better off by just adding new oracles. Even though methods that rely on finding out a majority opinion may sometimes help, they make substantial assumptions about the reliability of the sources. For instance, according to the famous Condorcet Jury Theorem, if the sources are independent of each other and each source is more likely to give a correct answer rather than an incorrect one, then the answer of the majority will approach certainty when new sources are added. However, if the sources are generally unreliable then the majority will most certainly give us false information.

It seems that we are running in circles: In order to investigate the reliability of sources we need to have estimates of their reliability prior to the investigation. Of course, we typically do have prior estimates and we do prioritise certain sources over others: A naturalist may prioritise nature, a rationalist may prioritise reason or intuition, a phenomenologist experience, a theist holy scriptures, and so on. The point is that the model does not offer any guidance as to how these estimates are arrived at: The evaluation of sources is left as a strategic choice for the inquirer.

However, there is another way of assessing the oracles' answers, and that is justification understood in the dialectical sense discussed above. Upon receiving an answer from a particular source, we may ask the source for reasons for the answer. This does not resolve the theoretical problem that information only comes from oracles but it at least provides some principled ways of assessing sources. As Miranda Fricker (2010) has noted, the ability to support claims by offering reasons is a crucially important indicator property that helps the inquirer to distinguish good informants. In the case of nature we may perhaps not be able to ask for reasons directly but we may at least make more experiments to test the answer. In the case of human testifiers, we can ask how they know the answer or what makes them think it is correct. In the case of research reports and other literary sources, we expect to find descriptions of the experiments and other evidence supporting their results. In any case, if we want our inquiry to produce justified conclusions we should make sure that the sources we rely on are justified in theirs. The best way to find out is to interrogate them for the reasons they have for accepting the conclusions. Eventually, our aim is to find out whether we can integrate their results with our own inquiry, whether we can commit to the assumptions and methodological principles that have guided their research. If we can, then we may decide to accept their answers and rely on them in our own investigation. But if we doubt their conclusions, premisses, or methodological principles, and they cannot provide satisfactory reasons for them, then we may wish to bracket their answers and consult other sources.

Of course, we do not always go very far in asking for reasons, but the integration remains an ideal, especially in cases of collaborative research in which group members try to achieve knowledge together. Sometimes we are not even in the position to evaluate or understand the reasons that others have for their conclusions, and we can only rely on their expertise. This creates epistemic dependencies in which the reasons supporting one's conclusions are distributed over several sources (see Hardwig 1985). This dependence is illustrated by viewing inquiry and justification as interrogative processes.

Justification therefore enters inquiry on many levels. In fact, it can be suggested that questions of justification are inherently present in every stage of scientific practices, from choice of methods and basic assumptions to selection of questions to study, instruments to use, experiments to make, datasets to analyse, and so on. The justificatory principles that guide researchers in all these decisions may not come from highly general and idealised theories of rationality and justification studied in traditional epistemology. Rather they concern whether the decisions can be convincingly argued for to other researchers in the field sharing similar background assumptions. The aim of researchers is not to demonstrate infallible results following from absolutely certain first principles. Rather it is to produce well-argued but defeasible conclusions from reasonable background assumptions that are considered fruitful and maybe shared by other researchers in the discipline but only provisionally accepted.

The combination of interrogative model of inquiry and the dialectical model of justification illustrates the close relation between inquiry and justification but it still leaves room for seeing them as distinct activities. Even though questions of justification are present in every step of inquiry, inquiry can be seen as a process of searching for conclusions which combines forward steps of reasoning and interrogation and backward steps of revising strategies, bracketing and unbracketing previous steps represented in the tableau. Once the inquirers are satisfied with the current stage of the tableau, they will be able to assert their conclusions by constructing an argumentative line in which the various bracketed sidesteps are ignored. Typically this will then be used as the basic structure for a research talk or a written publication that is delivered to the scientific community in an argumentative form that exhibits the conclusions as justified in the form required by the dialectical principles: It presents the conclusions as backed up by reasons derived from principles and methods assumed to enjoy a default status of justification together with results obtained from oracles, that is, experiments and previous research, which are documented in accordance with generally accepted principles. A critical reader should then be able to find replies to challenges that may rise and sources for previous research that the study builds on. Should the critic find the reported evidence wanting, she may present her criticisms, but again in an argumentative form that provides reasons to doubt the alleged results.

This is why scepticism has no bite in science. The claims made by scientists are not meant to be absolute but conditional in nature: These are the results arrived at using these methods given these assumptions. Neither the Pyrrhonian sceptic who continues to ask for reasons beyond the generally accepted assumptions nor a Cartesian sceptic who says that there is a logical possibility that the assumptions may be false will be able to raise a positive reason to doubt the assumptions. Since they are not prepared to make any commitments themselves, they will not be able to argue that an alternative hypotheses might be more plausible than the ones made by the inquirers. Only other inquirers will be in a position to do that. If they are successful, revisions will be in place. The self-correcting nature of science follows from the interdependence between inquiry and justification: Inquiry aims to start from reasonable, default-justified premisses and to proceed by reasonable steps using acceptable principles in order to produce justified conclusions that survive critical scrutiny. However, sometimes the conclusions turn out to be problematic, in which case we may need to go back and revise or bracket some of our assumptions or the answers we have received from oracles. Justification in scientific context does not depend on static support structures between premisses and conclusions. Instead, science is a continuous self-correcting enterprise consisting of social processes of inquiry and justification continuously interacting and influencing each other.

5 Conclusions: Producing Scientific Knowledge

We have seen that, on the one hand, inquiry requires justification because its ultimate aim is to produce scientific knowledge, because scientific knowledge requires justification, and because the justification of the produced knowledge depends on the justification of its premisses and its methods. On the other hand, justification requires inquiry because justification is a product of inquiry. Moreover, processes of justifying one's conclusions may also create a need for inquiry because when an agent is trying to defend her views dialectically, it may turn out that existing evidence does not support them to a sufficient degree. Hence, more evidence is needed to settle the issue, which thus suggests new experiments and avenues of further inquiry, eventually leading either to finding stronger evidence for one's results or a revision of one's starting points and improvement of the theories.

Given the dialectical approach to epistemic justification and Hintikka's model of inquiry, both justification and inquiry can be seen as social activities in which agents dialectically pose questions and give answers to them. The picture that emerges displays science as a collaborative enterprise in which scientific knowledge is produced. Individual agents sometimes take the role of an inquirer in pursuit of new knowledge asking for questions and making challenges and sometimes the role of an oracle answering questions and justifying their results to other inquirers who are asking questions and making challenges. Various special sciences differ in their methods and practices, but it can be argued that they all share a common structure consisting of steps of reasoning and inquiry together with argumentative principles governing epistemic justification and knowledge production. The combination of the interrogative model of inquiry and the dialectical model of justification suggested here aims to model that shared structure. Anything more specific than that may demand detailed empirical study of actual scientific practices in specific disciplines if the target is a descriptive model, or substantial methodological recommendations if a prescriptive model is sought for.

This picture also illustrates the nature of scientific knowledge: It depends on theoretical and methodological assumptions which may sometimes have to be corrected in order to meet critical challenges. Dependence on assumptions does not lead to scepticism, however. We may still have knowledge, it is just that our knowledge is conditional in form. We may know that from these premisses and these methodological assumptions these conclusions follow. This is the form of scientific knowledge, and at least in principle, in the ideal case in which all the assumptions made explicit, it can be certain. It may turn out that one of the premisses or assumptions was not justified, or even that it was false. Still the conditional claim was and remains a piece of scientific knowledge. It is just not very interesting piece of knowledge once its antecedent turned out to be false, so we need to make corrections to our assumptions and inquire further.

Acknowledgements The comments of two anonymous reviewers are gratefully acknowledged. Part of the work was carried out while working at the University of Helsinki under a grant (number 1251076) from the Academy of Finland.

References

Annis, D. B. (1978). A contextualist theory of epistemic justification. *American Philosophical Quarterly, 15*(3):213–219.

Fricker, M. (2010). Scepticism and the genealogy of knowledge: Situating epistemology in time. In A. Haddock, A. Millar, & D. Pritchard (Eds.), *Social epistemology* (pp. 51–68). New York: Oxford University Press.

Genot, E. J. (2009). The game of inquiry: The interrogative approach to inquiry and belief revision theory. *Synthese, 171*, 271–289.

Hardwig, J. (1985). Epistemic dependence. *The Journal of Philosophy, LXXXII*, 335–349.

Hintikka, J. (2007). *Socratic epistemology: Explorations of knowledge-seeking by questioning*. Cambridge: Cambridge University Press.

Hintikka, J., Halonen, I., & Mutanen, A. (1999). Interrogative logic as a general theory of reasoning. In *Inquiry as inquiry: A logic of scientific discovery* (Volume 5 of Jaakko Hintikka selected papers, pp. 47–90). Dordrecht: Kluwer Academic.

Hookway, C. (2006). Epistemology and inquiry: The primacy of practice. In S. Hetherington (Ed.), *Epistemology futures* (pp. 95–110). New York: Oxford University Press.

Kiikeri, M. (1999). Interrogative reasoning and discovery: A new perspective on Kepler's inquiry. *Philosophica, 63*, 51–87.

Lammenranta, M. (2004). Theories of justification. In I. Niiniluoto, M. Sintonen, & J. Woleński (Eds.), *Handbook of epistemology* (pp. 467–495). Dordrecht: Kluwer Academic.

Levi, I. (2012). *Pragmatism and inquiry: Selected essays*. Oxford: Oxford University Press.

Williams, B. (1973). Deciding to believe. In *Problems for the self: Philosophical papers 1956–1972* (pp. 136–151). Cambridge: Cambridge University Press.

Williams, M. (2001). *Problems of knowledge: A critical introduction to epistemology*. Oxford: Oxford University Press.

Wittgenstein, L. (1969). *On certainty*. Oxford: Basil Blackwell.

The Interrogative Model of Inquiry and Inquiry Learning

Emmanuel J. Genot and Agneta Gulz

Abstract Hakkarainen and Sintonen (Sci Educ 11(1):25–43, 2002) praise the descriptive adequacy of Hintikka's *Interrogative Model of Inquiry* (IMI) to describe children's practices in an inquiry-based learning context. They further propose to use the IMI as a starting point for developing new pedagogical methods and designing new didactic tools. We assess this proposal in the light of the formal results that in the IMI characterize interrogative learning strategies. We find that these results actually reveal a deep methodological issue for inquiry-based learning, namely that educators cannot guarantee that learners will successfully acquire a content, without limiting learner's autonomy, and that a trade-off between success and autonomy is unavoidable. As a by-product of our argument, we obtain a logical characterization of serendipity.

Keywords Interrogative model of inquiry • Inquiry learning • Strategy theorem • Logic of discovery • Sherlock Holmes

1 Introduction

Epistemological models distinguish *contexts of discovery* from *contexts of justification*, and usually proceed from the assumption that inferences carried in the former cannot be rationalized. This is often expressed by saying that there can be no *logic of discovery*, only a *logic of justification*—where 'logic' is intended in a broad sense, including e.g. probability theory. However, some models of inquiry have explicitly tackled discovery of new facts, as part of problem-solving strategies. In particular, Hintikka's *Interrogative Model of Inquiry* (IMI) presents a formal approach to discovery, and describes inquiry as a two-player game where one player, *Inquirer*, asks 'small' instrumental questions to the other player, *Nature*, in order to

E.J. Genot (✉)
Philosophy, Lund University–LUX, Box 192, 221 00, Lund, Sweden
e-mail: Emmanuel.Genot@fil.lu.se

A. Gulz
Cognitive Science, Lund University–LUX, Box 192, 221 00, Lund, Sweden

C. Başkent (ed.), *Perspectives on Interrogative Models of Inquiry*, Logic, Argumentation & Reasoning 8, DOI 10.1007/978-3-319-20762-9_2

answer a 'big' research question. Within this framework, it may be shown that, for a wide variety of contexts, question-based discovery is grounded in deduction. Hintikka interprets the IMI as a vindication Sherlock Holmes' method, in which deduction guides interrogation.

For the above reasons, Hakkarainen and Sintonen (2002) argue that Hintikka's IMI offers an epistemological basis for *inquiry-based learning*. Proponents of inquiry-based learning consider that learners' progresses should not be assessed solely by evaluating whether they have acquired certain contents. Rather, evaluation should also take into account how well learners have developed analytical and experimental strategies to acquire new knowledge. The core assumption shared by proponents of inquiry-based learning is that children can actually develop autonomously highly sophisticated learning strategies, that mimic scientific method. If they are correct, designing learning environments that encourage children to develop such strategies would be more effective to prepare them to engage as adults in scientific inquiry, or at the very least in critical thinking, than e.g. relying on rote learning and normalized testing.

Hakkarainen and Sintonen present an empirical study that supports the descriptive adequacy of the IMI to inquiry contexts, and vindicates the core assumption of inquiry-based learning. Specifically, they claim that what the IMI characterizes as strategic reasoning actually occurs in an inquiry-based learning context involving elementary school children. Based on their observations, they suggest to mine the IMI for methodological principles, in order to develop new pedagogical practices and design didactic tools. However, and by their own admission, Hakkarainen and Sintonen rely on the conceptual apparatus of the IMI alone, and disregard the formal results which in the IMI characterize knowledge-seeking strategies. Whether this formal characterization actually supports Hakkarainen and Sintonen's methodological proposal thus remains an open question.

This paper addresses this question, and in so doing uncovers a deep methodological difficulty for inquiry-based learning. One the one hand, the study carried by Hakkarainen and Sintonen clearly shows that children engaged in cognitive processes that undoubtedly displayed the characteristics of discovery processes that the IMI describes formally as strategic and guided by deduction. On the other hand, in the light of the formal results of the IMI, these cognitive processes can also be shown to be such that they cannot be guaranteed to yield successful acquisition of a determined content. Moreover, the same formal results show that if inquiry-based learning is 'scaffolded' so as to guarantee successful learning of an intended content, the learner's autonomy is in fact virtually destroyed. The challenge for inquiry-based learning methodology, and the design of inquiry learning environments, is that a trade-off between success and autonomy is unavoidable.

We first introduce the formal model of the IMI (Sect. 2), explain how it relates strategic questioning to deduction (Sect. 3), and then turn to abduction in information-seeking strategies, and its relation to deduction (Sect. 4). Each of these section illustrates the model with one of Hintikka's favorite Sherlock Holmes example (the Case of Silver Blaze). Once the model in place, we outline the study presented by Hakkarainen and Sintonen and discuss whether its conclusions are actually supported by the IMI (Sect. 5). Finally, we conclude on the Socratic method, and how it illustrates the difficulty to promote learners' autonomy through question-driven learning.

2 The Game of Inquiry

2.1 *Learning and Information-Seeking as Questioning*

Early formulations of the IMI date back to the 1980s but we will consider the model (for this exposition) as a generalization of algorithmic learning-theoretic models that appeared in the 1990s, esp. the 'first-order paradigm' of Martin and Osherson (1998). Schematically, the latter model characterizes a *problem* as a pair $\langle T, Q \rangle$, where T is a background theory expressed in some (first-order) language $\mathcal{L}$[1]; and Q is a (principal) *question*—usually, but not necessarily, a binary question—that partitions possible states of Nature compatible with T, denoted hereafter $\mathbf{S}(T)$. Nature chooses a state $s \in \mathbf{S}(T)$ and a *data stream* (an infinite sequence of basic sentences of $\mathcal{L}$) that in the limit fully characterizes the features of s expressible in $\mathcal{L}$; then Nature reveals one datum at a time. A learning strategy is a function taking as arguments finite segments of the data stream, and returning either an answer in Q or '?' (suspension of judgment).

The model of Hintikka et al. (2002) generalizes the above by dropping some idealizing assumptions. Nature, instead of a complete data stream, chooses a set A_s of *available answers* in s, that can be expressed by sentences in $\mathcal{L}$ of arbitrary complexity (and may then be analyzed by 'analytical' moves). A_s determines which properties and entities are resp. observable and identifiable. The data stream is built by Inquirer, using instrumental questions to supplement the information T gives her about s, and may therefore remain incomplete.[2] An *interrogative learning strategy* takes as argument a finite sequence of data, and outputs a (possibly empty) subset of 'small' questions (aimed at generating the extension of the data sequence) along with the current conjectured answer to Q (or suspension of judgment). Finally, Q may be a *why*- or *how*-question about some $q \in \mathcal{L}$, in which case Inquirer *assumes* that q holds, and aims at finding conditions which, together with T, entail

[1]A first-order language $\mathcal{L}$ can express statements about individuals, their properties and relations; combinations of such statements (with Boolean operators *not*, *and*, *or*, and *if… then…*); and their existential and universal generalizations (with quantifiers *there exists …* and *for all…* respectively). A *basic* sentence of $\mathcal{L}$ contains only individual names and relations symbols, i.e. no Boolean operator other than (possibly) an initial negation, and no quantifier. In what follows, we implicitly restrict the meaning of 'deduction' to 'first-order deduction'—i.e. relations between premises and conclusions couched in some first-order language.

[2]Introducing A_s weakens the assumptions that: (*a*) data streams are always complete in the limit; (*b*) all predicates (names) of $\mathcal{L}$ denote observable qualities (identifiable objects); and: (*c*) a datum needs no analysis. The IMI also drops the idealization that: (*d*) Nature always chooses s in $\mathbf{S}(T)$, and: (*e*) all answers in A_s are true in s. Cases where (*d–e*) hold define the special case of *Pure Discovery* (cf. Sect. 3.1).

q. The answer to such a *why*- or *how*-question 'compacts' the whole line of inquiry whereby q is shown to be entailed by T together with *ad explanandum* conditions (Hintikka and Halonen 1997; Hintikka 2007, ch. 7) (also, Sect. 4.2).

The success of Inquirer's strategy depends in part on the set of questions she is ready to ask at a given point (which evolves throughout inquiry), and in part on A_s. Hintikka calls *range of attention* the set of *yes-no* questions Inquirer considers at any given time (Hintikka 1986), but the role of this set of questions is left implicit in the results presented by Hintikka et al. (2002). We will make it explicit, since it is critical to understand how the IMI bears upon learning practices of empirical agents.

Together with T, the answers to instrumental questions induce an *information bi-partition* over $\mathbf{S}(T)$: the first cell comprises scenarios compatible with the answers, and the other, those which are not. At the outset, the first cell is identical with $\mathbf{S}(T)$: all possible states compatible with T are *indiscernible* from each other, and s is assumed to be one of them. The partition is refined when new answers are accepted. Answers gradually 'hack off' scenarios incompatible with them. The assumptions that T and A_s are truthful may be revised in the course of inquiry, thereby reopening possibilities. Instrumental questions may also trigger 'sub-inquiries' (e.g. *why*- and *how*-questions, or questions with statistical answers requiring parameters estimation) about some problem $\langle T', Q' \rangle$—where T' extends T with some of the answers already obtained from A_s when investigating $\langle T, Q \rangle$—possibly suspending investigations of $\langle T, Q \rangle$ proper.

An inquiry about $\langle T, Q \rangle$ terminates when Inquirer is able to tell whether the first cell of the partition (compatible with the answers and T) is identical with some $q_i \in Q$, i.e. suffices to identify s 'enough' to answer Q. This may sometimes be impossible (e.g. for inductive problems) but one can then strengthen T with additional assumptions (including e.g. extrapolations for unobserved values). It is also sometimes possible to devise methods that rather than waiting for an answer to Q, emit an initial conjecture and adopt a policy for changing it later in face of new data.[3] The model handles retraction of answers by 'bracketing' and excluding them from further information processing, which may re-open Q by preventing identification of s. Bracketing can also be extended to handle revisions of T (Genot 2009). Reasoning probabilistically from answers known to be uncertain is discussed in Hintikka (1987). Bracketing and probabilistic reasoning will be discussed in more details in Sect. 3.1.

[3] An example is the *halting problem*, in which one must determine whether the current run of a program p, that may execute either finitely many instructions, or loop an instruction indefinitely, is finite or infinite. An 'impatient' method that conjectures that p is currently at the beginning of an infinite run, and repeats this conjecture indefinitely unless p stops (in which case the method changes its assessment) *solves* the problem in the above sense on every possible run. Kelly (2004) discusses in details the relation between the halting problem and empirical inductive problems.

2.2 The Sherlock Holmes Sense of "Deduction"

An example from Sherlock Holmes inquiry in *The Case of Silver Blaze* ideally illustrates the type of reasoning the IMI captures. In this short story, Holmes assists Inspector Gregory in the investigation of the theft of Silver Blaze (a race horse) and the murder of his trainer. The principal question is: *who stole Silver Blaze and killed his trainer?* During the night of the theft, a stable-boy was drugged and Silver Blaze's trainer was killed. Gregory holds a suspect, Fitzroy Simpson, and has already settled the following (instrumental) questions: *Does Simpson have motive? Did Simpson have an opportunity to commit the theft and the murder? Does Simpson own a weapon that could have been the murder weapon?* and *Can Simpson be placed at the crime scene?* All these questions have received a positive answer. Simpson is indebted from betting on horses. He visited the stables the evening before the theft, stopped the maid carrying the food, and was eventually driven out by the stable-boy and a watchdog. He owns a weighted walking stick that could have been the murder weapon. And finally, a scarf has been found near the victim's body, that the stable-boy and the maid recognized as Simpson's.

Gregory's questioning strategy is a staple of crime fiction: it's a by-the-books strategy, that may be applied to any case of homicide, as it uses questions applicable to almost every potential suspect, once some descriptions ("the murder weapon", "the crime scene") have been specified for the current investigation. This strategy keeps questioning simple, as there are no strategic dependencies between questions. It gives a basis for quasi-probabilistic inferences, as a high 'yes' count increases suspicion (culprits usually have one), and a high 'no' decreases it (innocents usually have one). Although the former count may result from a coincidence, the probability remains low as long as answers are statistically independent. A conclusion put forward as a consequence of applying this strategy is acceptable provided that scenarios where answers would not be independent—i.e. when either the high 'yes' or 'no' counts have hidden common causes—are ruled out. In such scenarios, the method is known to be unreliable, as it may conclude to the guilt of a innocent who has been framed, or to the innocence of a culprit who has carefully premeditated and executed his plot. But as long as hidden common cause are not suspected, the hypothesis of Simpson's guilt is strengthened by Gregory's reasoning.

Holmes describes the case as one where "[t]he difficulty is to detach the framework of fact—of absolute undeniable fact—from the embellishments of theorists and reporters" (Conan Doyle 1986, p. 522). Holmes' own expectations are instrumental in his decision to investigate,[4] but he does not favor any hypothesis, even for the sole purpose of testing it first. In particular, although Holmes conceded that Simpson's guilt is the 'natural' hypothesis, he does not consider it as the first to be investigated. Instead, he proceeds trying to identify the thief, narrowing

[4]Holmes confesses that "[he] could not believe it possible that the most remarkable horse in England could long remain concealed [and] expected to hear that he had been found, and that his abductor was the murderer" (Conan Doyle 1986, p. 522).

down the range of suspects without explicitly listing them, attempting instead to find discriminating properties, using *yes-no* questions. One of them is whether the dog kept in the stables has barked at the thief. Holmes does not ask the question explicitly, but obtains an answer from Gregory in the following dialogue:

> "Is there any point to which you would wish to draw my attention?" "To the curious incident of the dog in the night-time." "The dog did nothing in the night-time." "That was the curious incident," remarked Sherlock Holmes." (Conan Doyle 1986, p. 540)

The definite description "*the* curious incident" can refer to either of two circumstances: the watchdog's barking at the thief, or failing to do so. However, only one circumstance is compatible with Simpson's guilt, since the watchdog kept in the stables is the very dog that the stable-boy set after Simpson in the preceding evening. Eventually, Holmes sums up the conclusions he drew learning that the dog had barked against Simpson in the evening, and remained silent during the night:

> I had grasped the significance of the silence of the dog, for one true inference invariably suggests others. The Simpson incident had shown me that a dog was kept in the stables, and yet, though someone had been in and had fetched out a horse, he had not barked enough to arouse the two lads in the loft. Obviously the midnight visitor was someone whom the dog knew well. (Conan Doyle 1986, p. 540)

Holmes' instrumental question may seem irrelevant to those who do not anticipate his reasoning, and Holmes' reputation plays a role in their judgment: the horse's owner does not consider the incident significant, but Gregory and Watson do, knowing that Holmes seldom attends to insignificant facts. Holmes trusts his assumptions and reports about the facts, and conservatively so: the 'yes' count vs. Simpson could make one doubt that the dog is a good watchdog, but Holmes never contemplates 'bracketing' this assumption. Finally, Holmes' conclusion reduces the set of potential suspects by ruling out Simpson without tracking probabilities, because there is no range of suspects over which distribute them.

3 Deduction in Inquiry

3.1 *Pure Discovery*

The inquiry game described in Sect. 2.1 is with asymmetric information: Inquirer does not know whether her assumptions are correct (formally, if $s \in \mathbf{S}(T)$), nor which answers are available (in A_s), and whether those available are reliable. Nevertheless, as illustrated by Sherlock Holmes' method in *The Case of Silver Blaze*, one can take evidence at face value as long as possible, then follow a line of deductions, possibly taking educated guesses, rather than considering from the outset several cases in parallel. Indeed, Holmes usually reconsiders his grounds for accepting evidence, or relying on background assumptions, only in the face of contradictory evidence. His method amounts to address (at least initially) any problem-solving situation as what Hintikka calls a problem of *Pure Discovery* (PD):

> [Pure discovery] means a type of inquiry in which all answers are known to be true, or at least can be treated as being true. If so, all we need to do is to find out what the truth is; we do not have to worry about justifying what we find. (Hintikka 2007, p. 98)

A distinctive feature of the IMI is to take Pure Discovery (hereafter PD) as the 'default' mode of inquiry: PD reasoning is maintained as long as it is possible to do so, uncertain answers are disregarded whenever possible, and attempts are made to reach conclusions that involve only whatever premises and answers one can 'treat as being true'. However, a given context can turn out not to be a PD-context in a variety of ways, and Inquirer's strategy must be modified accordingly. Contradiction may arise between expectations based on deductions from T, and answers to some questions. Or multiple sources may give incompatible answers to the same questions. Or some action undertaken on the basis of conclusions arrived at earlier stages of inquiry, may fail to produce the expected result. Even if none of the above occurs, it may prove impossible to deduce a unique answer to the principal question Q from T and answers to instrumental questions. One then may have to settle for partial answers, weighted by the amount of justification available for them.

The IMI handles contexts in which conflicts occur mainly through *defeasible* reasoning. When premises in T turn out to be unsafe, i.e. when grounds for justification cannot be ignored anymore, or when answers are deemed uncertain, they can be 'bracketed' (Hintikka et al. 2002; Genot 2009) so that no further inquiry step depends on them: no consequence is inferred from them, and no further question is asked using them as presuppositions. 'Bracketing' allows for the circumscription of a 'safe' PD subcontext, and for maintaining PD behavior for as long as possible, and is reversible: premises and answers can be reinstated in the light of further evidence. Moreover, if one's current evidence proves insufficient, and no complete answer can be obtained, the IMI accommodates probabilistic reasoning, as a 'logic of justification' (Hintikka 1987, 1992). Subsequently, the IMI addresses the issues arising in PD-contexts, before considering any other type of context.

Mismatch between Inquirer's range of attention and the contextually available answers (represented by A_s) is the prime issue of interrogative inquiry. Mismatch occurs when either Inquirer asks a question which has no answer in A_s, or fails to ask a relevant question whose answer is in A_s—as with Gregory, failing to 'ask' about the dog. A related issue is the strategic problem of choosing the next best 'small' question given one's current information (T and past answers). Mismatch is an issue in PD and non-PD contexts alike, as it encompasses the use of 'control' questions which can be answered given one's current information. How Inquirer addresses these problems depends on how she manages her range of attention.

3.2 Building Blocks of Interrogative Strategies

The IMI counts *inferential* and *interrogative* moves on a par with each other. Hintikka calls *presupposition* of a question the statement that opens a question, i.e. makes possible to ask it meaningfully. Specifically, disjunctions make *whether*-questions possible, by determining a range of alternatives, and existential statements make possible to ask *what-*, *where-*, *which-* and *who*-questions. Subsequently, the fundamental 'rule' of the game of inquiry is that a question can be asked as soon as its presupposition has been inferred (making it available for an interrogative move). With our extended notion of range of attention, the rule can be rephrased as: *a question enters the Inquirer's range of attention when its presupposition is obtained by an inferential move*. This 'rule' is critical in how the IMI captures the dynamics of discovery of new facts through 'small' questions, as a goal-directed process.

Questioning strategies supervene on one's current information (T and the answers accepted so far), which is mined out for open questions. Inquirer is *not* assumed to be aware of all the consequences of her current information. For example, Inquirer's information partition may exclude that "neither A nor B" holds in the state of Nature s, which in turn entails that "either A or B" holds in s. But the question whether A or B holds will not enter Inquirer's range of attention before she has established that T entails that "A or B" holds. Once Inquirer performs the inference, she may choose to raise the question "Which of A or B holds?"—or a sequence of *yes-no* questions about A and B—and use it to refine her information partition. If no answer is obtained, she may need to *reason by cases*, or mine T (and past answers) to find equivalences between A and B on the one hand, and some A' and B' on the other, so as to reformulate her questions. The same holds *mutatis mutandis* for statements like "There is an x s.t. $\phi(x)$"—where $\phi(\cdot)$ stands for some description which qualifies x. Such statements open *wh*-questions about the x (object, person, location, etc.) satisfying the description. If one fails to obtain an answer, one can introduce some 'arbitrary' name α standing for the (so far unknown) object satisfying the description, avoiding any other assumption about α other than $\phi(\alpha)$, until (possibly) a referent for α is identified. Again, it may be possible to mine T to obtain a description $\psi(\cdot)$ such that T (possibly together with past answers) entails that "If x is s.t. $\psi(x)$, then it is s.t. $\phi(x)$" and ask the question about $\psi(\cdot)$ instead.

In the case of Silver Blaze, Gregory's strategy is based on a deduction from his background knowledge, providing him with a testable reformulation of the question *Is Simpson guilty?* The derivation could be obtained from a general truth formulated as follows: *if x is a murderer, then x has a motive, had the opportunity, owns a murder weapon, and was present at the crime scene*. Gregory's strategy can be viewed as an application of *modus ponens*, that assumes the natural hypothesis (Simpson is the culprit) and derives observable consequences. It thus uses 'small' *yes-no* questions that test properties occurring in the consequent of the general truth. The strategy only warrants a *partial* answer, because the general truth is not an equivalence, as someone may satisfy the description in the consequent without being a murderer.

Holmes formulates a different question (*Who stole Silver Blaze and killed his trainer?*) and the way he arrives at the instrumental question that specifies it, and the conclusion(s) he draws from the answer, all proceed from deductive inferences. But Holmes' 'small' question has the form *Is it the case that A or not?*, where A is: "the dog barked at the thief", and the possibility to ask it depends on the language he uses alone (irrespective of the current information state). Generally, for some language $\mathcal{L}$, any grammatically correct statement A or description $\phi(a)$ built with the vocabulary of $\mathcal{L}$ (where a is a proper name or an indexical like 'this' or 'that') can in principle be built into a *yes-no* question without the need of further inference from one's current information.[5] How the question whether the dog barked entered Holmes's range of attention, but not Gregory's, is trivially deductive: the deduction that *A or not A* from *any* background theory T would be valid, and thus its being deductive does not suffice to explain how it was arrived at.

Two other aspects of the case of Silver Blaze will be significant for our comparison with empirical data. The first is that Holmes' initial principal question is based on a *false presupposition*—namely, that there is a single individual who stole Silver Blaze and murdered his trainer. Holmes' instrumental questions are selected in order to help answer that question. The information Holmes obtains after asking about the dog eventually leads him to revise this presupposition. Narrowing down the range of suspects that satisfy the condition of "not being barked at by the watchdog", Holmes comes to suspect, and later establish, that the answers to the questions *Who stole Silver Blaze?* and *Who killed Silver Blaze's trainer* cannot be the same. Interestingly, because the deduction of the presupposition of the *instrumental* question about the dog is trivial, it is *independent* of Holmes initially incorrect assumption that the thief and the murderer are the same individual, which served as presupposition for his *principal* question.

The second significant aspect is that Holmes' mention of "the curious incident with the dog in the night-time" can be viewed as an implicit suggestion to Gregory—to consider a control question (*Did the dog bark at the thief?*) and revise his conclusions in the light of its answers. At the time Holmes asks about the dog, Gregory has accepted the positive answer to the question *Is Simpson guilty or not?* But pending some assumptions about watchdogs shared by Gregory and Holmes, assuming that Simpson is guilty leads to expect that the dog *has* barked in the night (because the dog barked at Simpson earlier in the evening). This expectation is incompatible to what is known to have happened, and thus constitutes a *reductio* of the assumption that Simpson is guilty. Gregory needs then to revise either the background assumptions that the watchdog is well-trained, and barks at unauthorized visitors even after a first encounter; or the assumption that coincidences that would make Simpson appear guilty can be neglected. In the latter case, new questions may enter Gregory's range of attention; such as: *How did*

[5] If A or $\phi(a)$ include vague terms (or imprecise categories), disambiguation is needed to obtain an answer, but *sequence* of *yes-no* questions (further specifying a 'prototype' in the current context) will suffice.

Simpson's scarf ended at the crime scene?—a question that, incidentally, Holmes later raises and answers, considering as relevant the fact that it is a scarf, and not that it is Simpson's.

4 Deduction Abducted

4.1 Strategic Reasoning in Interrogation

The previous section has presented informally the relation between selection of questions, and deduction. Let us now consider how the IMI formally characterizes this relation. Hintikka describes the strategic problem of interrogative inquiry (neglecting the distinction between statements and propositions they express) in the following terms:

> Strategic knowledge will in interrogative inquiry ultimately come down to a method answering questions of the following form: Given the list of the propositions one has reached in a line of inquiry, which question should one ask next? In view of the need of presuppositions, this amounts to asking: Which proposition should one use as the presupposition of the next question? (Hintikka 2007, p. 98)

Hintikka et al. (2002) present three formal results that can be combined to answer this question: the *Deduction Theorem*, the *Yes-No Theorem*, and the *Strategy Theorem*. The *Deduction Theorem* simply states that if a statement expressing an answer $q_i \in Q$ can be established *interrogatively* to hold in s assuming T, then that statement can be established to hold *deductively* (without using questions) from T and a finite subset A_s' of A_s. Equivalently: answers act as additional premises, and interrogative reasoning reduces to *deduction from T strengthened by a finite set of answers*.[6] The *Deduction Theorem* is in fact rather trivial. It is an immediate consequence of the definition of what problems and solutions are, in learning-theoretic models. Nevertheless, it implicitly refines this definition, as solving problems requires to raise the 'small' questions, whose answers will be instrumental to solve a problem. The role of instrumental question generating the data stream is usually left implicit in learning-theoretic models. Notice that the Deduction Theorem shows how one can come to accept some answer q_i that *does not in fact hold* in s, i.e. if s is *not* in $\mathbf{S}(T)$, when e.g. $T \cup A_s'$ is consistent.

Perhaps more surprising, the *Yes-No Theorem* is no less straightforward. It states that a statement expressing an answer q_i can be established interrogatively from T and A_s iff that statement can be established interrogatively from T and A_s *using* yes-no *questions only*. The Yes-No Theorem is best understood as stating that every

[6]Because of the possibility of mismatch, the converse of the Deduction Theorem only holds on the condition that elements of A_s needed to obtain (interrogatively) q_i from T are answers to questions in Inquirer's range of attention.

interrogative argument can be *reconstructed* with *yes-no* questions alone.[7] But the *Yes-No Theorem* also implies that it is possible in principle to solve interrogatively a problem $\langle T, Q \rangle$ without any *non-trivial* deduction from T. Trivial deductions from T are also necessary to formulate *control* questions: if one 'goes along' with expectations based on T, and takes its consequences at face value, one will not test for potential contradictions (assuming that T itself is consistent). Hence, contradictions between T and facts can only be revealed using *yes-no* questions trivially deduced from T.

Finally, the *Strategy Theorem* rests on an observation about *deductive* proofs. Obtaining the shortest proof for a conclusion c from a set of premises P (when c actually follows from P) requires to: (a) examine the least number of cases; and: (b) introduce the smallest number of (arbitrary) names. Proof rules that open cases and introduce names in deductive reasoning, are *the same as* inferential rules that open questions in interrogative reasoning. Taking $P = T$ and c to be a statement expressing some q_i in Q, answers in A_s eliminate cases, and dispense from introducing arbitrary individuals. Given the Deduction Theorem, this means that, when q_i can be interrogatively established given T and A_s, the shortest *interrogative* derivation is identical with the shortest *deductive* derivation of a statement expressing q_i from T and a finite subset A'_s of A_s. More informally: the best selection of questions, which depends on the best strategy for obtaining presuppositions in T, mirrors the best strategy to select premises from $T \cup A_s$. Therefore, anticipations about deductions from a strengthened theory T can guide the selection of questions whose answers could actually strengthen T. In a slogan: *deductive skills carry over to interrogative skills.*

As long as some conclusion c and some set of premises P are formulated in a first-order language $\mathcal{L}$, there is always a finite proof that c follows deductively from P; when it does. However, first-order consequence is not fully decidable: there may not be a finite proof that c does *not* follow from P, when it does not. Subsequently, the Strategy Theorem entails that there cannot be any general mechanical (algorithmic) method for solving interrogative problems by: (1) trying first to deduce some a statement that expresses some $q_i \in Q$ from T; (2) use questions to strengthen T with A_s if step (1) is not successful; and: (3) if step (2) is also unsuccessful, reiterate (1) and, if necessary, (2) with some potential answer $q_j \neq q_i$ in Q. However, it *does* entail that having some idea about *which cases compatible with T would have to be ruled out* to deduce a statement that expresses some $q_i \in Q$ from a strengthened version of T, gives a good idea of *which question one should ask* to establish interrogatively q_i from T (if answers were obtained).

[7] This understanding eschews the issue of possible mismatch between A_s and Inquirer's range of attention. In the left-to-right direction, every *whether*-question about A or B, or *wh*-question about $\phi(\cdot)$, that receives (say) answer A or $\phi(a)$ suffices for the *yes-no* questions about A or $\phi(a)$ to enter Inquirer's range of attention for the purpose of reconstructing an argument. The antecedent of the right-to-left direction holds when the *yes-no* questions are already in the range of attention (the consequent is satisfied trivially).

4.2 *Abduction and* Yes-No *Questions*

Hintikka has suggested that the Strategy Theorem offers important insights about *abduction* (Hintikka 1988, 2007, ch. 2), esp. in contrast with inference to the best explanation (IBE). The latter occurs when Inquirer accepts (defeasibly) one of the answers, without having established it interrogatively. Such a reasoning can be rationalized, e.g. by assuming a probability distribution over the refined partition; and an acceptance rule that fires if probabilities are raised (conditional on past answers) over a fixed threshold. Gregory's strategy is an illustration of IBE so construed, where the acceptance rule 'fires' because the answers are independent, and the probability of a coincidence is low. If the probabilistic constraints are precise enough, the outcome of IBE can be uniquely determined, but involves (probabilistic) justification, and is definitely non-PD.

By contrast *abduction*, as Hintikka's understands it, routinely occurs in PD contexts (or contexts that Inquirer still assumes to be PD). Abduction occurs when Inquirer anticipates a (possible) deductive derivation from some strengthened version of T, and attempts to steer the course of the investigation towards obtaining the answers that strengthen T in the desired fashion. Abduction thus depends on the 'deductive insight' that answers to some instrumental questions will strengthen T enough to reduce the admissible states to those in which some $q_i \in Q$ holds.

Unfortunately, abduction involving *yes-no* questions cannot always be fully rationalized. In particular, *yes-no* questions that do not 'break down' questions whose presuppositions are inferred from T and previous answers, involve what looks like 'intuitive leaps'. The difficulty also affects probabilistic IBE: a relevant partition of cases, over which probabilities are distributed, depends on T, but on occasion must be imposed by 'abductive' *yes-no* questions (Genot and Jacot 2012). With respect to our reconstruction of Gregory's reasoning, asking about the dog would be as 'abductive' for the purpose IBE, as it is for reasoning deductively. Furthermore, introducing *yes-no* questions is, as we said, the only way to reveal inconsistencies, and can now be seen to be 'abductive' as well.

Let us illustrate that last point with the example of Holmes and Gregory. Either one accepts that Simpson is guilty, as Gregory does, or one does not, as Holmes does. Acceptance of an answer by a given inquirer i, given a set T_i of background assumptions for that inquirer, eliminates all the scenarios in $\mathbf{S}(T_i)$ that are incompatible with that answer. If T_{Gregory} includes only scenarios where the watchdog is well-trained, then the answer to Holmes' question about the dog rules out all the scenarios in which Simpson is guilty. Gregory could in principle bracket the assumption that the dog is well-trained, maintain acceptance of Simpson's guilt, and reshuffle probabilities. The same holds *mutatis mutandis* about T_{Holmes}, although Holmes has not accepted Gregory's guilt in the first place, and disregards (non-extreme) probabilities.

Whether one reasons deductively or probabilistically, *raising* a *yes-no* question about the dog depends on the insights into whatever effect the possible answers to that questions would have—which scenario they would eliminate, or how they would affect the probabilities of certain events. We said earlier that Holmes' question could be viewed as an implicit suggestion that Gregory should revise his current assumptions, and we can now be more precise: pointing out that the dog did not bark implicitly questions the grounds for the step at which Gregory 'jumped' from a high probability of Simpson's guilt, to full acceptance. It shows that Simpson's guilt may not be the best explanation of what has happened, after all. Holmes' actually suggests to Gregory another, different reasoning line, by (subtly) manipulating Gregory's range of attention.

Hintikka has explicitly reconstructed Holmes' reasoning in *The Case of Silver Blaze* as an answer to a *why*-question (Hintikka 2007, ch.7, §2). As we mentioned in Sect. 2.1, answering a *why*-question compacts a line of inquiry. In that case, the statement that "a dog was kept in the stables, and yet [...] had not barked enough to arouse the two lads in the loft" answers the question: *Why is the thief the dog's master?* Hintikka shows that the above statement can be extracted from the proof that the thief is the watchdog's master—the only person that "the dog knew well" that could have visited the stables. In Hintikka's reconstruction, this statement is an *interpolation formula*, i.e. a formula that follows from the premises, entails the conclusion, and comprises only vocabulary common to them. Hintikka's reconstruction furthermore uses an extremely parsimonious first-order language, with two properties, one relation, and two names. Let us consider an informal equivalent of this reconstruction. The information (*a*) that no dog barked at the thief and (*b*) that there was a watchdog, provide *ad explanandum* conditions, alongside the general truth that watchdogs bark at strangers, but not at their masters. Once the stable-boys are ruled out—one had been drugged, and the other two where asleep in the loft—the only individual fitting the description 'master to any watchdog kept in the stables' is Silver Blaze's trainer. Once Holmes has reached this conclusion, the principal question also changes. Learning about the dog incident makes Holmes 'bracket' his own expectations that the thief is an assassin (cf. footnote 4).

The crux of Holmes' interrogative reasoning is how he picks premises (*a*) and (*b*). Since (*a*) is vacuously true (and uninformative) if no dog is indeed kept in the stables, one needs (*b*) to draw a useful conclusion. Holmes explains that the incident with the dog barking at Simpson in the evening implied (*b*), and that then learning (*a*) implied, together with the general truth that watchdogs bark at strangers, that the thief was not a stranger. And while the Strategy Theorem allows to reconstruct Holmes' line of reasoning, it does so vacuously, because it depends on a *yes-no* question that enters Holmes' range of attention (but not in Gregory's) without being inferred from his background information. Actually Holmes' picking premise (*a*) and anticipating its effect also depends on anticipating the answer to that question. Although (*a*) is part of the common ground that Holmes, Gregory and Watson share, its usefulness (as constraint on the information partition) is only revealed after (*b*) is learned. The same goes for the 'general truth' that watchdogs abstain from barking at their masters alone.

5 Abduction and Collaborative Learning

5.1 The CSILE Study and Its Conclusions

The study reported by Hakkarainen and Sintonen (hereafter HS) in (HS 2002) followed elementary school pupils, who had to complete science projects presented as broad questions. Examples of such questions given by HS are: "how to explain gravity?", "how did the universe begin, and how will it evolve?" and "how do cells and the circulatory system in the human body work?". In order to foster collaboration, but also to gather process data, the pupils where tutored in the use of the CSILE software environment, that lets users register notes in a database, with either informative or interrogative content. Once registered, a note is accessible to all other users, even if it is addressed by one user to another specifically. Informative content is revisable, and constitutes a knowledge base for the group. Interrogative content is registered in notes labeled either as "Problem" or "I Need To Understand" (HS 2002, p. 32).

How-questions are similar to *why*-questions, and presuppose that what has to be explained is indeed the case. But children had first to make sense of the presuppositions of the *how*-questions submitted to them. Specifically, they had to recover definitions for terms such as "gravity" and "cells", identify what the definite description "the circulatory system" refers to, theories articulating those definitions, as well as a theory entailing that the universe has an evolution. Since the CSILE knowledge base was initially empty, the pupils' first entries were of interrogative content, aimed at breaking down the presuppositions of the broad *how*-questions into manageable 'small' questions, without a definite idea of the meaning of those presuppositions. And according to HS, one distinctive advantage of the IMI over other epistemological models, is its ability to capture the dynamics engendered by such circumstances:

> [In] actual problem-solving situations, an agent has to start generating questions and theories before all necessary information is available. In the interrogative process, initially very general, unspecified and "fuzzy" questions are transformed to a series of more specific questions. As a consequence, the process of inquiry often has to start with a 'theory to work with' that is transformed into a more sophisticated one as the process goes on. [...] The dynamic nature of inquiry is, further, based on the fact that new questions emerge in the process of inquiry that could not be anticipated when the principal question was first raised. (Hakkarainen and Sintonen 2002, p. 39)

The methodology of HS's study tracks the co-evolution of theories and questioning strategies, from the data collected within the CSILE environment. First, children's questions, entered in the "Problem" and "I Need To Understand" categories of the CSILE database, were classified as *principal* and *instrumental*. Principal questions included the initial questions of the science project, and questions that triggered subordinated lines of inquiry. Second, the evolution of the knowledge produced, i.e. the proposed answers to the initial questions—entered through notes category in the CSILE database—was correlated to the formulation of questions (both principal and instrumental). Third, a "*deepening of explanation* scale" was defined, which assigned scores to students based on whether "in-depth advancement in a student's search for explanatory scientific information" (HS 2002, p. 33) was observed. Finally, the scores were validated by appeal to experts, namely "three internationally regarded philosophers of science from well-known Canadian and Finnish universities" (HS 2002, p. 34). The aim of this evaluation was to determine whether children had moved from "initial intuitive theories [to] a new conceptual understanding" (HS 2002, p. 38) mirroring the scientific theories describing the phenomena they had to explain. Individual reasoning strategies were not explicitly studied, but the CSILE environment allowed to track how children monitored each others' questions. HS express the general conclusion of their study as follows:

> The study indicated that CSILE students participated in extended processes of question-driven inquiry and systematically generated their own intuitive theories. The epistemic value of CSILE students' knowledge-seeking inquiry seems partially to be based on a process in which social communication pushed a student to pursue question-driven inquiry further than he or she might originally have been able to go. [CSILE] appeared to foster engagement in higher-level practices of inquiry [and] epistemological awareness concerning the process of inquiry. (HS 2002, pp. 38–39)

Based on these conclusions, HS take the IMI to be empirically validated, as descriptively adequate. Furthermore, they express the view that the IMI should be considered a methodological basis by educators who often insist on the importance of encouraging questioning, and mined for suggestions on how to develop pedagogical models and didactic tools:

> It appears to us that what is new about the interrogative approach is to emphasize question-transformation as the very foundation of scientific inquiry. [...][W]e do not have well-developed culture of question asking at school and it is very difficult to get students to follow the questions that emerge through their process of inquiry. In this regard, pedagogical models and computer tools elaborated by relying on the interrogative approach appear to be very valuable. (HS 2002, p. 41)

HS do not give further suggestions as to what kind of features those tools should include, that could facilitate question-transformation, and the evolution of theory-formation. This lack of specific suggestion is actually not surprising, for the IMI cannot actually back any general recommendation.

5.2 *Range of Attention and Serendipity*

The conclusions that HS draw with respect to inquiry learning in general, actually generalize the experts' opinion about the outcome of the CSILE study. HS summarize the outcome of the expert evaluation as follows:

> According to the experts' overall evaluation, CSILE students' research questions were at a high level of sophistication, and, if successfully answered, were likely to produce new conceptual understanding. Moreover, two out of the three experts noticed the student-generated research questions formed a pattern, which allowed the students to answer their

> main research questions by generating a series of more specific questions. Although the third expert agreed with the other experts that many of the CSILE students research questions were valuable, he criticized some of the questions as being based on wrong presuppositions. (HS 2002, p. 39)

Our analysis of the case of Silver Blaze should make conspicuous that criticism of questions based on "wrong presuppositions" can be mitigated by adopting a means-end analysis of the process of discovery and problem-solving. Indeed, we have seen that Holmes' instrumental questions, in the case of Silver Blaze, were based on the wrong presupposition that some unique individual was both a thief and a murderer. But they nonetheless lead to a reformulation of the principal question and a revision of the initial assumptions. And once the problem redefined, answers to these questions crucially contributed to solve it. Similarly, the "pattern" that allowed children to answer the main research questions crucially included re-formulations of questions, that promoted better understanding. Interestingly, HS insist on the fact that such reformulations often occurred in the CSILE study under the influence of others:

> Many comments by others were apparently intended to show that a student did not genuinely focus on his or her principal research question but wandered unproductively around peripheral areas of the topic. Through social interaction pointing out inadequate presuppositions, these students were guided to focus on more productive research questions, for example: "I think that you should describe and tell more in your theory about how the UNIVERSE will change in the future, and less about how the people will change in the future and how they will know more about the universe in the future because that is not really the question you are researching" (HS 2002, pp. 38–39)

HS view such circumstances as an aspect that the IMI is conceptually better equipped to capture than other models. They are right, insofar as the above example, and similar observed cases, introduce explicit suggestions to alter the course of inquiry by formulating different instrumental questions. The effect of such interventions is similar to the intended effect of Holmes' mention of "the curious incident…" of which we have indeed shown that the IMI captures the strategic import. However, the descriptive adequacy of the IMI does not warrant the methodological conclusion that "pedagogical models and computer tools elaborated by relying on the interrogative approach appear to be very valuable". More accurately, the conclusion is unwarranted if "valuable" insights pertain to the ability of a group of inquirers to auto-regulate the course of inquiry. Let us see why.

The trigger of Holmes' line of reasoning can be characterized descriptively as an instance of *serendipity*, defined as "observing an unanticipated, anomalous, and strategic datum which becomes the occasion for developing a new or extending an existing theory" (Barber and Merton 2004, p. 260). The concept of serendipity has been introduced in the sociology of science in order to overcome the descriptive limitations of epistemological models which leave out discovery. Interestingly, the IMI is able to characterize *loci* of serendipity, and even to further qualify inferentially their "strategic" nature, which is generally taken to be self-evident, and is left largely unexplained, in sociological discussions. In our example, Gregory is not aware of the 'datum' that the dog did not bark, while Holmes is. However, there does not seem to be any discernible reason explaining why Holmes becomes aware of that datum by himself, or explaining why Gregory needs Holmes. Holmes suggests at one point that the issue might be Gregory's lack of imagination,[8] which can hardly be fixed by some systematic method. Holmes' own reasoning strategy can be vindicated on purely deductive grounds, and his 'abducted' deduction can be analyzed with the formal model of the IMI. But the model also supports the view that Holmes' discovery is not the outcome of some systematic method. Introducing *yes-no* questions is indeed informed by one's deductive skills, yet these skills cannot be mechanized in general.

The latter has some important consequences for the conclusions drawn by HS. The general case under which fall the problems they studied is the case of a problem $\langle T, Q\rangle$ where T is empty, Q receives a formulation in a language whose interpretation is not yet fixed for the Inquirer, and A_s is such that Q may actually be solved—i.e. one of the answers to Q is derivable from some subset A'_s of A_s. Because T is empty, the only presuppositions that can be derived from it are presuppositions of *yes-no* questions. $\langle T, Q\rangle$ will be solved when some subset A'_s of A_s is obtained, such that one of the answers to Q can be derived from that subset together with T *and* that answer is actually derived. In such cases, how T is strengthened depends exclusively on the range of attention of the Inquirer, which is in turn determined by the associations that the Inquirer will make on the basis of the linguistic formulations of Q—in Holmes' words, the Inquirer's imagination.

In a multi-agent setting, the interaction between inquirers induces a dynamics in the inquirers' ranges of attention that is absent from the single-agent case. And indeed this is why the likes of Gregory and Lestrade are willing to consult Sherlock Holmes, as his presence more often than not results in corrections in the course of inquiries in which they stall. However, transitioning from single-agent inquiry to multi-agent inquiry incurs no guarantee that pooling the ranges of attention of all the inquirers will result in an auto-regulated 'collective' range of attention sufficient to recover the set A'_s from which one then could derive an answer to Q in a solvable problem $\langle T, Q\rangle$ with empty T. To put it differently, increasing the number of inquirers does not mechanically increase the odds that serendipitous *yes-no* questions will enter the range of attention of inquiry learners reasoning from initially insufficiently specified theories. The IMI offers no formal vindication of the pre-theoretic intuition that collaborative inquiry improves upon solitary inquiry for the purpose of raising appropriate questions.

[8] Inspector Gregory, to whom the case has been committed, is an extremely competent officer. Were he but gifted with imagination he might rise to great heights in his profession. On his arrival he promptly found and arrested the man upon whom suspicion naturally rested. (Conan Doyle 1986, p. 527)

6 Conclusion

The formal results of the IMI can certainly help to understand *post hoc* the children's inferences in the CSILE study, but the Strategy Theorem cannot rationalize (in general) the occurrence of *yes-no* questions that one needs to complete an initially empty background knowledge. The methodological import of the IMI is not noticeably better that the methodological import of less dynamic epistemological models. The IMI certainly supports the conclusion that "science educators [should] focus more on engaging students in sustained processes of question-driven inquiry than just examining contents of their current beliefs so as to facilitate their conceptual advancement" (HS 2002, p. 41). However, it offers little guidance regarding the design of collaborative-learning environments that would promote and nurture the development of successful interrogative learning strategies and successful interrogative problem-solving strategies.

The IMI does however warrant the following conclusion: a guaranty that an inquiry learner will be able to solve interrogatively a problem can always be obtained by manipulating the learner's range of attention. But manipulation of the learners' range of attention is tantamount to the transmission of strategic knowledge. A paradigmatic example of this manipulation, is how Socrates teaches Meno's slave all the geometry the illiterate boy needs to demonstrate that the diagonal of the square is incommensurable to its side (Hintikka 2007, ch.4, §8). Socrates uses only *yes-no* questions when doing so, and nonetheless manages to convey the required knowledge in geometry. Each time the slave is probing the consequences of an erroneous guess, he could well be said to be progressing in the demonstration. But his progress can only converge to the correct solution if monitored by Socrates. Socrates' own range of attention builds upon deductive skills, namely his ability to find the best derivation of the solution to the problem at hand. The transmission of Socrates' strategic knowledge suffices for the slave to complete the demonstration, because the derivation is constructive, and Socrates transmits the skills required to perform the construction.

Thus, the IMI makes conspicuous the conundrum that the inquiry learning methodology has faced since Socrates. One the one hand, increased guidance—transmission of strategic knowledge—can help learners reach solutions, but incurs the risk that they will wait for tutors to formulate questions. On the other hand, lack of guidance favors autonomy, but incurs the risk of unproductive research, that proceeds from poorly grounded questions. *Pace* Hakkarainen and Sintonen, the conceptual apparatus of the IMI cannot warrant more substantial methodological conclusions. However, perhaps more surprisingly, the IMI can offer some insights as to why one cannot in general leverage epistemological models to obtain general pedagogical and didactic principles applicable to inquiry learning. These insights are made possible by a deeper conceptual understanding into the nature and strategic role of serendipity. Indeed, it follows from the Strategy Theorem and the Deduction Theorem that, short of pre-existing knowledge, interrogative problem-solving requires not only deductive skills, but also ingenuity and good luck.

References

Barber, E., & Merton, R. K. (2004). *The travels and adventures of serendipity*. Princeton: Princeton University Press.

Conan Doyle, A. (1986). *Sherlock Holmes: The complete novel and stories* (Vol. 1). New York: Bantam Books.

Genot, E. J. (2009). The game of inquiry. The interrogative approach to inquiry and belief revision theory. *Synthese, 171*, 271–289.

Genot, E. J., & Jacot, J. (2012). How can yes-or-no questions be informative before they are answered? *Episteme, 9*(2), 189–204.

Hakkarainen, K., & Sintonen, M. (2002). The interrogative model of inquiry and computer-supported collaborative learning. *Science & Education, 11*(1), 25–43.

Hintikka, J. (1986). Reasoning about knowledge in philosophy: The paradigm of epistemic logic. In *TARK '86: Proceedings of the 1986 conference on theoretical aspects of reasoning about knowledge* (pp. 63–80). Monterey: Morgan Kaufmann.

Hintikka, J. (1987). The interrogative approach to inquiry and probabilistic inference. *Erkenntnis, 26*(3), 429–442.

Hintikka, J. (1988). What is abduction? The fundamental problem of contemporary epistemology. *Transactions of the Charles S. Peirce Society, 34*, 503–533.

Hintikka, J. (1992). The concept of induction in the light of the interrogative approach to inquiry. In J. Earman (Ed.), *Inference, explanation, and other philosophical frustrations* (pp. 23–43). Berkeley: University of California Press.

Hintikka, J. (2007). *Socratic epistemology*. Cambridge: Cambridge University Press.

Hintikka, J., & Halonen, I. (1997). Semantics and pragmatics for why-questions. *The Journal of Philosophy, 92*, 636–657.

Hintikka, J., Halonen, I., & Mutanen, A. (2002). Interrogative logic as a general theory of reasoning. In D. M. Gabbay, R. H. Johnson, H. J. Ohlbach, & J. Woods (Eds.), *Handbook of the logic of argument and inference* (Vol. 1, pp. 295–337). Amsterdam: Elsevier.

Kelly, K. T. (2004). Uncomputability: The problem of induction internalized. *Theoretical Computer Science, 317*(1–3), 227–249.

Martin, E., & Osherson, D. (1998). *Elements of scientific inquiry*. Cambridge: MIT.

Inquiry and Deliberation in Judicial Systems: The Problem of Jury Size

Staffan Angere, Erik J. Olsson, and Emmanuel J. Genot

Abstract We raise the question whether there is a rigorous argument favoring one jury system over another. We provide a Bayesian model of deliberating juries that allows for computer simulation for the purpose of studying the effect of jury size and required majority on the quality of jury decision making. We introduce the idea of jury value (J-value), a kind of epistemic value which takes into account the unique characteristics and asymmetries involved in jury voting. Our computer simulations indicate that requiring more than a >50 % majority should be avoided. Moreover, while it is in principle always better to have a larger jury, given a >50 % required majority, the value of having more than 12–15 jurors is likely to be negligible. Finally, we provide a formula for calculating the optimal jury size given the cost, economic or otherwise, of adding another juror.

Keywords Jury size • Bayesian model • Computer simulation • Deliberation • Voting

1 Introduction

The size of deliberating juries in court varies somewhat for different countries. In the English speaking world, the number is usually 12, except in Scotland which has a 15-juror system. Yet there is a growing debate regarding the possibility of downsizing juries. A bigger jury is more expensive and difficult to administer than a smaller one, and, at least in smaller countries, a big jury can be difficult to assemble given the constraint that the same juror should not serve in consecutive trials. The pressure to downsize has led to some court cases where it has been ruled that smaller juries are admissible. Thus in the case *Williams v. Florida* (399, U.S. 78, 1970), the US Supreme Court ruled that the relevant part of the constitution, the

S. Angere (✉) • E.J. Olsson
Department of Philosophy, University of Lund, Lund, Sweden
e-mail: staffan.angere@fil.lu.se; erik_j.olsson@fil.lu.se

E.J. Genot
Philosophy, Lund University–LUX, Box 192, 221 00, Lund, Sweden
e-mail: emmanuel.genot@fil.lu.se

C. Başkent (ed.), *Perspectives on Interrogative Models of Inquiry*, Logic, Argumentation & Reasoning 8, DOI 10.1007/978-3-319-20762-9_3

Sixth Amendment, does not require juries to be composed of any specific number of jurors. In particular, six jurors should be allowed because "the essential feature of a jury obviously lies in the interposition between the accused and his accuser of the common sense judgment of a group of laymen" and, furthermore, "[t]he performance of this role is not a function of the particular number of the body that makes up the jury". The court added: "And, certainly the reliability of the jury as a factfinder hardly seems likely to be a function of its size."[1]

This ruling, which overturned the earlier Supreme Court decision *Thompson v. Utah* (170, U.S. 343, 349, 1898) to the effect that the jury guaranteed by the Sixth Amendment consists "of twelve persons, neither more nor less", stands in stark contrast to a recent evaluation of the Scottish 15 jury system which found that system to be, in the words of Cabinet Secretary for Justice Kenny MacAskill, "uniquely right" (Forsyth and Macdonnell 2009). In the consultation process, some advantages of 15-person juries were noted as being that people still have confidence in the system, larger juries lead to fairer verdicts, they are less likely to be influenced by prejudice, they allow for majority verdicts and are composed of a greater cross section of the public. Against this were arguments that 15-person juries often lead to unwieldy discussions and that the juror pool is being stretched by the requirement of having so many jurors for each trial (Forsyth and Macdonnell 2009).

Given what seems to be a deep disagreement on the relationship between jury size and jury competence, it would be desirable to find a rigorous argument for either position, one than both parties to the debate were rationally obliged to accept. Obviously, we want jury deliberation to be as reliable a process as possible: we want someone to be convicted just in case he or she in fact did it. These considerations suggest the use of the famous Condorcet jury theorem, stating, among other things, that a larger voting body gives rise to a more reliable majority vote. It would seem, in the light of this mathematical result, that a deliberating body should be as large as possible, time and money permitting.

Unfortunately, the application of the Condorcet theorem to deliberating bodies is highly problematic. Condorcet's assumptions include that of independence of voting, which tends to be violated by deliberating bodies: in the process of deliberation, jurors will become increasingly influenced by each others' views. Furthermore, the theorem, in its standard formulation, requires everyone's likelihood of individually coming to the right answer to be above 50 %. While one may, optimistically, hold that individual jurors tend, on average, to be right more often than not, it is not clear how the presence of the occasional statistical outliers affects the result. It is obviously not enough that a majority of the jurors have a chance of more than 50 % to be right, since this is compatible with almost 75 % of the votes finally cast to be wrong.[2]

In an effort to overcome some of these limitations this paper proposes a different model, called Laputa, which allows for a process of group deliberation and inquiry. The model does not assume that jurors cast their final votes independently but

[1] *Williams v. Florida*, reprinted as pp. 3–70 in Jacobstein and Mersky (1998).

[2] See List and Goodin (2001) for generalized versions of the Condorcet theorem. See also Goodin (2003) for an extended discussion.

only that jurors, where they contribute to the deliberation process, do so based on their own evidence rather than based on the evidence they received from others in the group.[3] Laputa is fundamentally Bayesian and decision-theoretic in nature. Naturally, the jury process has been investigated from similar perspectives before, beginning with Kaplan (1968). However, these studies, as far as we can tell, have not taken into account the deliberation process and its possible effect on the voting outcome which is not surprising given the mathematical complexity any such study would have to grapple with. In the present article, the computational problem is solved by focusing on the method of computer simulation rather than on that of analytical proof. In our understanding of juror inquiry, we settle for a model which in certain respects generalizes Jakko Hintikka's well-known interrogative model of inquiry. We will offer some remarks about the relations between Hintikka's model and our modeling assumptions, and give further details in the discussion section.

2 A Probabilistic Model of Jury Deliberation

There are several features that set juries apart from many other deliberative bodies and that will play a role in motivating our model:

1. *Random selection of jurors*. While the exact process whereby the jurors are selected varies widely, the usual case is that they are selected randomly from a precompiled list of eligible jurors. There may be various screening processes designed to exclude jurors that whose impartiality could be questioned. Also, it is considered desirable that the jurors come from varied backgrounds and provide a representative sample of the population. For example, a jury consisting of only Wall Street bankers, or only Mexicans, or only women, would be considered inappropriate.
2. *Layman jurors*. The jurors are supposed to be laymen and not experts.
3. *Binary question*. The jury's task is to deliberate on the question whether the accused is guilty or not. There is, in general, no third alternative.[4]
4. *Restricted evidence*. There are some restrictions on the evidence that the jury can appeal to in the process of deliberation. The jury is supposed to be present in court to hear all the evidence presented there. This evidence includes not only the written or spoken material presented but also the observed reactions of the

[3]For more details on Laputa and its interpretation, see Olsson (2011, 2013). See also Olsson and Vallinder (2013) and Vallinder and Olsson (2013a,b).

[4]In the Scottish legal system, a jury can also give the verdict "not proven". As some commentators (e.g. Luckhurst 2005) have noted, including this verdict alongside the not guilty verdict has no legal consequence: in both cases the accused goes free and cannot be tried again for the same offence. Instead it is common to argue that the value of the not proven verdict is not legal but social: it allows the jury, for better or worse, to acquit the defendant while leaving a stain on his or her character. Alternatively, it can be used to "expose a poor investigation and highlight the failings of an incompetent prosecutor" (Luckhurst 2005). Since the "not proven" verdict has no legal consequence we have decided not to take it into account in this study of legal decision making.

accused, the witnesses, and so on. Juries are often instructed to avoid learning about the case from any source other than the trial (such as from media accounts) and to refrain from conducting their own investigations (such as independently visiting a crime scene). Parties, lawyers, and witnesses are not allowed to speak with jury members. Jurors are, however, allowed to appeal to their own general life experience in the process of deliberation.

5. *Public announcements within the jury*. Finally, while in the deliberation room, any contribution to the discussion made by some juror is available to all the other jurors. It would be unusual, and probably inappropriate, for some jurors to discuss matters "in private" without the knowledge of the other jurors.

As we propose to model jury deliberation, at every point in time a juror may, with varying degrees of competence, conduct inquiry, communicate with the other jurors, or both. Conducting inquiry here means consulting memory or notes about what happened at the trial or about other relevant things, such as the juror's own life experience. It does not include conducting investigations outside the court. Inquiry results in a reason for or against the guilt of the accused. As we conceive of reasons, they need not be interpreted as conclusive. If a juror has conducted inquiry, he or she may announce the result to the other jurors in the form of a pro or con reason (vis-à-vis guilt). These other jurors will react to the information by updating their cognitive states. This process will continue until time is up, at which point the jurors cast their individual votes.[5]

In the light of this initial characterization of the jury deliberation process we need to represent the following in the language of probability theory: (a) a juror's reliability, (b) a juror's cognitive state, and (c) how a juror's cognitive state is updated as the effect of receiving a pro/con reason. Let us start with jurors' reliability. A juror can be more or less reliable in retrieving information from memory or notes. A juror's reliability in this regard can be modeled as the (objective) probability that any result of inquiry is true. At the outset, we allow for different jurors to have different levels of competence—from being wrong all of the time, to being right all of the time, and everything in-between.

We assume that a juror's cognitive state consists of three things: an assessment of the accused's guilt/innocence, a self-assessment, and an assessment of others. The assessment of guilt or innocence is represented as a subjective probability ("credence") in the proposition that the accused is guilty, i.e. a number between 0 and 1. A number close to 1 means that the juror thinks the accused is probably guilty. A number close to 0 means that the juror thinks the accused is probably innocent. The self-assessment records how reliable (trustworthy) the juror considers his or her own inquiry to be. Here we generalize a common assumption of Hintikka's

[5]In some jury systems, such as the American, the condition specifying when the deliberation has come to an end does not refer to time but to some other feature of the situation, such as the jurors having reached a unanimous verdict. We have decided to leave the study of such jury systems for another paper. Having said this, the simulation results we present below count indirectly against the American system, and it seems unlikely, in light of these results, that the latter should be a serious competitor to e.g. the Scottish jury system as regards the quality of collective decision making.

interrogative model of inquiry by allowing an inquirer to be less than fully confident in the results or her inquiry (see Sect. 6 for a detailed discussion). The assessments of others record, for each other juror, how reliable (trustworthy) the juror in question considers those other jurors to be.

While it is easy to represent the assessment of the accused's guilt or innocent in probabilistic terms, it is less clear how to model probabilistically a juror's self-assessment or assessment of others. Our main idea is that a juror's trust in a source (own inquiry or other jurors) can be represented as a *credence in the reliability of the source*. Thus, a juror's self-assessment can be thought of as the juror's credence in the proposition that she is a reliable inquirer. We assume that a juror's trust in a source to be represented as a *trust function*, i.e. an assignment of a credence to every possible degree of reliability. For instance, a juror may assign a credence of 0.7 to the hypothesis that the source is telling the truth 90 % of the time. Trust functions offer a probabilistic representation of a critical aspect of Hintikka's interrogative model, namely that reasoning from any evidence whatsoever always takes into account the evidence (cf. Sect. 6).

Let us now turn to the question of how juror's cognitive states should be updated. A juror reacts to reasons emanating from inquiry or other jurors by only taking into account (a) whether the reason is a pro or con reason (vis-à-vis guilt), (b) her own (prior) credence in the guilt of the accused, and (c) her (prior) trust in the source. Internal details of reasons or arguments are abstracted from. This is an idealization yet one without which the model would probably become utterly, and unworkably, complex. Here, our model departs slightly from Hintikka's own, which usually emphasizes the fine structure of reasons in insisting on strategic aspects of reasoning. But this apparent departure actually allows us to generalize Hintikka's model, as will be explained in Sect. 6. Independent support for making this idealization can be found in the Persuasive Argument Theory (PAT) tradition in social psychology, as explained in Olsson (2013).[6] Moreover, it receives some support from the fact that jurors are supposed to be laymen and not experts: experts are more likely to care about the fine structure of reasons than are laymen. Above all, this way of construing the updating of cognitive states in response to reasons is supported by our statistical approach to the jury problem, as soon to be explained.

The single source case. Let g be the proposition that the accused is guilty. Suppose that a juror receives a pro reason from a source α. We can then compute the posterior credence in g (i.e. the credence in g after receiving information from some source) as well as the reliability of the source:

$$C_{t+1}(g) = C_t(g \mid \alpha \text{ gives a pro/con reason })$$

$$C_{t+1}(\alpha \text{ is reliable to degree } r) =$$
$$C_t(\alpha \text{ is reliable to degree } r \mid \alpha \text{ gives a pro/con reason})$$

[6]For more on the PAT tradition see Isenberg (1986).

The many sources case. Suppose that a juror receives information from many sources $\alpha_1, \ldots, \alpha_n$ at the same time. How can we calculate the following probabilities?

$$C_{t+1}(g) = C_t(g \mid \alpha_i \text{ gives a pro/con reason }, \ldots, \alpha_n \text{ gives a pro/con reason })$$

$$C_{t+1}(\alpha_i \text{ is reliable to degree } r) = C_t(\alpha_i \text{ is reliable to degree } r \mid \alpha_1 \text{ gives a pro/con reason }, \ldots, \alpha_n \text{ gives a pro/con reason})$$

We recall that the jurors have been chosen randomly from the population of eligible candidates that are representative of the entire population. In the normal course of events, this selection process should ensure a certain degree of independence of thinking among the jurors, so that the fact that one juror at a given point in the deliberation notes or remembers something from the trial will not by itself make it more likely that another juror will note or remember that same thing. We also recall that jurors give pro/con reasons directly as they find evidence in their own notes or recollections. These two considerations together justify assuming a principle we call *source independence*:

(*SI*) *Each juror assumes that the other jurors are reporting independently, conditional on the truth/falsity of* g.

Using source independence, the result of receiving information from multiple sources is calculable from data about the individual sources, just as in the single-source case (cf. Olsson 2013). The bottom line is that assuming source independence makes the model computationally workable and at the same time it seems reasonably realistic given the way in which jurors are selected and assumed to interact.

Now that we have a probabilistic model of the deliberation process, let us return to our main problem: to evaluate the effect of jury size on the jury's competence.

Clearly we cannot solve this problem by looking at just a few deliberation processes while varying the size of the jury. If we do, we would not know whether the effect of adding more jurors was due to the size or to something else (difference in initial credence, individual competence, and so on). We need a way to study *the effect of size per se*. The solution to this problem is to study a large number of varied deliberation processes for a jury of a particular size and assess the average competence over all these processes. The competence pertaining to the jury size under consideration is the average, or expected, competence over all these particular deliberation processes.

This suggestion raises a worry regarding the practical possibility of performing all these competence calculations by hand. We propose to solve the computational issue by means of computer simulation. Our Laputa model has been implemented in a computer program that bears the same name and which automatically generates juries, allows the members to deliberate, in the idealized sense previously described, and, finally, collects data about the average reliability of the juries of the given size. Laputa can study millions of juries and deliberation processes in this fashion. Such considerations of scale also give an additional justification for treating reasons as "black boxes" without any internal structure because any persuasive effect that derives from the internal structure of reasons will be but a drop in a vast statistical ocean, or so we conjecture.

When Laputa generates a jury and a deliberation process it has to select initial values for various parameters. These parameters are, for each juror:

- prior credence in g, i.e. credence in g after court proceedings but before jury deliberation
- competence, i.e. probability that a result of inquiry is correct
- inquiry activity level
- communication activity level
- trust function for inquiry
- trust functions for other jurors

We configured Laputa to select these values according to a beta distribution with mean $2/3$ and mode $3/4$. This corresponds to the values $\alpha = 4$, $\beta = 2$, and its shape is plotted below.

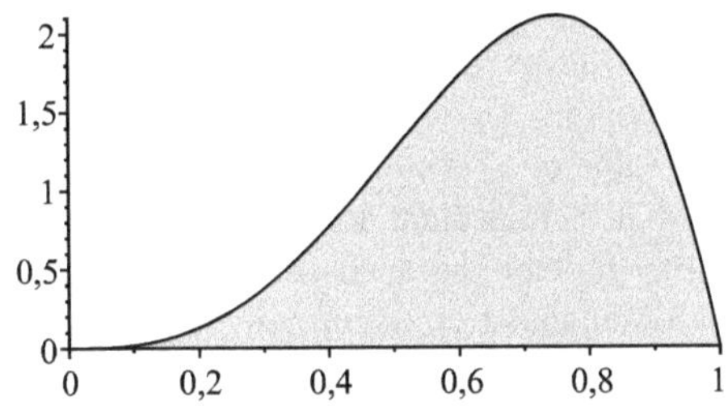

The Beta distribution is congenial to Bayesianism, and has several useful properties:

- Unlike the normal distribution, it is naturally clamped to $[0, 1]$, and so does not need to be truncated. The normal distribution is not, as it is, possible to use to generate numbers in the interval $[0, 1]$, but beta distributions with $\alpha \approx \beta$ are similar to normal distributions.
- It simplifies several calculations, since it interacts well with conditionalization.
- It has a straightforward statistical interpretation: for an inquirer beginning with a uniform distribution on all possible frequencies of a property P in a population, the beta distribution with parameters α, β gives the credence that inquirer should assign each frequency, given that he or she has observed $\alpha - 1$ instances of P and $\beta - 1$ instances of not-P in that population.

For these reasons, we will use the above distribution whenever we want one whose expected value and peak are both between $1/2$ and 1, symbolizing "somewhat better than average." This modeling decision corresponds to the limited degree of optimism embodied in applications of the Condorcet jury theorem, although it does not place any restrictions on the competences of individual jurors, but only on their statistical mean.

3 Epistemic Value in a Jury Situation

We will refer to the kind of epistemic value we aim to study as *Jury value* (J-value, for short). J-value should take into account: (i) the fact that it is the final state and not the difference between the final and initial states that is important, (ii) the fact that it is the majority's opinion that counts, rather than the average opinion, and (iii) the fact that the jury situation is importantly asymmetric, as embodied in Blackstone's principle "better that ten guilty persons escape than that one innocent suffer" (Blackstone 1769).[7]

Since we are dealing with majority voting it is important to settle on what we are to mean by "majority". Different justice systems differ in how large a majority is required for a verdict, from a simple >50 % majority up to unanimity. Requiring unanimity among 20 jurors will result in fewer verdicts than requiring unanimity among, say, three jurors. A justifiable expectation, therefore, is that the value of having a certain number of jurors may depend on the size of the required majority. Hence we will have to take into account different required majority sizes when we measure the expected J-value of a certain jury size.

Another parameter that is important for J-value is the credence required for voting for or against the guilt of the accused. In most legal traditions, a greater confidence is required for a conviction than for an acquittal.

In a survey of American judges, the mean credence associated with the concept "beyond a reasonable doubt" was about 90 % certainty (McCauliff 1982). For this reason we have chosen 0.9 as the credence in the guilt of a suspect required for a given juror to vote accordingly.

In the kind of trial we are dealing with, there are five possible relevant outcomes of a round of deliberations:

- conviction of the guilty (*CG*)
- conviction of the innocent (*CI*)
- acquittal of the guilty (*AG*)
- acquittal of the innocent (*AI*)
- no verdict (*NV*)

In the last case, we assume that the deliberations have to continue for another round. In epistemological terms, this corresponds to *status quo*, an outcome that

[7]This principle has reappeared in many guises both before and after Blackstone, with a varying number of guilty acquittals held to be better than one innocent conviction. Cf. Volokh (1997).

may itself be connected with various costs. We refer to the J-value of outcome X as $J(X)$. Since it is always better to get the right verdict than no result at all, and always better to get no verdict than to get the wrong verdict, we postulate that the conditions

$$J(CG) > J(NV)$$
$$J(AI) > J(NV)$$
$$J(NV) > J(AG)$$
$$J(NV) > J(CI)$$

hold. These inequalities give rise to the following qualitative structure among J-values, where an arrow from outcome O_1 to outcome O_2 signifies that O_2 has a higher value than O_1:

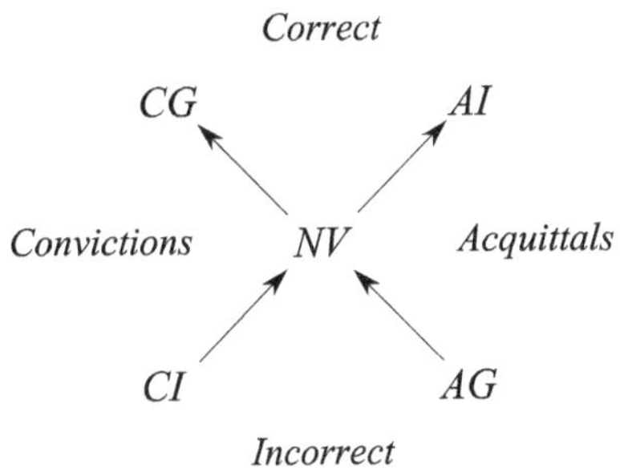

How can we determine the outcome values more specifically? We could, of course, simply assign them conventionally, but we think that a better approach would be to try to ground them in specific features of the jury process. Since J-value is to be interpreted as a kind of *epistemic* value, it is not the practical consequences of the various outcomes that are to be assessed. We can think of the epistemic value of an outcome as the value it would have, from the point of view of an idealized judge, to be told the corresponding verdict. Still, the practical consequences are connected to the epistemic ones: the judge is generally *obliged* to follow the verdict of the jury, so if the judge is given the verdict that the suspect is guilty, the judge has to convict him or her, purely on basis of the epistemic situation.

This means that, from the perspective of the idealized judge, epistemic and practical value coincide. This is fortunate for us since it means that we can identify the J-values using decision theory. In general, utilities are determined only up to an affine transformation, and so it should be possible to assign two of the values arbitrarily. Interestingly, the particulars of the jury situation suggest more structure. The Blackstone ratio says that we should prefer acquitting 10 guilty men to convicting one innocent. What does this mean in terms of utilities? In order for Blackstone's principle to be interpretable at all, we have to assume that these are additive across cases. Thus the combined J-value of two verdicts will have to be the sum of the J-values of the individual verdicts.

Additive quantities have a clearly defined zero, which is the value of a type of situation S such that $J(nS) = J(S)$, where nS is the occurrence of n instances of S. In our case, NV is such a situation: it gives the judge no information at all and two verdicts, both of which are uninformative, contain exactly the same information as one. Therefore, we may set $J(NV) = 0$.

We still have the freedom to choose a scale for J-value arbitrarily. For reasons of mathematical simplicity we settle for $J(CI) = -10$. Using this value, together with the Blackstone ratio, we may draw the conclusion that the value of AG must be such that

$$J(CI) < 10\,J(AG).$$

Since we assumed $J(AG) < J(NV)$, it follows that $J(AG)$ must be between 0 and -1. Given the intuitive disvalue in acquitting the guilty, we set $J(AG)$ to -1. While this is tantamount to judging that convicting the innocent is *exactly* as bad as letting 10 guilty men go, it only constitutes an infinitesimal deviation from the Blackstone principle.

$J(CG)$, the value of a correct conviction, is difficult to assess, and there seems to be little empirical work upon which one could rely for guidance. $J(CG)$ should certainly exceed $J(NV)$, the value of not arriving at a verdict, but how it should relate to $J(AI)$, the value of an innocent acquittal, seems impossible to determine on an a priori basis. Indeed, the literature contains arguments for $J(CG) > J(AI)$ (Tribe 1971) as well as for $J(CG) < J(AI)$ (Milanich 1981), and even for $J(CG) \approx J(AI)$ (Connolly 1987).

Since we have assumed additivity, there is an alternative way in which we characterize $J(CG)$. Let n be the total number of guilty suspects sent through the jury system for which a verdict is reached, and let c and a be the number of convictions and acquittals, respectively. By definition, we have $n = c + a$. The value $J(CG)$ can be calculated as the limit, as $n \to \infty$, of the ratio

$$\lambda = -\frac{c}{a}$$

such that one should be indifferent between (a) adopting the jury system in question and (b) not making any verdicts at all. In short, λ records the number of guilty convictions it takes to undo the disvalue of one guilty acquittal.

One J-value remains to be assessed: $J(AI)$, the value of acquitting the innocent. We have already decided upon a degree of reasonable doubt. As it turns out, this degree in conjunction with the other J-values are sufficient to fix $J(AI)$ as well. To be rational, any juror should vote for conviction whenever the expected utility of doing so is greater than that of acquittal. Letting p be the juror's credence in the suspect's guilt, we should therefore have that

$$p\, J(CG) + (1-p)\, J(CI) \;>\; p\, J(AG) + (1-p)\, J(AI)$$

iff $p > 0.9$. From this we derive that we therefore must have $J(AI) = 9\lambda - 1$.

Collecting our findings, we get the following table of J-values for the various outcomes:

	Suspect	
Verdict	Guilty	Innocent
Conviction	λ	-10
No verdict	0	0
Acquittal	-1	$9\lambda - 1$

Setting λ to 1, we get $J(AI) = 8$, corresponding to an assessment according to which each correct acquittal is as good as 8 correct convictions. For $J(AI) = J(CG)$, we need to set $\lambda = 1/8$. A lower value produces assessments for which a correct conviction is better than a correct acquittal. However, such low values of λ make the value of a correct conviction, as compared to an incorrect acquittal, strangely low, as pointed out in Connolly (1987).

Finally, the asymmetry between guilt and innocence means that the ratio of suspects who are actually guilty to those who are actually innocent will influence the result. Unfortunately, this is a figure which is extremely hard to assess in the present context. Despite its imperfections, the legal process is the best source we have for assessing the ratio in question. However, that source is unavailable in the present context because it is precisely the legal process that is currently under scrutiny. As an approximation, however, we may use the conviction rate, i.e. the percentage of cases brought to a jury which finally lead to conviction rather than acquittal. While this number varies from country to country, and also varies depending on the type of crime in question, it lies around 80 % both in the U.S. and the U.K. (United States Courts 2010; Ministry of Justice 2011) Even if the actual number of guilty defendants deviates from this number, we have no evidence to suggest that such deviation would vary systematically in either direction. Given our limited knowledge, using 80 % as an approximation of the percentage of guilty defendants seems to be at least a reasonable option.

4 Simulations Based on *J*-Value

We instructed the simulation program Laputa to compute, for each jury size, the average expected J-value over 1,000,000 juries of that size, each deliberating for 15 steps ("round table discussions"), with λ set to 1. We refer to such an expected value, for n jurors, as $E[J_n]$. Running the simulation, we get the graph depicted in

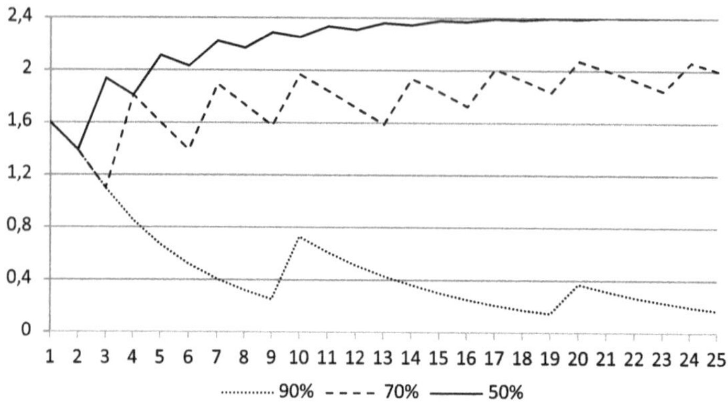

Fig. 1 Expected J-values of different majorities and number of jurors

Fig. 1 (with number of jurors along the x-axis, and the resulting expected J-value, for different majority sizes required, along the y-axis).

The addition of more jurors clearly increases the J-value, at least for >50 % and 70 % required majority. When we require a 90 % majority, the difficulty of getting a conviction means that fewer deliberations will lead to a verdict, and since this has a J-value of 0, the expected J-value will go to 0 as well. For a >50 % required majority, adding more jurors makes the J-value approach 2.4, which is the theoretical maximum for the case where 80 % of the defendants are actually guilty and $\lambda = 1$. For a 70 % required majority, the maximum seems to lie around 2.0. As we see, the advantage of adding more than 15 jurors should, in many cases, be negligible. One curious feature of the data is the "sawtooth" appearance of all curves in Fig. 1. We can explain this effect as follows. A >50 % required majority translates into a bigger majority required for a jury with an even, as opposed to an odd, number of jurors. With a 2-member jury, the only way to achieve >50 % majority is through unanimity, whence there will be fewer verdicts than with just a single juror. For 4 members, it translates into 75 %, while for 5, it requires only 60 %. Hence, there will be fewer verdicts for an even number of jurors. Since the J-value of no verdict is zero this will tend to decrease the expected J-value for cases involving an even number of jurors, thus accounting for the sawtooth appearance of the curve.

To substantiate this hypothesis, the probability of not reaching a verdict can be measured using Laputa. The results are given in Fig. 2.

As expected, higher requirements on majorities give rise to a greater probability of not reaching a verdict. What may not be quite as expected, however, is that this probability decreases as the number of jurors is increased, in sharp contrast to what would be the case if the inquirers voted independently.

Our results so far indicate that no more than a >50 % majority should be required for a conviction, even in criminal cases. We may further strengthen the support for this conclusion by showing that it holds independently of the proportion of

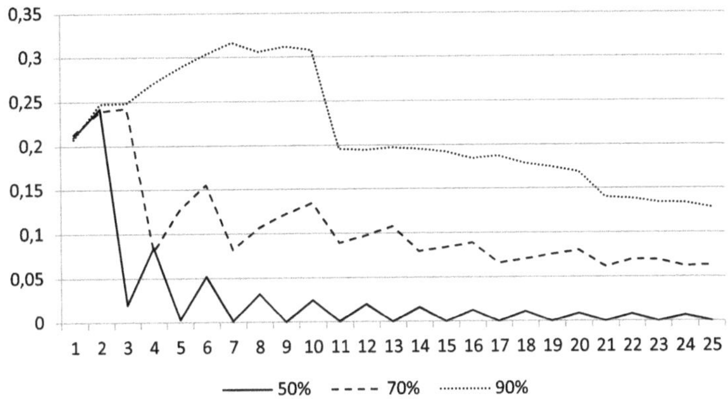

Fig. 2 Probability of *NV* for different majorities and number of jurors

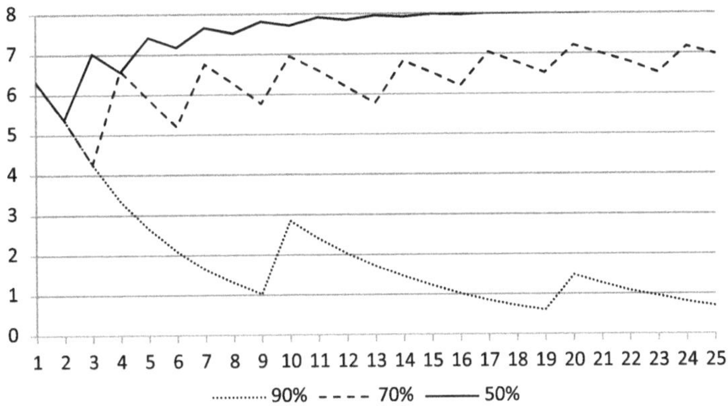

Fig. 3 Expected J-values when defendant is innocent

defendants who are actually guilty in relation to all defendants. In Fig. 3 we have plotted the same data as in Fig. 1 under the assumption that *no* defendants are guilty.

Apart from the maximum J-value being 8 (the value of a correct acquittal) in this case the curves are almost indistinguishable from those in Fig. 1. This adds further support to the validity of our method since, as we noted, the proportion of actually guilty suspects is difficult to approximate in a non-circular manner.

Altering the parameters so that $\lambda = 0.125 = J(AI)$ and rerunning the experiments gives the results presented in Fig. 4.

Here the scale is different and the maximum expected J-value attainable is 0.125 rather than 2.4. Apart from this, the graph is reminiscent of the one preceding it. The main difference lies in the fact that, when $\lambda = 0.125$, a very small number of jurors tends to give negative J-value, whereas a jury with a single juror (or with three jurors, in case we require only >50 % majority) is worse than no jury at all. This is due to the fact that, as λ decreases, correct convictions begin to affect the result more than correct acquittals. Since voting for conviction requires greater certainty

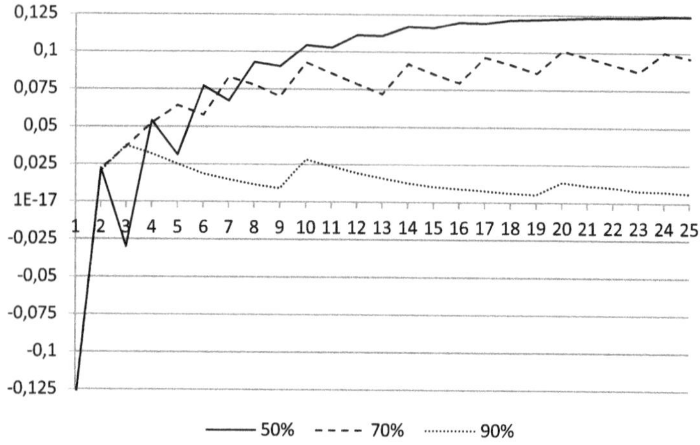

Fig. 4 Expected J-values for $\lambda = J(AI) = 0.125$

than voting for acquittal, there will always be fewer correct convictions than correct acquittals. Making the latter count for less will therefore make it harder to offset the cost of incorrect verdicts.

There are several reasons why adding more jurors is beneficial to jury competence. One of them is that since more jurors means more results of inquiry, and these results get communicated to the whole jury, everyone will be better informed. But there is also the factor that, generally, discussion tends to strengthen everyone's held opinions, and thus push their beliefs farther into certainty territory. Thus, after the deliberation process, more jurors will be willing to vote for guilt, reducing the number of unsuccessful attempts to reach a verdict as well as the number of erroneous acquittals.

The fact that discussion itself tends to strengthen prior opinion is obvious when a juror hears his or her own view echoed by the other jurors. But even hearing a divergent view can strengthen a juror's prior opinion, if he or she is willing to attribute the divergence to a general lack of credibility or even distrust on the part of the juror expressing the contrary opinion. For example, when a juror is convinced that g, hearing that not-g from some other juror may be interpreted by the first juror, via his or her trust function, as evidence to the contrary. This follows from the Bayesian treatment of trust used in Laputa and is, we believe, in accordance with human psychology.

5 Calculating the Optimal Jury Size

Since, at least in the case of a >50 % required majority, the addition of further jurors is conducive to epistemic jury competence, the question of an optimal jury size will have to involve a weighing against other values. While economy is an obvious value that may need to be given due weight, there are further values that concern the judicial process without being epistemological in kind. For instance, it is of interest for the defendant as well as the prosecutor that the trial proceeds as quickly as possible, and a greater number of jurors tends to slow down the process.

To simplify the problem, we will assume that the combined costs of adding more jurors are linear for each round of deliberation. When it comes to economic costs, this is probably indeed the case. With regards to other types of cost, it may at least be an admissible approximation. Let c be the non-epistemic disvalue of adding another juror; thus the total value of adding n jurors will be $-nc$. The interesting case will be when $c > 0$, as this will require an actual weighing of J-value against other values.

There is of course an extensive literature in value theory and economics about how to weigh or combine values.[8] A central theorem in this context was proved by Harsanyi (1955): when combining independent utilities, each of which satisfies the von Neumann-Morgenstern axioms, the only consistent choice is to use a weighted sum. We have already assumed J-value to be such a utility, and in the absence of any other well-developed theory of value, it is reasonable to take non-J-value to be in this class as well. Since we are only combining two forms of value, the weighing will be determined by a single number $w = wc/wJ$, where wJ is the weight attached to jury value, and wc the weight attached to other values. But this means that we can simply include w in c by measuring non-J-value using the same scale as J-value, so the total expected value of a practice, when applied to n persons, will be $V(n) = E[J_n] - nc$.

This is applicable primarily when the majority required is 50 %. For higher majorities, the probability of NV becomes significant, and each such verdict also carries the costs of another round of deliberations, so the full formula would be given by the equation

$$V(n) = E[J_n] - nc + P(NV)\ V(n)$$

which can be solved to yield

$$V(n) = \frac{E[J_n] - nc}{1 - P(NV)}$$

The probabilities $P(NV)$ were given in Fig. 2 above. In order to be able to calculate a maximum, we need to represent both these functions and $E[J_n]$ as a continuous and differentiable. This will, of course, involve a conventional choice on our part of which function to use. Among the usual functions available, those of the shape

$$A + Be^{Cn+D}$$

[8]See, for example, Keeney and Raiffa (1976) and Broome (1991).

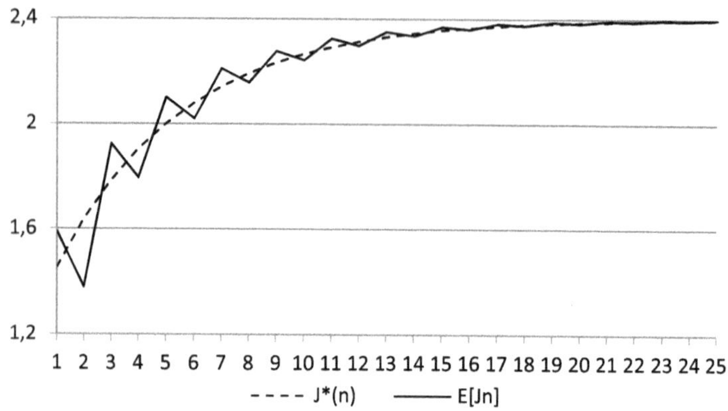

Fig. 5 $E[Jn]$ and $J^*(n)$ for 50 % majority

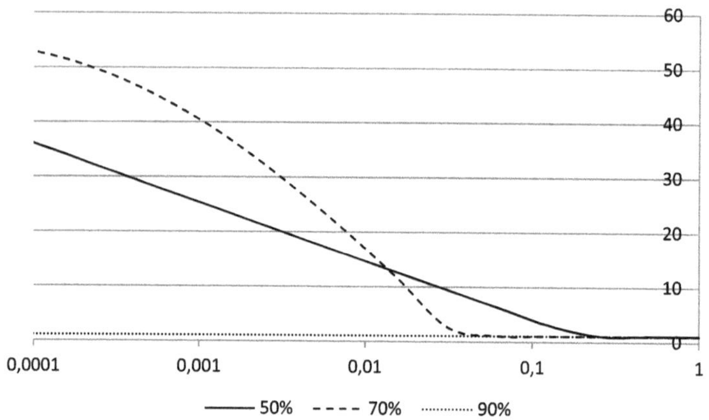

Fig. 6 Optimal Jury sizes depending on cost of adding a new juror

turn out to approximate the functions we want to model best. Fitting such an exponential functions to the data points of the >50 % required majority series of Fig. 1 gives a function

$$J^*(n) = 2.4 - 1.1753\, e^{-0.2150n}$$

with a root mean square error of 0.075. We have plotted both $E[Jn]$ and J^* in Fig. 5.

Using J^* and similar continuous approximations of the J-value, we can find the optimal jury size by a simple optimization. Differentiating $V(n)$ with respect to n and setting this to zero to find the maximum, for each possible cost c of adding a single juror, gives Fig. 6.

We have assumed that there has to be at least one juror. With a 90 % majority required, this is also the best number of jurors to have. For 70 % and 50 % majorities, the optimal number depends on c. For example, if the addition of a single juror has practical disvalue equal to a hundredth of the value of obtaining a correct conviction, i.e. $c = 0.01$ (remembering that we have assumed $\lambda = 1$), a 50 % majority system is best served by having around 15 jurors, and a 70 % majority system by having around 18.

As in the case of λ, the determination of c will depend on personal values as well as on particularities of the specific justice system, such as the expense involved in adding a further juror. For this reason, it may very well be the case that what jury size is optimal differs not only between different countries but also within the courts belonging to one and the same country. What the present model gives us is a way to calculate such optima in a way that depends on these particular circumstances.

6 Discussion

In this section, we first discuss the consequences of our model, and second, explain how our modelit can be seen as generalizing generalizes Hintikka's model of interrogative inquiry (IMI) in certain respects. As we noted, several legal theorists have proposed to use formal decision theory for the purposes of investigating the jury process (Kaplan 1968; Connolly 1987; Arkes and Mellers 2002). Such attempts were severely criticized in Tribe (1971) for illegitimately disregarding the ritual aspects of a trial. This objection may indeed be well-founded so long as the purpose of a formal treatment is to replace the jury system, in this case with one based on decision theory. The purpose of our study is not to replace judicial procedure but to suggest possible ways in which that procedure could be improved.

For instance, our study indicates that requiring more than 50 % majority should be avoided. This is a very stable recommendation which holds even if we count an incorrect conviction as a hundred times worse than a correct one. For another example, we suggested that having more than 15 jurors should be expected to add little perceptible epistemic value to the deliberation process. In the same vein, we could ask what degree of certainty should be required for a juror to vote for guilt. In the American justice system, jurors are informed about the "beyond reasonable doubt" requirement. In some states, they are, in addition, instructed how to interpret it (see Diamond 1990). Such instructions could potentially be based on simulations of the type we have been studying.

Since J-value is interderivable with the degree of certainty required for conviction through eq, changing this value affects the relationship between the values of $J(CG)$ and $J(AI)$ as well. When we allow p (the required credence in question) to vary, we have the more general determination

$$J(AI) = \frac{p(\lambda + 1)}{1 - p} - 10$$

of the value of acquitting the innocent, given a value of λ. This is useful, since despite the fact that people generally report 90 % certainty as what they require for reasonable doubt, actual studies show that they tend to vote on much lower certainties. According to Dane (1985), measuring the jurors' value judgments and then calculating the threshold from these results in an astonishingly low threshold of roughly 52 %. As shown in Dhami (2008), the same result is obtained even if the jurors were told to judge the defendant innocent unless they were 90% certain of his truth. Not only is this an excellent illustration of how badly we tend to estimate our own degrees of belief; it also highlights the importance of doing experiments with a wide range of parameter values, especially if we are interested in measuring the effectiveness of actual juries as opposed to merely ideal ones.

If, following the findings (Dane 1985; Dhami 2008), p is set to 5 %, we get the following relationship between λ and $J(AI)$:

$$J(AI) = \frac{13\lambda - 107}{12}$$

From this it follows that as long as $\lambda \geq 8\ {}^{3}/_{13}$, $J(AI)$ will be positive, and at $\lambda = 107$, $J(CG)$ and $J(AI)$ will be equal. The resulting expected J-values for the latter case are given in Fig. 7, for the majority amount of 50 %.

The shape of the curve is certainly similar to the shape of the >50 % required majority curve in the earlier figures, which means that our choice of an inverse exponential function as an approximation for use in the optimization problem remains valid.

However, because of the connection between p and λ, it is hard to compare cardinal values with the case $p = 0.9$. At first sight it might, for instance, seem like setting $p = 0.52$ would be much better than setting it at 0.9, since the expected J-values are significantly higher for each possible number of jurors. But which part

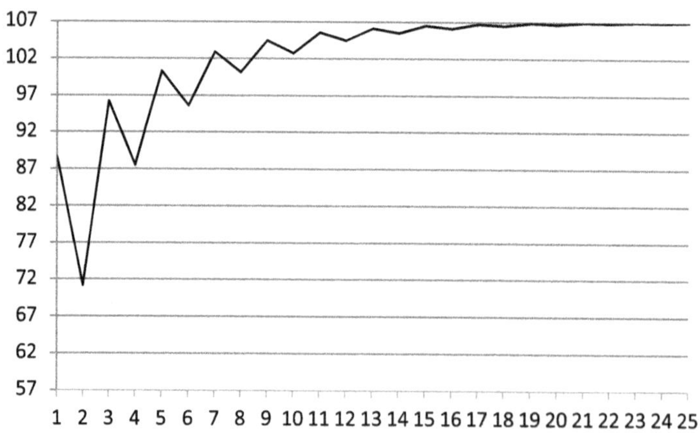

Fig. 7 Expected J-values when $p = 0.52$

of this increase is caused by lowering p and which part is caused by increasing the values of CG and AI? There seems to be no way to separate these factors.[9]

So what if we were *not* to adjust λ, but only p? This would give us J-values in the same interval as before, but it would mean that we require jurors to systematically contradict decision-theoretic rationality. It also would not solve the fundamental problem: subjective probabilities and values are conceptually linked, so an adjustment of probabilities is generally impossible unless we adjust our values as well (cf. Jeffrey 1990).

It is important to see why this does not affect the conclusions we have reached so far: we have only compared jury methods using the *same* J-value assignments to one another, and in these cases the method we have given for calculating the optimal size of a jury remains valid. The difficulty arises only when we try to evaluate scenarios not only on the basis of the values the jurors *have*, but also on the basis of the values the jurors *should* have. Then it seems that we would need some kind of second-order value judgment which might be difficult to elicit in an objective manner.

Now for the second topic in this discussion. Let us explain why we consider our model to be a generalization, in certain respects, of the interrogative model of inquiry. In Hintikka's 'standard model', a lone inquirer attempts to answer some principal research question, using her background knowledge, and answers to instrumental questions. The model essentially deals with the case of pure discovery, "a type of inquiry in which all we need to do is to find out what the truth is [and] we do not have to worry about justifying what we find" (Hintikka 2007, p. 98). In such cases, inquiry terminates when the inquirer's background knowledge, together with the answers to instrumental questions she has gathered, implies deductively one of the answers to the principal question. The IMI illuminates the strategic role of deduction in the selection of questions and how the goal of inferring deductively an answer from strengthened assumptions guides the selection of instrumental questions.

Jury deliberation, as modeled here, departs from pure discovery in at least two respects. The first concerns an assumption of restricted evidence. Evidence is essentially restricted to what transpired in court. In IMI terminology, at the time of deliberation, it is neither neither possible to ask new instrumental questions, nor to obtain answers to such questions previously asked. The second—the potential unreliability of information sources—is captured by assigning a credence to information coming from inquiry or other jurors. Simply put, jury deliberation, unlike pure discovery, requires taking into account information which is both incomplete and uncertain.

While the IMI already accommodates reasoning from uncertain answers, it does so by either introducing probabilities, attached to uncertain answers, as reflecting their relative justification (Hintikka 1987), or by introducing means to disregard

[9]It is, of course, always possible to *scale* the J-values so that they have the same maximum and minimum, thereby achieving an illusion of compatibility. But without an independent argument for why these maxima and minima *should* be the same such an approach seems woefully ad hoc.

(possibly provisionally) some background assumptions or instrumental answers when their justifications are questioned (Hintikka et al. 2002; Genot 2009). Thus there is a sense in which IMI, unlike the present model, pays attention to the "finer structure of reasons". A common feature of these mechanisms, though, is that they encapsulate information about the sources of these answers. It has been argued that tracking multiple sources, IMI style, can in particular account for reasoning patterns that *prima facie* violate Bayesian rationality (Hintikka 2004), or vindicate some of the controversial axioms of AGM-style belief revision in some contexts, but not in others (Genot 2009).

An approach to jury deliberation based on the above mechanisms is possible in principle, but would in practice require tracking the many parameters that contribute to a single juror's epistemic evaluation. Our model represents this the step using only three parameters: the (current) credence assigned to the proposition that the accused is guilty, the (current) self-assessment of reliability, and the (current) assessment of other jurors' reliability. These three parameters allow us to abstract from the finer structure of reasons in the case of individual reasoning, but it is presumably more a change in the level of process description, than a true divergence between models.

Abstracting from the details of the process by which jurors arrive at possibly uncertain answers to the principal question of guilt allows us "zoom out" to features that are specific to the multi-agent case, and to represent them explicitly. Simply put, one juror's preliminary answer to the principal question, at a given stage of deliberation, is at the next stage publicly announced, and becomes for all jurors part of the evidence to consider. New items of evidence are considered in the light of the trust one has in their sources (modeled by a trust function), and the total information is aggregated into a new preliminary answer, and a new assessment of trust. Hence, our model remains, we believe, compatible with the main tenets of Hintikka's interrogative model. In addition, it also genuinely generalizes Hintikka's model to the multi-agent case, and is to our knowledge the first systematic attempt at proposing and implementing such a generalization formally.

7 Conclusion

We have given a Bayesian model of deliberating juries for the purpose of studying the effect of jury size on group competence. We introduced the notion of J-value which takes into account the unique characteristics, asymmetries and values involved in jury voting. Our simulation results indicate that requiring more than a >50 % majority should be avoided. Of the jury systems currently in use, it seems that only the Scottish system does not require more than a >50 % majority. The British system, by contrast, requires a 10–2 (or 83 %) majority, whereas the American prescribes unanimity. A further result of our study is that while it is in principle always better to have a larger jury, given a required majority of >50 %, the value of having more than 12–15 jurors is likely to be negligible. More specifically, the optimal size of a jury appears to depend logarithmically on the non-epistemic cost of adding another juror. The Scottish system could potentially be further motivated by setting the value of a correct conviction to be the same as the disvalue of an incorrect acquittal, and the disvalue of adding a further juror to be a tenth of the value of a correct conviction. However, when different values are considered, different jury systems emerge as optimal.

These remarks are meant to be little more than suggestive hints as to how our approach could be relevant in practical cases. The extent to which our results apply to actual jury systems is an open question that we hope to be able to pursue in future work. Such an investigation would presumably involve addressing two limitations of our study. One concerns the fact that a jury trial is naturally divided into two stages: one stage at which the jurors listen to evidence presented at the court proceedings, and another at which they engage in closed room deliberations. It would be interesting to try to mimic these two stages in future simulations. A second limitation has to do with the problem of freeriding. Forming an independent judgment as to whether or not the defendant is guilty requires the weighing of evidence for or against the proposition in question, which in difficult cases can be a time and resource consuming activity. It is therefore attractive for a juror to decide to rely on the judgment of the other jurors rather than to form an independent opinion. If every juror delegates responsibility to the others, we have a serious freeriding problem, which may make the jury unable to reach a reliable majority verdict. Conceivably, as the size of the jury grows, the temptation to free ride increases, thus negatively affecting group competence. Various measures can be taken to counteract this mechanism of social psychology, e.g. regularly reminding the jurors during the deliberation process of the great responsibility involved in serving in a jury, the importance of making an independent assessment and the dangers of group think. Our model as presented presupposes that such steps have been successfully taken. However, it might be interesting to take a more general strategy where the possibility of freeriding is part of the model.[10]

Acknowledgements This paper was written by Angere and Olsson, except the second part of Sect. 6, which was written by Genot.

References

Arkes, H. R., & Mellers, B. A. (2002). Do juries meet our expectations? *Law and Human Behavior, 26*, 625–639.

Blackstone, Sir W. (1769). *Commentaries on the laws of England*. Oxford: Clarendon Press.

Broome, J. (1991). *Weighing goods: Equality, uncertainty and time*. Cambridge: Blackwell.

Connolly, T. (1987). Decision theory, reasonable doubt, and the utility of erroneous acquittals. *Law and Human Behavior, 11*, 101–112.

[10]We owe the observation that there might be a free-riding problem in larger juries to Andrzej Wiśniewski.

Dane, F. C. (1985). In search of reasonable doubt. *Law and Human Behavior, 9*, 141–158.
Dhami, M. (2008). On measuring quantitative interpretations of reasonable doubt. *Journal of Experimental Psychology: Applied, 14*, 353–363.
Diamond, H. A. (1990). Reasonable doubt: To define or not to define. *Columbia Law Review, 90*, 1716–1736.
Forsyth, J., & Macdonnell, H. (2009). Scotland's unique 15-strong juries will not be abolished. In *The Scotsman*. New York: Bantam Books.
Genot, E. (2009). The game of inquiry: The interrogative approach to inquiry and belief revision theory. *Synthese, 171*, 271–289.
Goodin, R. E. (2003). *Reflective democracy*. Oxford/New York: Oxford University Press.
Harsanyi, J. C. (1955). Cardinal welfare, individualistic ethics, and interpersonal comparisons of utility. *Journal of Political Economy, 60*, 309–321.
Hintikka, J. (1987). The interrogative approach to inquiry and probabilistic inference. *Erkenntnis, 26*, 429–442.
Hintikka, J. (2004). A fallacious fallacy? *Synthese, 140*, 25–35.
Hintikka, J. (2007). *Socratic epistemology*. Cambridge/New York: Cambridge University Press.
Hintikka, J., Halonen, I., & Mutanen, A. (2002). Interrogative logic as a general theory of reasoning. In D. M. Gabbay, R. H. Johnson, H. J. Ohlbach, & J. Woods (Eds.), *Handbook of the logic of argument and inference* (pp. 295–337). Amsterdam: Elsevier.
Isenberg, D. (1986). Group polarization: A critical review and meta-analysis. *Journal of Personality and Social Psychology, 50*, 1141–1151.
Jeffrey, R. (1990). *The logic of decision* (2nd ed.). Chicago: University of Chicago Press.
Jacobstein, J. M., & Mersky, R. M. (1998). *Articles and bibliography from the literature of law and the social and behavioral sciences*. Littleton: Rothman.
Kaplan, J. (1968). Decision theory and the factfinding process. *Stanford Law Review, 20*, 1065–1092.
Keeney, R. L., & Raiffa, H. (1976). *Decisions with multiple objectives: Preferences and value tradeoffs*. New York: Wiley.
List, C., & Goodin, R. E. (2001). Epistemic democracy: Generalizing the condorcet jury theorem. *Journal of Political Philosophy, 9*, 227–306.
Luckhurst, T. (2005). The case for keeping 'Not Proven' verdict. *The sunday times*.
McCauliff, C. M. A. (1982). Burdens of proof: Degrees of belief, quanta of evidence, or constitutional guarantees? *Vanderbilt Law Review, 35*, 1293–1335.
Milanich, P. G. (1981). Decision theory and standards of proof. *Law and human behavior, 5*, 87–96.
Ministry of Justice. (2011). Criminal justice statistics. Quarterly update to December 2010. Available online at http://www.justice.gov.uk/downloads/publications/statistics-and-data/criminal-justice-stats/criminal-stats-quarterly-dec10.pdf.
Olsson, E. J. (2011). A simulation approach to veritistic social epistemology. *Episteme, 8*, 127–143.
Olsson, E. J. (2013). A Bayesian simulation model of group deliberation and polarization. In F. Zenker (ed.) *Bayesian argumentation*. Dordrecht/New York: Synthese Library, Springer.
Olsson, E. J., & Vallinder, A. (2013). Norms of assertion and communication in social networks. *Synthese, 190*, 1437–1454.
Tribe, L. H. (1971). Trial by mathematics: Precision and ritual in the legal process. *Harvard Law Review, 84*, 1329–1393.
United States Courts. (2010). U. S. district courts–criminal defendants disposed of, by type of disposition and offense (excluding transfers), during the 12-month period ending March 31, 2010. Available online at http://www.uscourts.gov/Viewer.aspx?doc=/uscourts/Statistics/FederalJudicialCaseloadStatistics/2010/tables/D04Mar10.pdf.
Vallinder, A., & Olsson, E. J. (2013a). Do computer simulations support the argument from disagreement? *Synthese, 190*, 1437–1454.
Vallinder, A., & Olsson, E. J. (2013b). Trust and the value of overconfidence: A Bayesian perspective on social network communication. *Synthese, 190*, 1437–1454.
Volokh, A. (1997). *n* guilty men. *University of Pennsylvania Law Review, 146*, 173–216.

Inquiry, Refutations and the Inconsistent

Can Başkent

Abstract In this paper, I discuss the connection between Lakatosian method of proofs and refutations, Hintikkan models of interrogative inquiry and paraconsistency. I bridge these different schools with dialectic, and their underlying reliance on the inconsistent.

Keywords Lakatos's proofs and refutations • Hintikka's interrogative models of inquiry • Paraconsistency

1 Introduction

In this paper, I argue that Lakatos's methodology of scientific research programs as exemplified in *Proofs and Refutations* and Hintikka's interrogative models of inquiry share various epistemic and logical qualities. I furthermore claim that paraconsistency is one of such qualitative similarities between the Lakatosian and the Hintikkan research programs even though neither of the philosophers was explicitly committed to this view.[1]

The organization of this paper is as follows. First, I discuss the epistemic and methodological similarities between Hintikka's inquiry and Lakatos's research program. Then, I analyze those similarities from the view point of inconsistency-tolerant, paraconsistent logical approach.

What I claim here does not reject Lakatos's or Hintikka's results, but it questions the choice of underlying logic (which is the classical logic) which they used in their frameworks. My arguments unearth the hidden logical commitments of both philosophers, which I think is evident in their works but not widely discussed.

[1]It is important to note that Hintikka recently made some suggestions to combine IF logic – which does not entirely fall within the scope of this paper – with paraconsistent logics (Hintikka 2009; Carnielli 2009).

C. Başkent (✉)
Department of Computer Science, University of Bath, Bath, UK
e-mail: can@canbaskent.net; c.baskent@bath.ac.uk

C. Başkent (ed.), *Perspectives on Interrogative Models of Inquiry*, Logic, Argumentation & Reasoning 8, DOI 10.1007/978-3-319-20762-9_4

I am not directly arguing that both philosophers favor inconsistency-tolerant logics. Instead, I claim that their methodological frameworks make me question their commitment to classical logic, and that their systems have some aspects that intrinsically admit paraconsistency.

I now start with reviewing Lakatos's and Hintikka's frameworks from inconsistency – tolerant point of view.

2 Hintikka and Lakatos

Hintikka's model of interrogative inquiry is a well-known example of a dynamic epistemic procedure that results in knowledge increase. Simply put, in an interrogative inquiry, the inquirer is given a theory and a question. He then tries to answer the question based on the theory by posing some questions to nature or an oracle. In an interrogative inquiry, the inquirer has two options. He is allowed to ask questions to nature/oracle, conceived as a truthful source of information, or alternatively draw conclusions by using the given base theory and the answers he has already received.

The interrogative models of inquiry has largely been studied by the *Helsinki School*, and the major arguments of this research program can be found in a series of articles (Hintikka 1984, 1987, 1988, 2007; Hintikka and Harris 1988; Hintikka et al. 2002; Halonen and Hintikka 2005; Garrison 1988; Genot 2009). Recently, Carnielli studied the connection between interrogative models and paraconsistency, which also influenced the current paper (Carnielli 2009). Carnielli, after Hintikka's recent *sympathy* towards paraconsistency (Hintikka 2009), remarks that "the problem of coping with contradictory information belongs to interrogative games", which seems to agree with our perspective in this work (Carnielli 2009).

The procedure that interrogative inquires follows is simple. Yet, it admits some hidden assumptions that are not widely discussed. The first hidden assumption of Hintikkan inquiry is its reliance on classical logic and its rules of derivation. However, the epistemic procedure of interrogative inquiry does not require such a commitment to classical logic by- and in-itself.

In order to illustrate our argument, consider the following aspect of inquiry. In inquiry, players are allowed to *bracket out* some answers to eliminate them from the procedure if they think those answers are not relevant or do violate the consistency of the system. Hintikka writes:

> An important aspect of this general applicability of the interrogative model is its ability to handle uncertain answers – that is, answers that may be false. The model can be extended to this case simply by allowing the inquirer to tentatively disregard ("bracket") answers that are dubious. The decision as to when the inquirer should do so is understood as a strategic problem, not as a part of the definition of the questioning game. Of course, all the subsequent answers that depend on the bracketed one must then also be bracketed, together with their logical consequences. Equally obviously, further inquiry might lead the inquirer to reinstate ("unbracket") a previously bracketed answer. This means thinking of interrogative inquiry as a self-corrective process. It likewise means considering discovery and justification as aspects of one and the same process. This is certainly in keeping with

> scientific and epistemological practice. There is no reason to think that the interrogative model does not offer a framework also for the study of this self-correcting character of inquiry.
> (Hintikka 1962, p. 3)

In an earlier paper, I focused on the epistemological redundancy of bracketing in Hintikkan inquiry where I argued that the existence of inconsistencies is natural (and even desirable) in a dialogical inquiry. Yet, we can still make meaningful deductions under the presence of inconsistencies rendering the working system a paraconsistent one (Başkent 2014). Other problems of the bracketing in Hintikkan inquiry include epistemic, game theoretical and heuristic problems where the heuristic issues are quite central also for Lakatos.

Epistemically, there seems to be a major problem in bracketing. In an inquiry or a dialogue game, how can we know which answers to ignore beforehand? How can we know what to reject or accept? This epistemic problem empties the notion of bracketing. In other words, if inquiry is a procedure during which we want to acquire and learn some information, this implies that we *did not* have that information before. In an epistemic inquiry, we are supposed to be searching and looking for some information that we did not have before. We cannot discard some responses in favor of or against some questions or propositions – simply because we do not know the answer. If we knew, we would not ask.

A game theoretical response can be given to eliminate this problem, arguing against my point. Namely, in an inquiry, we simply choose the assumptions and responses that help us *win* the game. If we can win the game with a particular set of assumptions, then we adopt these assumptions as they give us a win. If we fail to win the game with that particular set of assumptions and the previous answers we received in the inquiry, we simply select another set of assumptions and answers, and keep playing, and repeat the procedure if necessary.

However, this objection undermines the *agency* of the players. In a game theoretical setting, each player follows a *strategy* to choose their moves. By definition, a strategy is predetermined and preset before the game based on some understanding of rationality and players' priors (and perhaps some probabilistic calculus). Borrowing the concepts of traditional game theory, therefore, a player's strategy considers *all* possible ways of plays for the opponent, and includes ways to respond to them (to counter-act the possible attacks). A strategy is pre-determined, and fully inclusive of all the possibilities – at least theoretically. An *unexpected move* of the opponent, a *new piece of information* and its consequences and many other possibilities, should therefore be already included in the strategy, by definition. Players decide, and set their strategy, and determine how they will play *before* they start playing the game. If we allow them to exercise their choice of moves based on their a posteriori success, that means that they did not have an a priori strategy before the game-play. Simply put, a game theoretical player is rational, and constructs a strategy based on his priors, as opposed to deciding how to play during the game. Therefore, such an objection clashes with the basic definition of a strategy – a function that tells the player which move to make at each state based on what moves the other players have made (Başkent 2011).

Finally, bracketing suffers from various central problems from a heuristic point of view. First, let us remember the Lakatosian concept of "proofs that do not prove" which is directly relevant and helpful to our investigation. Lakatosian methodology of proofs and refutations, as exemplified in *Proofs and Refutations* for instance, discusses the significant roles of (unsuccessful) thought experiments, informal proofs and unsound deductions in mathematical reasoning among many other things (Lakatos 1979, 2005; Başkent and Bağçe 2009). "Proofs that do not prove" are the proofs that are wrong in some ways, yet help us develop better proofs or improve the current false proof. Lakatos discusses this idea in detail, and explains its role in concept formation with many historical examples. For Lakatosian epistemology, in an evolutionary and practice based sense, mathematical concepts develop, improve and then they are falsified, proven and disproven along their conceptual development. Mathematical activity continues, and the concepts are redeveloped, the proofs are re-examined. In short, "proof attempts" help us improve the proofs. However, if we bracket "proofs that do not prove", we risk the growth of (mathematical) knowledge, and lose the opportunity to *learn from our mistakes* (Başkent 2014).

I already discussed the above points in an earlier work (Başkent 2014). Now, my focus is the *self-correcting character of inquiry* which bears some similarities to Lakatosian methods that include informal proofs, thought experiments and quasi-empirical view of mathematical activity, bridging the two as we shall see.

In my understanding, what Hintikka alludes in the above lengthy quote is that a scientific theory revises itself to exclude inconsistencies or incoherencies, and interrogative inquiry, as a special case of this phenomenon, follows a similar procedure. In Hintikka's perspective, this is the point that prevents him from being a pluralist logician – disallowing multiple conclusions in the deductive relation of the logic he uses. In short, whenever there seems to be a problem within the theory, the theory utilizes its own internal tools to fix itself. Some call it *belief revision*, some call it *epistemic updates*, there are various other logical methods which operate with a similar method to achieve a similar goal (Genot 2009; Garrison 1988).

However, note that this procedure itself is paraconsistent even though it aims at preserving the consistency at the end. Recall that paraconsistency is the umbrella term for the logical systems where inconsistencies do not trivialize the system. In paraconsistent systems, we can have $\varphi, \neg\varphi \not\vdash \psi$ for some φ, ψ. Dialogues can be thought of an example of paraconsistent phenomena (Rahman and Carnielli 2000; Rahman and Tulenheimo 2009). A careful approach to terminology is in order here. Paraconsistency is usually confused with *dialetheism* which is the view that suggests that some contradictions are true. Paraconsistency is a rather proof-theoretical approach whereas dialetheism is a semantical one. Additionally, it would be wise to underline the fact that logicians often distinguish *contradictions* from the *inconsistent* (Carnielli et al. 2007). For the purposes of this paper, we will assume that contradictions create inconsistencies. We will not suggest that every inconsistency is caused by a contradiction. Moreover, for the technically oriented reader, as they will realize throughout the paper, we will refrain ourselves from explicitly committing to a specific form of paraconsistent logic. Paraconsistent logics form a broad spectrum of logical formalisms motivated by various philosophical insights, and produce relatively different mathematical results. It should be clear that our philosophical treatment of the subject, at this stage, does not necessarily require any explicit commitment to a specific branch or understanding of paraconsistent school of logic, and more importantly we are, at least currently, *not* suggesting a paraconsistent logic for Hintikkan inquiry or Lakatosian method of proofs and refutations.

For Hintikka, an inquiry, in its broadest generality, can have some inconsistent statements which might have arisen from the dialogue or inquiry, yet, we must not include them in our deductive process. However, this means that, under the presence of inconsistencies, we still make some meaningful deduction – even if this deduction attempts at excluding those very inconsistencies and contradictions. We will perhaps ignore inconsistencies epistemologically, yet, logically they are simply there in the form of a set of contradictory answers perhaps. There can be thought of various choice mechanisms that determine which propositions and responses we need to include or exclude from the deductive process of the inquiry. Moreover, the decidability of the logical system (if it is first-order or propositional) makes a distinctive difference whether we can determine which responses to include or exclude from the procedure in order to maintain a coherent and consistent system. Yet, aside from the computational aspects of it and its difficulties, the very decision of *bracketing* some of contradictory statements is taken under the very existence of the same contradictory statements. This is a working paraconsistent procedure.

The crucial point here, as I underlined earlier, is that Hintikka thinks that the system will eventually correct itself. For him, after some thought-experiments or quasi-empirical observations, we will reach the true statements with an inquiry even if we may have hit some inconsistencies along the way. Here, again, notice that the very existence of the inconsistencies along the way does not trivialize the model. Hintikka does not seem to enjoy epistemic inconsistencies, yet he does not logically exclude them from his system in a convincing way.

A very similar issue appears in Lakatosian methodology as well. First, let us briefly recall Lakatosian method of proofs and refutations. Lakatosian methodology follows a simple yet well-defined road map which consists of the following methodological steps which I borrow from Corfield (1997):

1. Primitive conjecture.
2. Proof (a rough thought experiment or argument, decomposing the primitive conjecture into subconjectures and lemmas).
3. Global counterexamples.
4. Proof re-examined. The guilty lemma is spotted. The guilty lemma may have previously remained hidden or may have been misidentified.
5. Proofs of the other theorems are examined to see if the newly found lemma occurs in them.
6. Hitherto accepted consequences of the original and now refuted conjecture arc checked.
7. Counterexamples are turned into new examples, and new fields of inquiry open up.

As the above account identifies, Lakatos's method of proofs and refutations is a quite systematic account of mathematical discovery with a strong emphasis on mathematical practice. There are various strong criticisms towards Lakatos from mathematical angles, yet I will now dwell into them in this paper (Koetsier 1991).

One of my favorite passages of *Proofs and Refutations* discusses the Cauchian revolution of rigor in mathematics versus axiomatic Euclidean methodology.

> The Cauchy revolution of rigour was motivated by a conscious attempt to apply Euclidean methodology to the Calculus. He and his followers thought that this was how they could introduce light to dispel the 'tremendous obscurity of analysis'. Cauchy proceeded in the spirit of Pascal's rules: he first set out to define the obscure terms of analysis - like limit, convergence, continuity etc. - in the perfectly familiar terms of arithmetic, and then he went on to prove everything that had not previously been proved, or that was not perfectly obvious. *Now in the Euclidean framework there is no point trying to prove what is false* (My emphasis), so Cauchy had first to improve the extant body of mathematical conjectures by jettisoning the false rubbish. (...) What was considered by the rigourists to be hopeless rubbish, such as conjectures about sums of divergent series, was duly committed to the flames. 'Divergent series are' wrote Abel, 'the work of the devil'. They only cause 'calamities and paradoxicalities'. (...) The idea of a proof which deserves its name and still is not conclusive was alien to the rigourists.
> (Lakatos 2005, p. 137, footnotes are omitted)

Even though the above quote is taken from a discussion which is quite different than ours, it is still clear that Lakatos endorses the importance of contradictions for the increase of mathematical knowledge. The legitimate presence of such "paradoxicalities" do not collapse or trivialize the system. For Lakatosian methodology, under these circumstances, mathematicians still prove theorems – even sometimes with "proofs that do not prove" or with informal proofs. The existence of contradictions is therefore central for Lakatosian methodology to operate. At the end, contradictions perhaps are not included in the final theory for various metaphysical commitments that I shall not discuss here, yet, during the *course of their development*, the contradictions are appreciated and acknowledged, and perhaps even expected and desired in Lakatosian methodology.

There can be suggested various ontological and epistemological reasons why contradictions, thus inconsistencies, are carefully excluded from the final theory. To the best of my knowledge, neither Lakatos nor Hintikka discusses the origins of their ontological commitment to classical Boolean logic, and the role of this commitment in their methodology in detail. Nevertheless, this commitment does not constitute an essential and unchangeable component of their methodology and research programs. The dialectic and discussive nature of their methodology necessarily requires an inconsistency-tolerant framework.

Now, going back to the similarities between Lakatosian and Hintikkan methodologies, one of the most important similarities between Lakatosian method and Hintikkan method becomes obvious after a brief look at the aforementioned road-map of Lakatosian methodology: Lakatosian methodology is also a self-correcting inquiry under the presence of inconsistencies. As we observed, for Hintikkan methodology that is an important aspect of an interrogative inquiry.

For Lakatos, similarly, the process of mathematical discovery corrects itself by dealing with counter-examples, *proofs that do not prove* and similar *anomalies* and *monsters*. Lakatos goes further and introduces various methods for the self-correcting procedure. He employes three main strategies to implement the method of proofs and refutations: monster-barring, exception-barring and lemma incorporation (Başkent 2012).

The method of monster-barring deals with the objects which are not *in mind* when the conjecture is first suggested. The method of exception-barring accepts that the theorem in its stated form is not valid due to the emergence of some genuine counterexamples targeting the correctness of the theorem itself. Lemma incorporation depicts the way we turn the counterexamples into new examples, and how those new examples are helpful for the modified and re-formulated version of the theorem. Note that even if these methods try to maintain a consistent and coherent logical system for the theory, in an a priori fashion they *accept* inconsistencies first, and go on with further deductions in a coherent way – this is what makes this system paraconsistent. *Proofs and Refutations* provides various cases and examples for Lakatosian reasoning with inconsistencies. In *Proofs and Refutations* various contradictory situations are discussed, solved, discussed again and resolved.

Now, Hintikka alludes to similar notions when he considers the Socratic method of *elenchus*: it is a dialogue, it is dialectic and there is a strategic component similar to Lakatos's. In Hintikka, the strategic and game theoretical elements are clearer and carefully underlined.

> Another main requirement that can be addressed to the interrogative approach - and indeed to the theory of any goal-directed activity - is that it must do justice to the strategic aspects of inquiry. Among other things, it ought to be possible to distinguish the definitory rules of the activity in question from its strategic rules. The former spell out what is possible at each stage of the process. The latter express what actions are better and worse for the purpose of reaching the goals of the activity. This requirement can be handled most naturally by doing what Plato already did to the Socratic *elenchus* and by construing knowledge-seeking by questioning as a game that pits the questioner against the answerer. Then the study of the strategies of knowledge acquisition becomes another application of the mathematical theory of games, which perhaps ought to be called "strategy theory" rather than "game theory" in the first place. The distinction between the definitory rules - usually called simply the rules of the game - and strategic principles is built right into the structure of such games.
> (Hintikka 2007, p. 19)

The terminology and the context are different between the Hintikkan inquiry and the Lakatosian method. Yet, as the above quote illustrates, the strategic element is obvious in both. Additionally, there is another underlying tone of paraconsistency in *elenchus*, yet, in order to maintain our current focus, we will not dwell on this connection in this work (Carnielli 2009).

Lakatosian and Hintikkan methods share various qualities including their reliance on inconsistency. Yet, I need to argue somehow more on their understanding of inconsistency. I will achieve it in the next section.

3 Hintikka, Lakatos and the Inconsistent

In another work, I argued that Hintikka's approach to inquiry in his interrogative models is misleading in excluding inconsistencies. I claimed that inconsistencies are epistemically central for knowledge increase in dynamic epistemic procedures such as dialogues and dialectics (Başkent 2014).

A similar approach can be taken to analyze the Lakatosian methodology in the context of philosophy and methodology of mathematics. For this, we first need to remember the dialectical roots of Lakatosian method of proofs and refutations (PR, for short), and then the intrinsic relationship between dialectic and paraconsistency. In short, I will claim that Lakatosian methodology, via dialectic, is paraconsistent in nature – even though Lakatos himself did not make such a claim. Moreover, what renders Lakatosian philosophy paraconsistent also applies to Hintikkan method of inquiry. Let me now elaborate.

The relationship between PR and dialectic has been pointed out earlier by several authors (Kiss 2006; Kvasz 2002). For Lakatos, to improve the proof and the theorem, we need counter-examples and *disproofs* or *proofs that do not prove*.

Proofs that do not prove hint out an essential element of Lakatosian method of PR. For increase in knowledge, to improve the theorem and its proof, to revise the theory, we indeed rely on a proof that does not prove what it is set out to prove. In Lakatosian method, proofs are generally examined by raising counter-examples to them which in effect create a contradiction, thus an inconsistency. The proof is put forward, then after some quasi-empirical testing, some counter-examples are developed. At this moment of the method of PR, the method itself admits an inconsistency. Alas, PR chooses a strategy in which the proof, the proof that does not prove, is revised and improved. Granted, Lakatos strives to achieve consistency and coherence by his method. Any application of the method of proofs and refutations, with its negative and positive heuristics and protective belt, aims at a consistent and a coherent theory. I call this the meta-logical commitment of Lakatosian methodology. In other words, Lakatosian methodology is not committed to paraconsistency or dialetheism for that matter. Nevertheless, it needs inconsistencies to operate at the object level. They can be counter-examples, they can be various components of the theorem, their lemmata or their concepts which create an inconsistency. In Lakatosian methodology, when the proofs do not work as intended, it is not because of a simple error. Lakatos details them carefully in his work (Lakatos 2005, 1979).

What the method of proofs and refutations suggests as a next step *after* coming across to inconsistencies is not a counter-argument to my claim that Lakatosian methodology is paraconsistent in essence. The reason is quite simple. The decision to revise the theory by using the method of proofs and refutations (and more importantly to determine the *specific* ways to achieve this revision based on the mathematical object theory at hand) is taken *under* the very existence of inconsistencies. I argued along these lines earlier.

Another way of looking at this issue is to investigate the dialectic roots of Lakatosian method. As mentioned in Corfield's outline of the method of proofs and refutations (Sect. 2), the occurrence of counter-examples is an indispensable aspect of the method of PR. We can see the counter-examples as *anti-theses* where the initial proof attempts and immature theorems are the *theses*. Then, the Lakatosian dialectic operates and produces a *synthesis* using both thesis and anti-thesis. Lakatos himself often explicitly employs Hegelian method in his work as well (Lakatos 2005, p. 145–6).

However, the very same Hegelian method is paraconsistent. The observation that dialectic is a paraconsistent methodology can be traced back to Hegel himself (Ficara 2013; Kvasz 2002; Priest 1989). The core idea, as we already applied to Lakatosian methodology, is the fact that dialectic requires the presence of contradictory opinions, and operates under the very inconsistencies, yet produces a sound output. In this paper, I will not repeat the arguments in detail as to why dialectic can be considered as a dialetheic (and a paraconsistent) system. Yet, I will underline why dialectic, and in general dialogical systems are paraconsistent following Jaśkowski's argument for discussive logics (Jaśkowski 1999). In a dialogue, assume that a player received two answers p and $\neg p$ at different times. Nevertheless, it is completely possible that there exists a proposition q which is nowhere true in the model. Thus, q may not be deducible under the presence of a contradiction. Therefore, for some p and q, we observe $p, \neg p \nvdash q$. Thus, the dialogue is paraconsistent. It does not entail that in *all* dialogues we have contradictory answers and a proposition that still does not follow. Yet, it means that the logic we use to formalize such systems should be in fact inconsistency-friendly. This is a call for extending the classical logic to an inconsistency-friendly, paraconsistent logic. In a paraconsistent logic, the classical logic can be a special case of the paraconsistent system, which serves our aim here. The argument we presented here for logical systems applies to dialectic and to logics that can describe dialectic reasoning as well, which after all applies to Hintikkan inquiry and Lakatosian method of PR. Notice that we are not describing a logic of dialectics here, instead, we use the fact that any formal system that uses dialectical reasoning intrinsically can descriptively be analyzed within a paraconsistent logical framework. Thus, it would not be wrong to claim that procedures and processes that use dialectical way of reasoning *fit* and *embed* in paraconsistent logic. In short, if the Lakatosian method has dialectic roots, and dialectic itself is paraconsistent in nature, then the method of proofs and refutations enjoys being a paraconsistent methodology. This argument (via dialectic) indirectly shows that Lakatosian method of PR is paraconsistent.

Another argumentation from paraconsistent logic can also be given (Priest and Thomason 2007). An intriguing aspect of paraconsistency is the view that it considers the "consistent" as a special case of the "inconsistent" as I briefly pointed out earlier.

> The Euclidean conception of proof cannot characterise the history of mathematics. Lakatos' conception of proof as a fallible enterprise, starting from things that appear to be true, but which are subject to revision in the light of counter-examples, appears much more plausible. (...) Mathematicians and logicians are undoubtedly much more self-conscious about formulating the starting points, their axioms. But the axioms are no infallible epistemological bedrock. They are merely places where proof may stop, *pro tem*; they are

> still liable to be challenged by appropriate counter-examples. And this is just as true of the axioms of logic as those of mathematics. The development of paraconsistent logic can be seen as a clear case of this.
> (Priest and Thomason 2007)

This line of thought constitutes another argument for the paraconsistency of Lakatosian methodology. Namely, even if its overall goal is to establish a consistent and coherent theory, proofs and refutations may admit inconsistencies, and the consistent case is merely a special case for the broader inconsistency-tolerant framework of proofs and refutations.

This establishes that the Lakatosian method of proofs and refutations is inconsistency-tolerant and in fact paraconsistent.

*

So far, I have discussed the Lakatosian method of proofs and refutations (PR, for short) and its relations to paraconsistency. Now, I will argue that the same elements that render Lakatosian method paraconsistent applies to Hintikka's interrogative models of inquiry (IMI, for short) as well.

In order to achieve this, I will explicitly identify *some* of the common elements in PR and IMI that relate them to paraconsistency and dialetheia.

- Both PR and IMI is about knowledge increase caused by (quasi-)empirical testing.
- When the empirical test produces a contradictory result, both PR and IMI has a constructive strategy to follow instead of rendering the model trivial, and resetting the procedure.
- Both PR and IMI have some erotetic aspects where questions themselves are central to the inquiry.
- Both PR and IMI are seen as *activities*.

Notice that the above list is not exhaustive and it can easily be applied to various other dialogical, erotetic and discussive systems.

Let us now elaborate more on those points.

Both PR and IMI is about knowledge increase caused by empirical testing In PR, testing the hypothesis is essential. In fact, this is the point where Lakatos's philosophy converges to empiricism. Lakatosian approach tests the hypothesis, experiments on it, produces counter-examples that are directed towards the theorems, the hypothesis or its concepts or definitions.

In IMI, the hypothesis or the initial question is tested by asking questions to the oracle or nature from whom the right answers are collected. It can be argued that the empirical aspects of IMI are not as strong as in PR. Yet, this line of criticism mistakenly considers IMI as an analytical method where questions essentially support the deductive procedure.

What distinguishes PR as a methodology in mathematics is its *quasi-empirical* aspects that diverge from analyticity. In IMI, on the other hand, Hintikka distinguishes two ways to increase knowledge. One is the deductive and analytical method based on the previous answers obtained in the inquiry and the rules of logic. Second, and the most important one for our purposes here, is the *inquiry* part where the inquirer poses questions to the nature or oracle. This breaks the chain of analyticity, and constitutes an empirical or quasi-empirical test. A rational inquirer would not ask analytical or deductive questions. He simply would ask the question for which he needs answers for. Therefore, those answers cannot be a part of his original theory.

I must emphasize that my understanding of "quasi-empiricisim" extends to formal sciences as well. In IMI, a question to the oracle constitutes a quasi-empirical testing if the subject matter is a mathematical theorem or a theoretical physical result.

When the empirical test produces a contradictory result, both PR and IMI has a constructive strategy to follow The purpose of the (empirical or quasi-empirical) experiments in PR and IMI is indeed to test the hypothesis. In some cases, the tests can produce some results that may contradict the hypothesis which is being tested. This is a perfectly routine *modus operandi* for PR and IMI. Namely, in questioning and in experimentation, the inquirer/tester can be wrong, and this is perfectly understandable and expectable. Yet, from a formal perspective, this creates, what I call, an instant contradiction. At that particular moment when the results of the tests are received, what we have is an inconsistent system. Yet, as we have emphasized throughout this paper, this contradiction does not render neither PR nor IMI trivial. In fact, both PR and IMI has a well-defined strategy to follow under such instant inconsistencies.

Both PR and IMI have some erotetic aspects Both PR and IMI posit a metaphysical stand when it comes to question generation. In PR, for example, it is not clear or precisely defined, how one can develop the *right tests and quasi-experiments* that can produce the clever counter-examples. Similarly, in IMI, it is not clear how the initial question(s) directed to the nature/oracle are formulated in the first place. Such ontological aspects of PR and IMI fall outside the domain of this paper, yet, both PR and IMI does not explain how those questions are generated. Question generation is what separates PR and IMI from analytical or purely deductive procedures. Notice that some of such questions – the ones that cause revisions or updates – cause inconsistencies. Thus, taken as a metaphysical and formal system, PR and IMI *can* produce those questions which create inconsistencies. This means that both are inconsistency-tolerant and paraconsistent.

Both PR and IMI are seen as *activities* Lakatos's emphasis on mathematics as a quasi-empirical science and an activity can be traced throughout *Proofs and Refutations* (Lakatos 2005). The broader picture of the game of proofs and refutations points to an activity which is continuous, perhaps never ending process of constructing, deconstructing and reconstructing the concepts, theorems and proofs. From a dialectical perspective, PR being an activity is crucial as well. The activity continues, concepts are dialectically formed, and de-formed, and reformed *ad-infinitum*. Moreover, mistakes happen, theorems are falsified, concepts are redefined. Activity also takes the form of quasi-experimentation as we already mentioned.

*

Now, let me elaborate how the features above appear in IMI, and render it inconsistency – tolerant.

First of all, I argue that IMI also conducts empirical testing as part of its methodology. IMI has two methods for knowledge increasing: deduction and questioning. In this paper, we leave the analytical discussions on deduction and knowledge increase aside, and focus on the questioning aspect of IMI. In IMI, questions, in fact, answers to those questions, introduce new elements to the inquiry, furthermore these questions/answers are the only way to introduce new information. It is an entirely different question how the answers and their data are processed, selected or omitted in an inquiry (Hintikka 2007, p. 221). Moreover, it can also be argued that selecting the data just to maintain the consistency cannot be incorporated to interrogative inquiries (Başkent 2014).

However, the question – answer procedure of inquiry contains empirical elements. Even if the way that the questions are generated requires a metaphysical commitment, the way that they are *answered* is empirical and a posteriori in a broad sense. Otherwise, epistemically and game theoretically, then questioning makes no sense – why would a rational agent ask a question whose answer does not have the potential to bring along new information or ask an irrelevant question? Clearly, our argument does not entail that *all* answers require such an empirical procedure. Yet, our thesis simply point out that question – answer protocol *allows* empirical testing, even if it may not necessitate it per se.

Second, I briefly discussed *bracketing* in Hintikka's IMI as a strategy to avoid contradictions. Either with bracketing, or instead without using bracketing and replacing it with some choice procedure, IMI functions *with contradictions*. Even if the end-result for Hintikka is ideally a consistent system without contradictions, the very existence of bracketing acknowledges their role, existence and emergence in IMI. Similar to Lakatos's various methods to maintain the consistency, Hintikkan IMI has its own slightly less sophisticated way of maintaining the consistency and coherence of its system.

Third, the erotetic aspects of question generation is a crucial point of both IMI and PR. However, Hintikka himself does not say much about it when it comes to IMI. Yet, we believe, question generation in IMI is directly related to rationality of the inquirer. Clearly, the inquirer can raise any questions that the oracle can answer with yes/no answers. This does not rule out that the inquirer shall direct trivial or analytical questions to the oracle. What restricts the inquirer from asking trivial questions is the rationality element of the player, the inquirer. Assuming that he is committed to winning the game of inquiry, the inquirer will try to ask relevant and non-trivial questions, and try to maximize his gain from the questions. Ideally, he will receive consistent and coherent answers. However, in reality, in an empirical or computationally challenging inquiry, the inquirer can receive contradictory answers, and it is perfectly normal. Similar to Jaśkowski's argument we mentioned earlier, IMI admits inconsistencies (Başkent 2014).

Hintikka also discusses the probabilistic aspects of the question-answer activity of IMI (Hintikka 1987). This portrays a bit more realistic picture of IMI, and in a different way underlines the role of questions in IMI.

Finally, as Garrison also emphasized, Hintikkan IMI has some similarities as an *activity* to Laudan and Lakatos (Garrison 1988). It can be argued that in Hintikka, the activity aspect of the process can be most easily seen in the question formation. After all, the deduction is straight-forwardly defined, and the only *creative* room in the process is the activity of asking and forming questions. This creativity can perhaps be overshadowed by a know-it-all oracle, and this most certainly shortens the period of the activity. Instead of experimentation and various back-and-forth questioning, the oracle – ideally – produces the correct answer immediately and instantly. Nevertheless, this procedure renders still IMI as a dialog and an activity.

Notice that the activity aspect of Lakatosian PR is much more evident than that of Hintikkan IMI, and in fact the process of PR relies on the quasi-empirical activity as the generator of counter-examples. Yet, knowledge generation as an activity is a quite broad approach to various formalisms, and what I have tried to accomplish in this paper can be considered very similar to Garrison's attempt to unite Hintikkan IMI with Laudan's conception of science as a problem-solving, and question-answering activity (Garrison 1988).

In conclusion, I argued that Lakatosian PR and Hintikkan IMI share various aspects that render both inconsistency-tolerant frameworks.

4 Conclusion

Lakatos's and Hintikka's methods differ on a variety of points. Yet, within the scope of this paper, they are united on their approach to the inconsistent. However, I argued that their reading of the inconsistent, within their own goals and framework, is misleading, even if Hintikka later showed some interest towards paraconsistency. In fact, both PR and IMI rely heavily on the existence of (perhaps temporary) inconsistencies and contradictions.

The role of dialectics both in Hintikka and Lakatos is an interesting direction to pursue, and we restricted ourselves to briefly touching to that issue. Much more can be said, and especially in Lakatosian case studies, a more detailed outline of Lakatosian dialectic can be given within a broader framework which goes beyond the limits of a single research paper.

Also, more importantly, philosophers change their opinions and they revise their ideas – sometimes paraconsistently, sometimes classically perhaps. So did Hintikka. In Hintikka (2009), the Hintikka we read is quite different than what is represented in this paper as he considers (even remotely) the possibility of combining IF logic with paraconsistent logics to create a common framework.

Finally, the ideas we presented in this paper can easily extend to broader issues in philosophy of mathematics suggesting a paraconsistent view of the subject. We leave such investigations to a future work.

Acknowledgements I acknowledge the suggestions of the two anonymous referees. The paper has benefited a lot from the feedback of Marco Panza.

References

Başkent, C. (2011). A logic for strategy updates. In H. van Ditmarsch & J. Lang (Eds.), *Proceedings of the third international workshop on logic, rationality and interaction (LORI-3)*, Guangzhou (LNCS, Vol. 6953, pp. 382–3).

Başkent, C. (2012). A formal approach to Lakatosian heuristics. *Logique et Analyse, 55*(217), 23–46.

Başkent, C. (2014). Towards paraconsistent inquiry (under review).

Başkent, C., & Bağçe, S. (2009). An examination of counterexamples in *proofs and refutations*. *Philosophia Scientiae, 13*(2), 3–20.

Carnielli, W. A. (2009). Meeting hintikka's challenge to paraconsistentism. *Principia, 13*(3), 283–297.

Carnielli, W. A., Coniglio, M. E., & Marcos, J. (2007). Logics of formal inconsistency. In D. Gabbay & F. Guenthner (Eds.), *Handbook of philosophical logic* (Vol. 14, pp. 15–107). Dordrecht/London: Springer.

Corfield, D. (1997). Assaying Lakatos's history and philosophy of science. *Studies in History and Philosophy of Science, 28*(1), 99–121.

Ficara, E. (2013). Dialectic and dialetheism. *History and Philosophy of Logic, 34*(1), 35–52.

Garrison, J. W. (1988). Hintikka, Laudan and Newton: An interrogative model of scientific inquiry. *Synthese, 74*, 145–171.

Genot, E. J. (2009). The game of inquiry: The interrogative approach to inquiry and belief revision theory. *Synthese, 171*(2), 271–289.

Halonen, I., & Hintikka, J. (2005). Toward a theory of the process of explanation. *Synthese, 143*(1), 5–61.

Hintikka, J. (1962). *Knowledge and belief.* Ithaca: Cornell University Press.

Hintikka, J. (1984). The logic of science as a model-oriented logic. In *PSA: Proceedings of the biennial meeting of the philosophy of science association* (Vol. 1, pp. 177–185). Chicago: The University of Chicago Press.

Hintikka, J. (1987). The interrogative approach to inquiry and probabilistic inference. *Erkenntnis, 26*, 429–442.

Hintikka, J. (1988). What is the logic of experimental inquiry? *Synthese, 74*, 173–190.

Hintikka, J. (2007). *Socratic epistemology.* Cambridge/New York: Cambridge University Press.

Hintikka, J. (2009). If logic meets paraconsistent logic. In W. A. Carnielli, M. E. Coniglio, & I. M. L. D'Ottaviano (Eds.), *The many sides of logic* (pp. 3–13). London: College Publications.

Hintikka, J., & Harris, S. (1988). On the logic of interrogative inquiry. In *PSA: Proceedings of the biennial meeting of the philosophy of science association* (Vol. 1, pp. 233–240). Chicago: The University of Chicago Press.

Hintikka, J., Halonen, I., & Mutanen, A. (2002). Interrogative logic as a general theory of reasoning. In D. Gabbay, R. H. Johnson, H. J. Ohldbach, & J. Woods (Eds.), *Handbook of the logic of argument and inference* (Studies in Logic and Practical Reasoning, Vol. 1, pp. 295–337). Amsterdam/Boston: North-Holland.

Jaśkowski, S. (1999). A propositional calculus for inconsistent deductive systems. *Logic and Logical Philosophy, 7*(1), 35–56 (translated from the 1948 original).

Kiss, O. (2006). Heuristics, methodology or logic of discovery? Lakatos on patterns of thinking. *Perspectives on Science, 14*, 302–317.

Koetsier, T. (1991). *Lakatos' philosophy of mathematics: A historical approach*. Amsterdam/New York: North-Holland.

Kvasz, L. (2002). Lakatos' methodology between logic and dialectic. In G. Kampis, L. Kvasz, & M. Stölzner (Eds.), *Appraising Lakatos: Mathematics, methodology and the man*. Dordrecht/Boston: Kluwer.

Lakatos, I. (1979). *Mathematics, science and epistemology*. Cambridge: Cambridge University Press.

Lakatos, I. (2005). *Proofs and refutations*. Cambridge: Cambridge University Press.

Priest, G. (1989). Dialectic and dialetheic. *Science & Society, 53*(4), 388–415 (Winter).

Priest, G., & Thomason, N. (2007). 60% proof – Lakatos, proof and paraconsistency. *Australasian Journal of Logic, 5*, 89–100.

Rahman, S., & Carnielli, W. A. (2000). The dialogical approach to paraconsistency. *Synthese, 125*, 201–231.

Rahman, S., & Tulenheimo, T. (2009). From games to dialogues and back. In O. Maher, A. Pietarinen, & T. Tulenheimo (Eds.), *Games: Unifying logic, language and philosophy* (pp. 153–208). Dordrecht: Springer.

The Heterogeneity of Mathematical Research

Jean Paul Van Bendegem

Abstract The core thesis of this contribution is that, if we wish to construct formal-logical models of mathematical practices, taking into account the maximum of detail, then it is a wise strategy to see mathematics as a heterogeneous entity. This thesis is supported by two case studies: the first one concerns a mathematical puzzle, the second one concerns Diophantine equations and belongs to mathematics proper. The advantage of the former is that the connection with logical modeling is pretty clear whereas the latter mainly demonstrates the difficulties one will have to overcome. A link is made with Hintikka's method of analysis and synthesis.

Keywords Heterogeneity in mathematics • Logical modeling • Analysis and synthesis • Explanation

1 Introduction

In recent years enormous progress has been made in the field of the logical modelling of knowledge and how knowledge is shared. Not only do we have completely worked-out logics for the epistemic states of an individual agent but also of a group of agents that can have common knowledge, that can rely on external resources and other related properties.[1] The success of these logics is to a large extent, though not solely, determined by their applicability in computer sciences and economical games where the notion of agent is pretty well described and reduced to its relevant epistemic features. However, if we turn to the 'real' sciences then a different story needs to be told. Any real episode in the history of the sciences is a true challenge for these logical models as so many factors enter into the picture. In addition, the interesting part of the scientific process is not

[1] It is a futile attempt to present an exhaustive list of references, but let me just mention Van Benthem (2011) as a nice overview of a major part of the field.

J.P. Van Bendegem (✉)
Vrije Universiteit Brussel, Center for Logic and Philosophy of Science, Brussels, Belgium
e-mail: jpvbende@vub.ac.be

C. Başkent (ed.), *Perspectives on Interrogative Models of Inquiry*, Logic, Argumentation & Reasoning 8, DOI 10.1007/978-3-319-20762-9_5

so much the sharing of knowledge but the obtaining of such knowledge, i.e., the discovery process. One might argue, and rightfully so, that for that process too, many logics have been developed, ranging from inductive logics over abduction logics to logics of questions (and answers) and logics of inquiry.[2] Again the problem seems to be that too many factors enter into the picture and that, as far as discovery is concerned, all too often historical records are lacking that describe any such event in sufficient detail. If, instead of the sciences, we now turn to mathematics then, more or less, a similar story needs to be told unfortunately. Although one might have hoped that mathematics is sufficiently different from the sciences so that perhaps the task of developing logical models might turn out to be somewhat easier or more straightforward, such is not the case.[3] As an illustration, I quote here Johan Van Benthem (2010):

> In this brief note, I put together current logics of agency with mathematical activities, and discuss what issues arise. I have no deep results to offer, and indeed, I mainly find challenges to my own dynamic logics, rather than sweeping insights into mathematics. (pp. 278–279)

The complexity of the task is thus an important obstacle to confront and the central thesis of this paper will be that a crucial factor that contributes to this complexity is the heterogeneity[4] of the field of mathematics that makes a uniform logical treatment as good as impossible. Or, conversely, unless we develop models that take into account this heterogeneity, chances seem slim for interesting applications of dynamic (social) epistemic logics to mathematics. In addition, a case will be made for different forms of heterogeneity that can occur, e.g., in the search process for a proof, in the connection between theorem and proof or between theorem and background theory, and also in the search for an explanation of a proof or theorem. In short, heterogeneity is itself heterogeneous.

The paper is structured as follows. In the next section, the most elaborate part of the paper, I present two problems. The first problem is a small-scale mathematical question that stands more or less on its own, and does not require full-fledged mathematical resources but already indicates (different forms of) heterogeneity within one single mathematical issue. Nevertheless a lot of logical details can be derived from this simple example as will be shown. The second problem is situated within 'real' mathematics and this generates a different picture where

[2]The comment in the first footnote applies here as well.

[3]Although the relevant literature in this case is far more manageable than that mentioned in the previous footnotes, I will nevertheless restrict myself to the work of Jaakko Hintikka relevant for this paper and that, in first instance, are the book and the paper on the method of analysis and synthesis, resp. Hintikka and Remes (1974) and Hintikka (2012). For a more general presentation, see Van Bendegem (2014).

[4]I prefer the term 'heterogeneity' over 'diversity' because in contexts where we use 'diversity' it is not a priori excluded that all the items that are supposed to be diverse share some common characteristics, whereas the usage of 'heterogeneity' takes into account the possibility that such common elements need not be present or, if nevertheless they are, are deemed less important than the differences.

(again different forms of) heterogeneity is (are) fully present and only a listing can be presented of ingredients necessary to enrich the logical models so as to be applicable. These two case studies should be seen as an invitation to logicians to try and capture these elements in their models. The third and final section discusses some mainly philosophical consequences of the heterogeneity thesis thus inviting philosophers of mathematics, and especially those involved with the study of mathematical practice, 'to join forces'. The appendix to the paper briefly discusses a third problem that I did not include into the core of the paper as my analysis of the problem was mistaken, a fact that I considered worth reporting.

2 Two Case Studies

2.1 The First Case Study

The first case study, as mentioned above, concerns a rather simple, self-contained, not so challenging and straightforward mathematical problem.

Given is the following sequence:

- $a_0 = 0, a_1 = 1, a_2 = 2$ and $a_3 = 6$
- $a_{n+4} = 2a_{n+3} + a_{n+2} - 2a_{n+1} - a_n$ (*)

It is required to prove that every a_n is divisible by n.

The status of this problem is, among mathematicians, rather clear, I would assume: this is a nice puzzle, rather than a genuine mathematical problem, that probably requires some ingenuity to find the answer but only presupposes general mathematical knowledge.[5] The reason why I believe I can make this claim is because this problem was presented in a Flemish journal *Wiskunde & Onderwijs* (*Mathematics & Education*) whose primary audience is mathematics teachers in (mainly) secondary schools. In addition the problem has been taken from a rubric in the journal, labelled *Zoekersrubriek* (a sort of problems corner).

What follows is a description of my search for a proof. I do not claim that it is paradigmatic in any sense. The only thing I need is one possible scenario to see what ingredients I will minimally need for such a description to be as complete as possible.[6] I have divided that search into separate episodes as each part required a different look on the problem. This is already a first manifestation of the heterogeneity I am referring to: as we progress in our search for a solution we

[5]Corresponding to a MSc degree in mathematics.

[6]That being said, in one of the following issues of the journal the solutions that readers had sent in are discussed and presented. My solution corresponded to the solution presented there so it was not a 'bizarre' attempt but rather what one might expect. Interestingly enough, there was a remarkable difference: the proof presented in the journal used mathematical induction. I will come back to this point later on in the paper.

change strategies and end up with different questions and different methods. Let us call this ‘type I heterogeneity’. We do not seem to be dealing with a single problem but with a connected chain of related but sufficiently different subproblems.

The *first strategy* that comes to mind is to translate the condition ‘a_n is divisible by n’ into a workable formula. The obvious answer is to assume that the general form of a_n must then be $k_n.n$—which leads to the equality $a_n = k_n.n$—, and then examine what properties the k’s must have. That however turns out not to be helpful at all for the recurrence relation for the a_n’s becomes more complicated for the k_n’s. The reason is obvious: if we want to replace a_n by $k_n.n$, a_{n+1} by $k_{n+1}.(n + 1)$, up to a_{n+4} by $k_{n+4}.(n + 4)$, we will find a recurrence relation that involves both the k’s, indexed by n, and the n’s themselves. A single unknown has now been replaced by a set of two (related) unknowns.

The *second strategy* is to see whether there is a pattern to be found among the k’s for the initial values. And that produces an intriguing picture.

Calculate the first terms of the sequence:

- $a_0 = 0 = 0.0$, so $k_0 = 0$ (some arbitrariness is present here, as k_0 could be anything, but let us ignore this for the moment)
- $a_1 = 1 = 1.1$, so $k_1 = 1$
- $a_2 = 2 = 1.2$, so $k_2 = 1$
- $a_3 = 6 = 2.3$, so $k_3 = 2$
- $a_4 = 12 = 3.4$, so $k_4 = 3$
- $a_5 = 25 = 5.5$, so $k_5 = 5$
- $a_6 = 48 = 8.6$, so $k_6 = 8$
- $a_7 = 91 = 13.7$, so $k_7 = 13$
- …

A few remarks are in order. One might interpret this strategy as a form of ‘career induction’, whereby a finite number of initial cases are examined to see whether the property, viz., the divisibility of a_n by n, is indeed present. However the main object of this second strategy is not to check this property but to find indications for a pattern in the k’s. This has an important consequence as it means that we are now dealing with a different kind of problem: given the initial values of a particular series, what could the general form of that series be? Notice how different this question is from the original question where a pattern is given and one has to show that the pattern has a particular property.

The *third strategy* to answer this new question is to rely on general mathematical knowledge and, once these initial values have been calculated, I assume that every mathematician will produce the same answer: the values

$$0, 1, 1, 2, 3, 5, 8, 13, \ldots$$

are the initial values of the Fibonacci series (with or without the initial 0 but that does not matter). If that would be the case, then we do have a pattern for the k’s, namely

$$k_{n+2} = k_{n+1} + k_n$$

If the initial pattern were not recognized directly, it is interesting to note that today dedicated websites exist, such as https://oeis.org/, the *On-Line Encyclopedia of Integer Sequences*, that allow one to enter an initial series of values and the program produces possible patterns that satisfy these values. This third strategy, being successful, now leads to yet another problem, namely to *prove* that a_n must have the form $k_n.n$, where k_n is an element out of the Fibonacci series. However, in this particular case, the problem can be inverted: assume that $a_n = k_n.n$, where k_n is an element out of the Fibonacci series, and prove that the original recurrence relation for the a_n's will be satisfied. This turns out to be a 'nasty' piece of work that I will not reproduce here in full, merely some initial and intermediate steps and then the endresult:

Start with $a_{n+4} = 2a_{n+3} + a_{n+2} - 2a_{n+1} - a_n$ and replace all a's by the explicit expression and, after some rearrangements, this formula appears:

$$k_{n+4}.n + 4k_{n+4} = n.(2k_{n+3} + k_{n+2} - 2k_{n+1} - k_n) + 6k_{n+3} + 2k_{n+2} - 2k_{n+1}$$

Suppose we would rearrange this formula such that it takes the form $A.n + B = 0$. This equation will certainly be satisfied if $A = B = 0$. This invites to look at the following two equations:

$$\begin{aligned} k_{n+4} &= 2k_{n+3} + k_{n+2} - 2k_{n+1} - k_n \qquad (**) \\ 4k_{n+4} &= 6k_{n+3} + 2k_{n+2} - 2k_{n+1} \end{aligned}$$

But, if the k's satisfy the Fibonacci series then that means that the above two equations are 'rewrites' of the basic recurrence relation, namely $k_{n+2} = k_{n+1} + k_n$. This turns out to be the case, a rather routine exercise. As an illustration take the first equation:

$$\begin{aligned} k_{n+4} &= k_{n+3} + k_{n+2} \\ &= k_{n+3} + k_{n+3} - k_{n+1} \\ &= 2k_{n+3} - k_{n+1} \end{aligned}$$

Add and subtract k_{n+2} on the right hand side:

$$= 2k_{n+3} + k_{n+2} - k_{n+2} - k_{n+1}$$

Finally replace the second occurrence of k_{n+2} by $k_{n+1} + k_n$ and the result follows. A similar calculation proves the other equation.

For the discussion that follows it is helpful to summarize the process in its major successful (thus ignoring the dead ends) steps:

- Step 1: Reformulate the problem so that it can be mathematically manipulated;
- Step 2: Find a pattern in a variable relying on 'career induction';

- Step 3: Use external resources to identify the pattern;
- Step 4: Prove that the pattern does indeed satisfy the premisses of the problem.

Let me comment on each of these steps.

- Step 1: What we are asked to show is a statement of the form

$$(\forall a_n)A(a_n)$$

where $A(a_n)$ is the statement that 'a_n is divisible by n'.[7] This statement can be reformulated into an equivalent statement of the same form, namely,

$$(\forall a_n)B(a_n)$$

where $B(a_n)$ is now the statement that '$a_n = k_n.n$'. It is now clear that $(\forall a_n)(A(a_n) \equiv B(a_n))$, and one might think that little has been achieved, as a proof of A must also be a proof of B and inversely so.

So what is there to gain in reformulating a problem into an equivalent version? Clearly the answer must be sought in the fact that different statements deal with different predicates and concepts and this may prove to be important in the search for a proof. What does seem exceptional in this particular case, is that B(x) is an explication or definition of A(x): B(x) simply tells us what it means to be divisible. That being said, this process invites us to reflect upon the following matter: given a statement A(x), what are the B(x)'s that are equivalent? The straightforward answer must be: an infinite number of them.[8] A possible restriction could be to look in this first phase of the proof search at those B(x)'s that are 'close' to A(x).[9] This invites us to consider a notion of distance. How could we determine what the distance is between two equivalent statements? One possibility is to define the distance in terms of the length of the proof that shows A(x) and B(x) to be equivalent. As it must be clear, this is a tricky notion. Must we not talk about the shortest proof? And can we determine such a thing? Even in the case of a well-defined formal language, the choice and formulation of axioms and the choice of the underlying logical

[7]This is a slightly sloppy notation using a variable that itself contains an index, but no need at this point to have a totally correct presentation and I assume that everyone sees how it can be repaired quite easily I dare say.

[8]Given a statement A(x), it is easy to show that A(x) is equivalent to $A(x) \equiv (A(x) \equiv A(x))$. If we define the latter statement as $A(x)^{(3)}$ and $A(x)^{(n)}$ as $A(x) \equiv A(x)^{(n-1)}$, then all $A(x)^{(2n+1)}$ are equivalent to A(x). Of course, none of these statements carries any interest.

[9]There is no inherent necessity to start with this strategy. Perhaps here an important difference can be found between recreational mathematics and professional mathematics. In the latter case, I assume, one will not look for equivalent statements that are 'close' but also look for equivalent reformulations that 'transport' the problem from one mathematical domain into another.

machinery can have a tremendous effect on the length of a proof, witness the work of Parikh, especially his (1973). But what to do in the context of real mathematical practice, where even a well-defined formal language is not always available? There is definitely some vagueness lurking in the background here, but for cases where the proofs only count a small number of lines, this seems feasible. So the first step already introduces a concept that is important to include in an epistemology of the search for proofs.[10]

- Step 2 and step 3: Our attention has now shifted from B(x) itself to the 'behaviour' of the k_n's. The core question here now is how we can recognize a general pattern on the basis of an initial segment?

Just as in the first step, if the question is formulated in such a general way, then we face the classical (non-mathematical) induction problem: is not any initial segment compatible with an infinite number of continuations so how is one to make a choice? Again the issue of resources should be taken very seriously in this context. It is not the case that mathematicians consider every possible continuation but as soon as these particular numbers appear it is clear that the Fibonacci sequence 'forces' itself upon us. Of course, we do not have the guarantee that this will happen every time so what we have witnessed in recent times is the emergence of dedicated websites such as the already mentioned OEIS website that have become important aids in mathematical research. From the formal epistemological point of view, it is well-known how to deal with common and shared knowledge but such a database has, in relation to the community of mathematicians, a different structure and plays a different role. Individual mathematicians can store in their memories a set of sequences but this will only be a small part of the full content of such a database. Therefore the database is an external element and, as such not so much common knowledge, as common meta-knowledge, namely that mathematicians know that such a database exists and can be consulted. In addition, it requires specific tools how to query such an information source. In the case of OEIS it is quite simple: submit the initial finite sequence. Although in some cases, quite a number of alternatives are proposed, it remains a feasible task to see whether one

[10]Interestingly enough, whether or not one succeeds in formally pinning down such a distance measure, real mathematical practice is already dealing with this problem as the following example shows. Billey and Tenner (2013) argue for so-called fingerprint databases where a formula can be tested for equivalent formulations to save time and not fall into the trap of having seemingly discovered a novelty: "There are examples throughout mathematical history of theorems having been discovered, and subsequently rediscovered independently—sometimes over and over again" (p. 1035). The informal distance measure they employ is the number of lines of the proof that demonstrates the equivalence.

of them actually does the job.[11,12] There is more: the answer OEIS provides are possible continuations of the sequence plus a mathematical contextualization, i.e., what theorems are known about that sequence, to what domains does it belong, and so forth. This additional information will surely increase the probability of finding an answer to the original problem.[13]

- Step 4: The last step is almost trivial. Since we have an explicit form for the k_n's and thereby for the a_n's, it is now sufficient to prove that the original recurrence relations are satisfied, as this is equivalent to answer the original question.

There is however one very important remark to make: the endresult, i.e., the proof of the original question will mainly consist of this step.[14] The previous steps are not taken up in the proof, which makes it clear that the proof itself is not in any case a summary of the search process but a rendition of the final stage of that process and thus is highly uninformative (at least in this case). It is extremely typical that the solution mentioned in the aforementioned journal, *Wiskunde & Onderwijs*, starts with a definition of the Fibonacci series and then continues by

[11]It is undeniably an enormous task to set up such a database as the number of mathematically meaningful possibilities to continue a finite fragment can be staggering. Take, e.g., the initial sequence 1, 2, 4, 8, 16. Of course the first thing that comes to mind is powers of two. But another well-known continuation is 31, 57, 99, 163, ..., where the numbers are equal to the maximum number of regions one can divide a circle into, given all the lines connecting n points on the circumference of the circle. Now the entry for this sequence gives 47 possibilities. This is, as said, tractable but at the same time it is extremely interesting to see in what other mathematical contexts the sequence appears. This is a second-order effect of the use of such databases that should be taken into account in a formal model.

[12]The need for such dedicated databases is clearly becoming a matter of prime importance in the development of mathematics, witness a recent study of the National Academy of Sciences, see National Research Council (2014).

[13]The few remarks made here are just the beginning of a far-reaching exploration. One of the anonymous referees of this paper made a number of important suggestions concerning this matter. I list a few of them. Is it necessarily the case that every mathematical problem includes such a search phase? It is a deep question and I do not have a convincing answer at the moment either way. Are there philosophical and computational implications? There I am quite confident that the answer must be positive. No database, if sufficiently large, escapes the 'big data' issue: how should one organize the data to make efficient data mining possible? Philosophically, such issues have a direct connection with the way(s) a mathematical community is organized, who is having access to data sources and who can change, improve and delete data. This, by the way, relates nicely to work being done recently on the Polymath phenomenon, see, e.g., Nielsen (2012). Finally, one may wonder whether this type of search process is proper to mathematics? I think not. Is it proper to the exact sciences? Probably, since the problem how one should store qualitative data is far more complicated than the storage of quantitative data. In short, much work needs to be done.

[14]This point will be taken up again in Sect. 3.2, where Hintikka's approach is discussed in relation to the analysis and synthesis process in mathematics. I will not develop this point any further in this paper but a connection can and should be made between on the one hand the distinction between the search process for the proof and the proof itself and on the other hand the well-known and strongly debated distinction between the context of discovery and of justification.

mathematical induction. It is truly striking that throughout the search no mention was made of mathematical induction, but rather of a form of scientific induction, namely to guess or derive a general pattern on the basis of a finite set of data. This implies that in a model for a community of mathematicians, it cannot be solely (finished) proofs that circulate among them but it must be much more than that.

To summarize, as far as this case study is concerned, if we want to develop formal models of mathematical practice, we will need formal counterparts for (a) a concept of proof-related distance of equivalent statements, (b) a structured notion of searchable resources or, more generally speaking, of databases, and (c) the 'translation' for the proof search to the final proof (as it usually appears to the community of mathematicians). I see no intrinsic reason for the impossibility of successfully implementing these three tasks. If, however, as will be done in the next subsection, we move to 'real' mathematical problems the size of the task does, I believe, become impressive (although I would continue to claim it remains manageable, hence possible).

2.2 *The Second Case Study*

This case study concerns Diophantine equations and illustrates a quite curious property that mathematicians are very familiar with but not necessarily non-mathematicians, namely the fact that there need not be any structural similarity between the theorem that needs to be proven and the proof itself. This is what I consider to be a form of heterogeneity but now between statements of theorems and proofs. Let us call this 'type II heterogeneity'.

Consider the following group of equations:

$$x^3 + y^3 + z^3 = n \quad \text{for} \quad 29 \leq n \leq 33$$

Obviously the five equations are highly correlated as there is a simple and neat way to formulate them in a single statement, as I have done. I first list the results without comments:

- $x^3 + y^3 + z^3 = 29$ has at least two simple solutions: $x = 3, y = z = 1$ and $x = 4, y = -3, z = -2$;
- $x^3 + y^3 + z^3 = 30$ has a smallest solution: $x = -283059965, y = -2218888517, z = 2220422932$;
- $x^3 + y^3 + z^3 = 31$: no solutions;
- $x^3 + y^3 + z^3 = 32$: no solutions;
- $x^3 + y^3 + z^3 = 33$: as it happens this problem is still open and, apparently, no one seems to have an idea how to handle it.

Why have I chosen this specific example? Basically because I do not happen to be the only one to be struck by this curious phenomenon, see, e.g., Poonen (2008) and Stoll (2010), inspired by Poonen, and the Cut-the-knot website (http://www.cut-the-knot.org/): problems that, when formulated, are really close[15] together, turn out to be entirely different in terms of their solutions. Actually, it even seems to be worse: one has the impression that there is no pattern at all present here. Just ask yourself how you would handle the cases n = 28 or 35?[16] But there is more: how these results have been obtained are as diverse as well. Let me briefly go through the proofs (if indeed that is what we can call them).

The easiest cases are n = 31 and 32. The fact that there are no solutions is simply based on modulo arithmetic, in this case modulo 9. Write an arbitrary number n as 9k + m, then n reduces to m (mod 9), where $0 \leq m \leq 8$. If we take the third power of n then, modulo 9, only m^3 will remain so we only have to check what the residues are of m^3 for $0 \leq m \leq 8$:

m	0	1	2	3	4	5	6	7	8
m^2	0	1	4	9	16	25	36	49	64
m^3	0	1	8	27	64	125	216	343	512
m^3(mod9)	0	1	−1	0	1	−1	0	1	−1

So m^3 (mod 9) is to be found between –1 and 1. Therefore if we add three third powers, their sum modulo 9 will be between –3 and 3. As 31 and 32 are equal to 4, resp. 5 (mod 9), they can never be the sum of three cubes. That is easy.

The cases n = 29 and 30 are the outcome of computer searches, i.e., extensive computations. Of course not that extensive for the n = 29 case where the solutions are relatively small. However for the n = 30 case, really clever algorithms had to be used to find this solution that still required a quite serious amount of calculating time. See Beck et al. (2007) for details about the algorithm. To be sure, we have no proofs here, just an answer to the question: is there a solution? If the question would be whether we know all solutions to a particular equation, then the best result to date is that for the cases n = 1 and 2, we have an explicit parameterization thus generating all possible solutions:

For the case n = 1 (Mahler 1936):

$$(9t^4)^3 + (3t - 9t^4)^3 + (1 - 9t^3)^3 = 1$$

[15]Note that the meaning of 'close' is not the same as used before in this paper (when discussing the 'distance' between equivalent statements). A possibility for determining a distance between two formulae A(x, c) and B(y, d) where x and y are a set of variables and c and d a set of constants is to simply count the number of symbols that need to be replaced to transform one formula into the other. For the formulas we are looking at here, the distance is minimal as only one constant needs to be replaced. To define such a measure for arbitrary formulas is, of course, quite another matter and will not be tackled here.

[16]I have skipped the case n = 34 for a small search immediately leads to the solution $n = 34 = 27 + 7 = 27 + 8 - 1 = 3^3 + 2^3 - 1^3$, hence x = 3, y = 2 and z = –1.

For the case $n = 2$ (attributed to Werebrusov in 1908 according to Mordell (1942)):

$$(1 + 6t^3)^3 + (1 - 6t^3)^3 + (-6t^2)^3 = 2$$

It is highly typical for such problems that from time to time another solution is found for some particular n. This is related to the fact that the algorithms can sometimes be speeded up if the number n has particular properties. So, e.g., there is a solution known now for $n = 52$:

$$x = 60702901317, y = 23961292454, \text{ and } z = -61922712865$$

The situation we are faced with here can be best summarized, I believe, by the fact that we have no idea how to handle the open case, $n = 33$. What is one supposed to do, apart from a massive and clever calculation? There seem to be no general strategies available, no overarching concepts that have a uniting force and no general theory that groups all these equations.[17] And yet that last statement is not entirely true. There is another way to look at these problems.

I started out by presenting this problem as belonging to the domain of Diophantine equations. But instead of writing down the formula in the form

$$x^3 + y^3 + z^3 = n$$

we can simply inverse it (fully realizing that since identity is supposed to be symmetric this should make no difference but notation in this case is not without its importance) and then, I claim, we see something else[18]:

$$n = x^3 + y^3 + z^3$$

What we have here now is a problem about the decomposition of natural numbers and the question is not whether this equation has Diophantine solutions but rather what natural numbers can be written as the sum of three cubes, and that is an altogether different question (about basically the same equation). This claim is supported by the fact that a series of ideas and proof techniques enter into the picture that were not directly associated with our previous approach. Let me just sketch some such elements.[19]

The more general problem, well known in number theory is this: given a number k, how many kth powers does one need to represent any natural number n? The

[17]This observation will be further developed in Sect. 3.3, where I discuss briefly the problem of mathematical explanation.

[18]'We see' here means that the equation in this form will be identified in the mathematical literature as belonging to a different domain than the equation in its original form.

[19]See Watkins (2014), pp. 207–209, for a nice summary.

answer is usually indicated by the function g(k) = the number of kth powers needed to represent n. For k = 2, we know that g(2) = 4, i.e., any natural number can be written as the sum of four squares, the famous result of Lagrange. Edward Waring in 1770 asked the general question stated above. Waring himself proposed an explicit formula for g(k), without proof:

$$g(k) = \lfloor (3/2)k \rfloor + 2k - 2$$

where $\lfloor x \rfloor$ is the so-called floor function, i.e., the largest integer smaller than x. However a second function appears in this context and that changes things in a rather dramatic way. The function G(k) = the smallest number of kth powers needed to represent n from a certain finite number N onwards. Why is such a function interesting? Here is one reason: if it turns out that G(k) << g(k) then it is more interesting to work with G(k). After all, we are interested in all natural numbers and, if there is an initial finite fragment where behaviour is different from the long-run perspective, then, since it is finite, this can be dealt with separately. In the case k = 3, we now know that g(3) = 9 and G(3) ≤ 7, for a given N, and the conjecture is that G(3) = 4, at present known to be the lower limit of G(3) (in the sense that there is no N such that all numbers, larger than N are the sum of three cubes).

It is indeed the case that we have a more general framework to deal with the original problem and general theorems and the like but it is clear what the price is to be paid: our original question simply disappears in the background as no longer interesting. The cases we have been discussing for n = 29 up to n = 33 are in the finite part where the G-function does and will not care about. So, although we have a theory available, it does not help us with our original problem as there will be no theorems or computational results for such small values.[20] I would consider this to be another manifestation of heterogeneity: a shift in theoretical background can reduce the importance of a problem (or, of course, the inverse, i.e., enhance it). Let us call this 'type III heterogeneity'. Let me end here the presentation of this second case study and see where a similar thought exercise as in the first case study will lead us.

To be honest, I would not know where to start. This example seems so far off from existing logical models (up to my knowledge) that it is hard to see how one could deal with them. Every case for n = 29 up to and including n = 33 seems to require a different treatment. Some are easy to solve (with proofs), some are results of calculations that do require proofs to show that the shortcuts in the algorithm do what they claim to do, some are unknown. Cases can be formulated in different theories and approaches that do not really simplify matters for problems that are important and relevant in the one framework cease to be so in the other one. All that being said, I do stick with my original claim about the feasibility of logically

[20]This does not exclude, of course, that the proofs of those theorems use interesting concepts and proof methods that might turn out to be relevant for the original problem.

modelling what is going on here in its full complexity. I do not see any fundamental reason why such an undertaking could not be successful. My strongest argument is this: in previous publications, e.g., Van Kerkhove and Van Bendegem (2004), we have proposed a(n informal) model for understanding mathematical practice, based on an earlier proposal of Philip Kitcher.[21] It consists of a seventuple <M, P, F, PM, C, AM, PS>, containing the following elements:

- a mathematical *community* M of individual *mathematicians* $m_1, m_2, \ldots, m_i$;
- a *research program* P within the framework of which specific problems $p_1, p_2, \ldots, p_j, \ldots$ can be formulated;
- a *formal language* F, wherein axioms, definitions, and a body of *formal proofs* $f_1, f_2, \ldots, f_k, \ldots$, can be expressed, that provide typical answers to the above problems; note that here too metamathematical considerations can play their part;
- a set PM of *proof methods* $pm_1, pm_2, \ldots, pm_l, \ldots$
- a set C of *concepts* $c_1, c_2, \ldots, c_n, \ldots$
- a set AM of *argumentative methods*: $am_1, am_2, \ldots, am_s, \ldots$
- a set PS of *proof strategies* $ps_1, ps_2, \ldots, ps_t, \ldots$

I will not do the exercise here but it seems obvious that the second case study can be accommodated in such an extended model or, at least, certain parts of it. Let me just mention one reason why I believe that such models are well suited to accommodate heterogeneity. The elements of the seventuple are not linked to a particular mathematical problem but rather form the ingredients that constitute the problem. One might expect that several proof strategies and methods will be used, that different concepts will occur and that the background theory and the language wherein it is expressed have an impact as well. To remain within the kitchen metaphor: a cookbook may appear quite homogeneous in its direct appearance—after all, recipes do tend to have a fixed schema that occurs over and over again—but on the level of the ingredients, it is quite heterogeneous and, once the recipe has to be executed, that heterogeneity surfaces as many of the ingredients require separate and specific treatment.[22] Thus the challenge will be to bring the logical models together with Kitcher-like less formal or informal models to obtain (probably) some hybrid form wherein mathematical practice in all its heterogeneity can be expressed. Let me now turn to philosophical matters.

[21]Kitcher (1983) proposes a model consisting of a quintuple <L, M, Q, R, S>, containing:a *language* L, a set of *accepted statements* S, a set of *accepted reasonings* R, a set of *important questions* Q, and a set of *philosophical or metamathematical views* M.

[22]It is not an unreasonable thought to equate the cookbook with a foundational theory such as ZFC and the daily activities of a mathematician or group of mathematicians with the actual cooking. Or, to put it in other words, the homogeneity that characterizes such theories as ZFC does not transfer to the daily practices. I briefly return to this matter in the final paragraph of the conclusion of this paper.

3 Some Philosophical Thoughts About Heterogeneity and Mathematical Practice

3.1 About Problem-Solving

No doubt many readers will have wondered why I ignored the vast literature about problem-solving, specifically in mathematics. Where is Georg Pólya, to name but one of the founding fathers? Should he not have been included? The answer is of course yes, if we would have been aiming at a full-fledged presentation of what mathematicians do when they do mathematics. But the aim of this paper is more modest: what elements are needed to make existing logical models richer (and thereby closer to actual practice), taking into account the heterogeneity of the mathematicians' activity? It would however be unwise to put all this material aside as irrelevant. As it happens, some elements that occur in problem-solving literature have already been included into logical models. Take, e.g., the very basic idea of splitting up a problem P into a set of subproblems P_i, such that, if all P_i are solved, thereby the original problem is solved.[23] This idea is to be found not merely in problem solving contexts, but also in the domain of artificial intelligence, where distributed problem solving is a core issue, with or without cooperation and argumentation. However, without going into details here, it is my impression that such proposals go together with some form of homogeneity. If we think in terms of a community of agents or mathematicians in our particular case, then it is clear that every agent is interchangeable with every other agent: the only characteristics that matter are those that identify that agent's position in the network and its access to other agents. That does not seem to hold in real-life situations. So, granted that all the literature about problem-solving strategies and about artificial networks with distributed knowledge is indeed important and relevant and needs to be studied closely and in depth, one should not expect to get final answers here. These models too will need to be made richer in order to deal with the case studies we have presented here.

In addition very often the focus is on mathematical problem-solving in educational context (as was the case originally for Pólya as well) and not often enough on professional mathematics. Of course, as I have tried to show by the second case study, on that level things do become more complex and more difficult to handle. And what is surely required is to combine this literature with personal experiences by mathematicians themselves. A recent fine example is the 'story' told by Cédric Villani in (2012). The book contains not only the genesis of the proof of a theorem but also includes conversations, e-mail exchanges, discussions, dreams,

[23]Note, incidentally that this is another variation on the theme of the equivalences that I mentioned in the first case study for in such a case $P \equiv (P_1 \ \& \ P_2 \ \& \ldots \& \ P_n)$ and the proof of the equivalence should be short, which is often the case. Just think of a problem about natural numbers where the problem is split up in the even case and the odd case. But do note that this does not imply that each P_i will be treated in the same manner.

wrong tracks, dead ends, partial successes and the final result, which won him the Fields medal in 2010. Although one must realize that such a story is to be considered more a reconstruction, a retelling than an actual, factual rendition of what happened, it does nevertheless contain valuable elements that need to be incorporated in the models we are looking for. Let me however look in the next subsection at another attempt that deserves our proper attention.

3.2 *Hintikka Method of Analysis and Synthesis*

The reason why I am having a closer look at the work of Jaakko Hintikka in relation to mathematical practice is that he is surely one of the principal researchers to have examined throughout his career closely the relations between logical models and mathematics.[24] In particular, I will have a look at the [2012] paper. A fuller analysis would also require at least the seminal [1974] book, jointly written with Unto Remes, to be discussed. The object of the paper is a logical analysis of the (Greek) method of analysis and synthesis. The commonly shared (but not necessarily completely correct) view is that analysis proceeds from the conclusion upwards to the premisses whereas synthesis makes the opposite move as it proceeds from the premisses downwards. If both happen to meet at a certain point in the reasoning then a proof has been found. Hintikka's claim is that the Beth tableau method is an excellent way of logically formulating this idea. A formal example is not really needed here: in a tableau we write down the premisses on the left-side and the conclusion on the right-side and then we reason in both halves of the tableau until the same formula appears at both sides.[25]

However, this method by itself is not sufficient:

> We have to introduce an epistemic element into the reasoning. In mathematical practice, this element is often tacit. It can be made explicit by adding to the usual first-order logic an 'it is known that' operator K. (p. 59)

I will return to this 'tacit' element in the conclusion of this paper. As the tableaus are extended with the K operator, Hintikka turns the tableau method as an instrument for the search of proofs into a problem-solving tool. This also happens by the

---

[24] An additional reason is that part of this paper has been presented at the LoQI conference (*Logic, Questions and Inquiry. A conference on Hintikka's Interrogative Model of Inquiry*), organized by the IMI project (*Interrogative Model of Inquiry*), funded by the ANR (*Agence Nationale de Recherche*), held in Paris, 30 May – 1 June 2013. For my purpose here, I have selected some of his works specifically relevant for the discovery and justification processes in mathematics.

[25] Note that I did not, as Hintikka indeed does not as well, refer to the premisses being true and the conclusion being false, though of course a tableau can always be construed in that fashion. The point here is that, if we forget about true and false, what we do in the left-side of the tableau is to reason from the premisses, whereas in the right-side of the tableau we reason starting from the conclusion. If a formula appears at both sides, a connection has been made between premisses and conclusion.

introduction of the possibility to ask questions, especially in those cases, where the conclusion is not necessarily known and can only be introduced as a question (thereby making the link with the topic of the previous subsection). Of special interest is the clarification by this extension between 'knowns' and 'unknowns' in a mathematical problem. It is mentioned a few times in the paper that geometry and algebra should not be treated on a par in this context. In geometry it is not clear how in a geometrical figure or diagram known and unknown can be brought together whereas in algebra known and unknown can occur together in a single equation. This distinction between the two domains must add to the heterogeneity that I am arguing for.[26] Let us call this 'type IV heterogeneity'.

What does seem clear is that, if we make the move from geometry to algebra, other extensions will be needed of the basic tableau method and of the extended method Hintikka proposes. To make my point clear: take another look at the second case study. What would be in the right-side of the tableau? Obviously the existential statement $(\exists x, y, z)(x^3 + y^3 + z^3 = n)$, for a particular n. This formula can be instantiated, producing $a^3 + b^3 + c^3 = n$, for some a, b and c, but it is not clear at all what further analysis can be done. Take one specific example: why would anyone come up with the idea of applying a modulo 9 reasoning to the problem? Or, more precisely, why 9, as modulo reasoning is fairly commonplace in this particular domain? Referring back to the extension of the Kitcher model we proposed, it would imply that at least search strategies should be incorporated. To achieve that, game semantics, another of Hintikka's projects, could be an excellent first start.

Let me now turn to a final topic in this section, a 'hot' topic as it were in present-day philosophy of mathematics, namely mathematical explanation.

3.3 A Brief Excursion About Explanation

Vital and essential for the one, nonexistent for the other, no matter what one's view is in this discussion, mathematical explanation needs our attention. I will not repeat here the two major proposals—Kitcher's seminal idea of unification and Steiner's equally seminal idea of a characterizing property, see Mancosu (2011) for details—that circulate at present, but I think that the two case studies show that these two will not prove to cover the whole domain, under the supposition, of course, that there is such a thing as mathematical explanation. And, if asked for a reason for that belief, my answer would once again be the heterogeneity of the mathematical enterprise. Let me have a look at the two cases.

---

[26] I must repeat that the focus of the paper is on geometry, therefore one should not expect any issue of heterogeneity being addressed here. And the particular subdomain of geometry Hintikka is looking is thereby a fairly homogeneous domain. This is definitely not meant as a critique! The object of the paper after all is to understand what it needs to better model the relations between geometrical figures and reasoning about those figures rather than presenting a full-fledged model of mathematical practice.

In the first case, while I was searching for the solution and the Fibonacci series appeared 'out of the blue' as it were, I was puzzled and did not understand why this was the case. At first sight there is nothing in the final proof that explains this curious phenomenon. At least, I could not identify any element in the proof itself that could serve as (part of) an explanation. But what I did not mention in Sect. 2.1 is that some mathematicians sent in a solution to the problem to *Wiskunde & Onderwijs* that used the *characteristic polynomial*[27] of the recurrence relation.

The above proof has no explanatory value whatsoever and it does not really matter what notion of mathematical explanation is being used. I do of course realize that this is a challenging and slightly provocative statement but I think it stands up. There is at first sight no unification present here or some overarching concept, so no Kitcher-like idea, and there is no essential or characteristic property involved, so no Steiner-like idea, therefore the two major views tell me this proof must be considered to be non-explanatory.

There is, of course, one very interesting feature that must strike any mathematician: the k's satisfy the very same equation as the a's, namely (**). That produces the idea that the a's are also somehow related to the Fibonacci series. How to show that? Relying on the general background knowledge of a (rather) well-trained mathematician, he or she will come up with the idea of the characteristic polynomial for a recurrence relation, as mentioned above.

This is based on the idea that the original equation can always be rewritten as follows:

$$\begin{aligned} a_{n+4} &= 2a_{n+3} + a_{n+2} - 2a_{n+1} - a_n \\ a_{n+4}/a_n &= 2a_{n+3}/a_n + a_{n+2}/a_n - 2a_{n+1}/a_n - 1 \end{aligned}$$

If the ratio a_{n+1}/a_n has a limit, say g, and if we replace a_{n+2}/a_n by $(a_{n+2}/a_{n+1})(a_{n+1}/a_n)$ and so forth for the other terms in the equation, and then take the limit, then we get:

$$\begin{aligned} &g^4 = 2g^3 + g^2 - 2g - 1 \qquad \text{or} \\ &g^4 - 2g^3 - g^2 + 2g + 1 = 0 \end{aligned}$$

This last equation can be rewritten as (this is elementary algebra):

$$(g^2 - g - 1)^2 = 0$$

and (one of) the solution(s) of the equation $g^2 - g - 1$ is precisely the golden ratio, which can also be defined as the limit of the ratio k_{n+1}/k_n, and the connection is made. So, after all, there is a core property, namely the characteristic polynomial, that gives (part of) an explanation. However, firstly, I did not use that property in

[27]Not to be confused with Steiner's use of characteristic!

the proof that I constructed, which is strange.[28] Secondly, it is not immediately clear how the original problem should be answered using that property. That in itself would generate another search process. It seems more likely to expect that a full explanatory proof will require more than this one concept (assuming that the above can already count as a partial explanation, because not everyone, mathematician and non-mathematician alike, shares this idea). For one thing, it is not clear at all how the characteristic polynomial relates to the divisibility of the a's by n.[29]

If we now turn to the second case study, it seems clear to me that here little or nothing can be said. The modulo 9 reasoning to exclude the cases for n = 9k + 4 or 9k + 5 can be taken to have explanatory power but for the other cases explanations of whatever sort seem really far away. Of course, in most cases, we only have calculations and not proofs but I see no immediate reason why a calculation by itself could not have explanatory power. In addition, it seems highly unlikely that some unifying account could be found that would do the job. Precisely due to the heterogeneity of this problem, explaining what is going on here seems a futile undertaking. This last statement should not be interpreted in a negative way: it provides us with examples where one can defend that the proofs and/or calculations do not explain why. One of the reasons why I discussed in Sect. 2.2 the reformulation of the original question into Waring's problem was to show that there could be a unifying theory. Unfortunately in that more general framework the original question became an unimportant element in the margin. That being said, the possibility was present that moving the problem from one domain to another might produce an explanation that was not available in the first domain. Can this be seen as anything else but another sign of the heterogeneity? Let us call this (derived) 'type V heterogeneity'.

Let me address one final matter in this section.[30] In Sect. 3.2 I discussed several possible extensions of the tableau method, primarily an analytical tool, changing it into a problem-solving strategic tool. Could the method be further extended to include the explanatory aspects of the proof one is looking for as well? On the one hand I see no principal or fundamental argument for a negative answer. On the

---

[28]I call this 'strange' because it reminds me of Sherlock Holmes (a character also very dear to Jaakko Hintikka) and the curious incident with the dog in the night-time: if the characteristic polynomial is indeed a core element in the explanation of what is going on here, why then does it not appear in the proof itself (or, formulated differently, why is there at least one proof where it does not play any part)? Or let me put matters in this way: if, instead of the Fibonacci sequence some other sequence P had appeared during my search, I would not have been amazed or surprised as I did not have any expectations at that moment. All I needed was to find some pattern such that the k's satisfy it.

[29]It is actually tempting to think that the designers of the problem worked backwards to find the initial recurrence relation. It should therefore not surprise us that Fibonacci appears but, even if that were the case, the explanatory question would remain. What we now would like to obtain is an explanation why the recurrence relation of the a_n's takes that particular form and not another.

[30]This paragraph is the result of a remark of one of the anonymous referees of this paper. In the first version there was no real link between Sects. 3.2 and 3.3. This, I believe, has now become clearer.

other hand, I do think that the analyticity will be severely weakened. When one is convinced that explanation is not a mere property of a proof but involves concepts that are related to the proof yet are not determined by it, then elements are introduced that are more likely to be synthetic rather than analytical. I refer to my paper Van Bendegem (to appear) where I discussed this matter in relation to the contingent nature of mathematical knowledge.

4 To Conclude

In Hintikka (2012), the paper I discussed in Sect. 3.2, we read the following:

> In general, it does not make much difference if an interpreter tries to evoke the holy cow called mathematical practice. If such practice is not haphazard, it must be governed by some tacit rules which must be discussed on a par with explicitly codified ones. (p. 51)

Whether or not we are dealing here with 'a holy cow' is not the issue, rather I believe that this quote makes two very important claims: the first one is that mathematical practice is governed by tacit rules and the second one that the tacit rules should be treated in the same way as the explicit ones. The fact that they are tacit entails that work needs to be done to make them explicit. One should not be amazed if mathematicians do not recognize them when faced with them. After all, if they are tacit, you are not supposed to consciously know that they are at work. But the fact that they have to be treated on a par entails the following. Since we use logical models for understanding the explicit practice and/or results of mathematical research, it follows that Hintikka subscribes to the idea that formal and logical models will be needed to understand the tacit rules. There is a clear agreement here between this view and what is proposed here in this paper. And, of course, on a more general level, Hintikka makes clear and defends the importance of the study of mathematical practice, no matter what animal, holy or otherwise, corresponds to it.

The core thesis of this paper is that, if we want to further explore the multiple relations between logic and mathematics, then it will be necessary to take into account what I have called at various places in the paper 'heterogeneity of mathematics'. I recall the five types that we already identified in this paper, merely on the basis of two small case studies:

- Type I: The search process to find a solution to a mathematical problem typically falls apart in different stages that require different strategies, including reformulations of the problem;
- Type II: The proximity of mathematical problems need not be related to a proximity of the corresponding proofs or similar problems can require different proofs and distinct problems can be solved by similar proofs;
- Type III: A mathematical problem can change drastically when transposed from one mathematical background to another, up to the point of its disappearance or becoming uninteresting;

- Type IV: Mathematical theories that form the background for a (set of) problems are to be considered different because of the different proof strategies and related concepts that are being used;
- Type V: Mathematical explanation, whatever it might be, depends (though perhaps not solely) on proof and it thus 'inherits' its heterogeneity.

If all these types are ignored, i.e., if homogeneity is too much emphasized, then inevitably we will turn back again to published proofs, the final outcomes of a process that suggests a homogeneity but in actuality has eliminated all the heterogeneous elements. This leaves us wondering where the result came from and, before one knows it, special realms, Platonic heavens and the like, have to be created in order to explain what is, after all, a human process. That being said, what I have not shown is that such homogeneity is to be avoided at all costs. Perhaps the detailed heterogeneity of everyday mathematical practice needs to be counterbalanced or complemented by something that allows us to get a larger view that unites rather than diversifies. Is that not precisely an implicit aim of foundational studies, e.g., set theory, category theory, univalent foundations or homotopy type theory? If so, then this provides an unexpected justification of such studies from the perspective of mathematical practice.

Appendix

This paper is the perfect occasion to set something straight. In previous publications, most notably in Van Bendegem (2004), I claimed that in mathematics one always had to deal with the 'unexpected'. One might think up very nice general schemes but trust mathematics to come up with exceptions that relativize the generality and its accompanying claim. (I guess that here was one of the starting points for thinking about heterogeneity). I call these proofs 'from the unexpected' and my prime example was the following:

Consider a real-valued function f from R to R. No special properties or requirements are needed. One is asked to prove an easily stated theorem about f, namely that f is always the sum of a symmetric function g, i.e. a function g such that $g(-x) = g(x)$ and an anti-symmetric function h, i.e., a function h such that $h(-x) = -h(x)$.

I did not manage to solve this problem when I first encountered it. There is very little material to use but on the other hand the fact that it applies to any function f, without any qualifications, seems strange. That being said, it does seem a really strong property. No matter what function you can come up with, it is decomposable into two functions with a highly specific property. That seems odd. The first strategy seemed to be to write f(x) as the sum of two functions g(x) and h(x),

$$f(x) = g(x) + h(x)$$

and further suppose that, e.g., g(x) is symmetric. The object would then be to show that f(x) – g(x) is anti-symmetric. However, that much is clear, at least at first sight, this is never going to work. Since f(x) can be any function at all, why would the difference between an arbitrary function, f(x), and a function with a specific property, g(x), itself have a specific property? I did not continue this line of attack and got nowhere. When I afterwards saw the solution to the problem, I felt 'cheated' in first instance, as the solution makes use of an algebraic identity, namely:

$$f(x) = [(f(x) + f(-x))/2] + [(f(x) - f(-x))/2]$$

Call the function between square brackets on the left side of the right hand side expression g(x) and the function between square brackets on the right side of the same expression h(x) and you are done. Of course, one understands immediately why f can be arbitrary: no specific properties are required. End of story. Though not exactly.

While writing this paper, I re-examined the problem and it turns out that my original strategy, that I abandoned too quickly, would have led me to the correct result by a completely straightforward argument. So suppose that you do want to investigate the function f(x) – g(x) and want to show it is anti-symmetric, or:

$$f(-x) - g(-x) = -(f(x) - g(x))$$

Given that $g(-x) = g(x)$ this simplifies to:

$$f(-x) - g(x) = -f(x) + g(x)$$

and this gives an explicit expression for g(x):

$$g(x) = (f(-x) + f(x))/2$$

which is precisely the answer we were looking for, if we now calculate what h(x) must look like. On the one hand, it means that I can no longer use this example, which need not be a problem as proofs from the unexpected are plentiful but on the other hand there is an important conclusion to be drawn from this example. Often we abort attempts too soon on the basis of a projected estimate and, once again, we are talking about resources: is it worthwhile to continue a reasoning or calculations if the prospects of success seem rather slim at that moment? Or, as we would say in everyday language: I gave up too quickly.

References

Beck, M., Pine, E., Tarrant, W., & Jensen, K. Y. (2007). New integer representations as the sum of three cubes. *Mathematics of Computation, 76*(259), 1683–1690.

Billey, S. C., & Tenner, B. E. (2013). Fingerprint databases for theorems. *Notices of the AMS, 60*(8), 1034–1039.

Hintikka, J. (2012). Method of analysis: A paradigm of mathematical reasoning? *History and Philosophy of Logic, 33*(1), 49–67.
Hintikka, J., & Remes, U. (1974). *The method of analysis: Its geometrical origin, its general significance*. Dordrecht: Reidel.
Kitcher, P. (1983). *The nature of mathematical knowledge*. New York: Oxford University Press.
Mahler, K. (1936). Note on hypothesis K of Hardy and Littlewood. *Journal of the London Mathematical Society, 11*, 136–138.
Mancosu, P. (2011). Explanation in mathematics. In E. N. Zalta (Ed.), *The Stanford encyclopedia of philosophy* (Summer 2011 ed.). Stanford: Stanford University Press. http://plato.stanford.edu/archives/sum2011/entries/mathematics-explanation/
Mordell, L. J. (1942). On sums of three cubes. *Journal of the London Mathematical Society, 17*, 139–144.
National Research Council (2014). *Developing a 21st century global library for mathematics research*. The National Academies Press: Washington, D.C.
Nielsen, M. (2012). *Reinventing discovery. The new era of networked science*. Princeton University Press: Princeton.
Parikh, R. J. (1973). Some results on the length of proofs. *Transaction of the AMS, 177*, 29–36.
Poonen, B. (2008). Undecidability in number theory. *Notices of the AMS, 55*(3), 344–350.
Stoll, M. (2010). How to solve a Diophantine equation. *ArXiv*:1002.4344v2 [math.NT].
van Bendegem, J. P. (2004). The creative growth of mathematics. In D. Gabbay, S. Rahman, J. Symons, & J. P. van Bendegem (Eds.), *Logic, epistemology and the unity of science (LEUS)* (pp. 229–255). Dordrecht: Kluwer Academic.
van Bendegem, J. P. (2014). The impact of the philosophy of mathematical practice on the philosophy of mathematics. In L. Soler, S. Zwart, M. Lynch, & V. Israel-Jost (Eds.), *Science after the practice turn in the philosophy, history, and social studies of science* (pp. 215–226). London: Routledge.
van Bendegem, J. P. (to appear). Contingency in mathematics: Two case studies. In L. Soler (Ed.), *Contingency in Science*. Pittsburgh: University of Pittsburgh Press.
van Benthem, J. (2010). Logic, mathematics, and general agency. In P. E. Bour, M. Rebuschi, & L. Rollet (Eds.), *Construction — Festschrift for Gerhard Heinzmann* (pp. 277–296). London: College Publications.
van Benthem, J. (2011). *Logical dynamics of information and interaction*. Cambridge: Cambridge University Press.
van Kerkhove, B., & van Bendegem, J. P. (2004). The unreasonable richness of mathematics. *Journal of Cognition and Culture, 4*(3–4), 525–549.
Villani, C. (2012). *Théorème vivant*. Paris: Grasset.
Watkins, J. J. (2014). *Number theory: A historical approach*. Princeton: Princeton University Press.

Interrogative Inquiry as Defeasible Reasoning

G. Aldo Antonelli

Abstract This paper presents an account of interrogative inquiry based on defeasible inference rules. With any such account, the main issue is the proper identification of the class of conclusions that are warranted on the basis of a set of such rules. In particular, the main formal features that any such account needs to satisfy are identified, and two different approaches are presented, the second one of which satisfactorily meets all desired properties. The approach is based on the author's previous work on defeasible logics.

Keywords Non-Monotonic Logic • Default Rules • Defeasible Inference • Models of Inquiry

1 The Original Model

Hintikka (1984) introduces the Interrogative Model of Inquiry (IMI) as a dynamic model of scientific inquiry, which, contrary to traditional approaches to the logic of science, is conceived as providing a *logic of discovery* rather than a *logic of justification*. According to the proposed model, science proceeds by asking questions and seeking answers to those questions, rather than by deriving deductively valid consequences from first principles.

In presenting Hintikka's IMI framework, we assume that the Inquirer works with a background theory, T, investigating properties of a given model M of T. The model plays the role of the external world being investigated and the background theory is assumed to be true in the model. Among the question that the Inquirer can pose, some are yes/no questions, which can be represented in the form "A?" for a given sentence A (in the language of T), whereas other questions can be characterized as wh-questions of the form "$\exists x B(x)$?".

From a more abstract point of view, we can conceive of IMI as introducing a ternary relation $T : M \Vdash A$, where T is theory, M a structure in the same signature

G.A. Antonelli (✉)
University of California, Davis, CA, USA
e-mail: antonelli@ucdavis.edu; aldo.antonelli@gmail.com

C. Başkent (ed.), *Perspectives on Interrogative Models of Inquiry*, Logic, Argumentation & Reasoning 8, DOI 10.1007/978-3-319-20762-9_6

as T, and A a sentence in the language of T. Here T plays the role of a *background theory*, and A represents the answer to a question which is asked with respect to a model M. The question receives a positive answer if the sentence A is true in the given model of T.

More formally, we can say that $T : M \Vdash A$ holds iff A can be obtained as the last member of a finite sequence of "moves" $A_1, A_2, \ldots, A_n$, each one of which is:

- A member of the *background* theory T; or
- A *deductive* consequence of previous sentences in the sequence (a "deductive" move); or
- A sentence A_i such that $M \models A_i$ (an "interrogative" move).

According to the model, the "Inquirer" is allowed to perform either a deductive or an interrogative move in order to reach the conclusion A. However, this model is quickly recognized to be too general, in that no restrictions are imposed on the kind of interrogative moves that the Inquirer is allowed to ask. On this model, for instance, we could recover *true arithmetic* (i.e., the set of sentences true in the standard model arithmetic $\mathfrak{N} = (\mathbb{N}, 0, 1, +, \times))$, by means of inquiries of the form $T : \mathfrak{N} \Vdash A$, where A is a sentence of arbitrary arithmetical complexity and T some appropriate arithmetical theory (e.g., Peano arithmetic). Accordingly, completely unrestricted inquiry is *not* a suitable model of scientific discovery, and (as Hintikka himself quickly recognized) one need to search for appropriate restrictions on the class of questions of the form "A?" that the Inquirer is allowed to pose. A natural approach is then to impose such restrictions based on the complexity of the question "A?:"

Restrict the question to sentences $A \in \Sigma_n$ for various quantifier prefixes Σ_n.

The most basic form of restricted inquiry is *atomistic* inquiry, in which interrogative moves are restricted to atomic formulas. This case is well understood from classical model theory, since it reduces $T : M \Vdash A$ to the notion of model consequence $T \cup \Delta(M) \models A$, where $\Delta(M)$ is the atomic diagram of M. But even this basic constraint may prove not to be restrictive enough in that the assumption that for each model M either $T : M \Vdash A$ or $T : M \Vdash \neg A$ (where only atomic queries are allowed) is, by a well known result, equivalent to the condition that every embedding between models of T is elementary.

A restriction to Π_2 inquiry is considered by Hintikka (1988). Whereas atomistic inquiry provides a model of *observational* science, Π_2 inquiry provides a model of *experimental* science. Scientists are interested in *correlations* established through *controlled experiments*. Such experiments are aimed at the discovery of a function $f(x) = y$ giving the mode of dependence of y on x, as in the case, e.g., of Gay-Lussac's law correlating temperature and pressure of an ideal gas. Clearly, the dependence of y upon x can be described by a Π_2 statement of the form $\forall x \exists y R(x, y)$, and so Π_2 inquiry can be construed as providing a model of a law-like correlation subjected to experimental verification. We know, of course, that no single experiment can pin down the whole graph of a function f, as only initial segments can be subject to direct confirmation, whereas proposed correlations *can* be ruled out by means of experiments. Thus, there are serious limitations to the usefulness of this kind of inquiry as well.

2 Presuppositions

Interrogative moves can be constrained by their *presuppositions*. Many different constructions can act as presupposition triggers (factives, definite descriptions, etc.). *Questions* are among the most extensively studied presupposition triggers. Consider the following "loaded" questions:

- When did you stop smoking?
- What is the force required to accelerate a body of mass 1 kg that is at rest in a vacuum to the speed $\boldsymbol{c} = 2.998 \times 10^8$ m/s?

Hintikka's IMI restricts interrogative moves to those whose *presuppositions* appear as previous steps in the interrogative game. This treatment of presupposition does not seem to do justice to their nature.

Presuppositions have been widely studied, since they are significantly different from both direct semantic entailments and Gricean implicatures. Like implicatures they are *cancelable*, but only when embedded. In the following example the presupposition trigger is embedded under a negation (and immediately canceled):

I didn't stop smoking — in fact I never was a smoker.

The presupposition of a yes/no question "A?" is usually identified with the disjunction of its possible answers, $A \vee \neg A$. Similarly, the presupposition of a wh-question "$A(x)$?" is identified with the corresponding existentially quantified statement $\exists x A(x)$. However, in the context of questions, at least, presuppositions are *meta-linguistic* in nature: they express necessary conditions for the question to be *asked*. To require that presuppositions appear as previous steps in the interrogative process is to treat them on a par with ordinary conclusions. This is a shortcoming that we try to address in what follows.

3 Defeasible Inquiry, I

Hintikka (1988) makes the case for defeasible inquiry by introducing the possibility that the output of interrogative moves—Nature's answers—might be considered *less than certain*. This corresponds to the possibility that the outcome of some experiment might later be determined to be invalid or contradicted by further experiments.

This possibility provides the motivation for developing a logic of defeasible inquiry. It is often suggested that inductive logic already provides such a model. However, the process of defeasible inquiry exhibits features that are significantly different from traditional inductive logic, in that while inductive logic deals with *uncertain inferences* from *indubitable premises* (observations), deafeasible inquiry deals with *certainty-preserving inferences* from *uncertain premises* (defeasible interrogative moves).

In order to accommodate such a model, Hintikka (1988) and Hintikka et al. (2002) develop a particular kind of sequent calculus. The first thing to notice about such a calculus is that the deductive component must be *subclassical*. In fact, the sequent $\vdash A \vee \neg A$ is not in general derivable (otherwise the presupposition of every yes-no question would be satisfied). The deductive component is supplemented by an interrogative component, which allows for the output of past interrogative moves to be pre-empted along with any later deductive moves that rely on it.

Rather than rehearsing Hintikka's proposal, in what follows we provide an account of defeasible inquiry which is explicitly based on *defeasible inference rules* (see Antonelli 2005), whose antecedents represent the presupposition that needs to be fulfilled for the rule to be applied. In this way, we will be closely following Hintikka's admonition that defeasible inquiry is certainty-preserving inference from defeasible premises.

There are, however, significant differences between the present proposal and Hintikka's. Model-oriented inquiry uses a classical model M as an *oracle*, with the consequence that the answer to each question is *definitely* true in M. It follows that the model-oriented paradigm needs to be abandoned to accommodate defeasible inquiry. Accordingly, we propose that we move from a model-based paradigm to one that is *rule-based*. According to the proposal, "nature" supplies a stock of *inference rules* that allow the tentative adjunction of certain propositions to the inquirer's knowledge base—but *only provided* the corresponding presupposition is met. The presupposition is here represented by the antecedent of the rule.

What leads to additional complexity in the case of the rule-based approach is the possibility of *conflicts*. These arise in two ways: we can have conflicts between tentative conclusions and "hard facts"; or we can have conflicts between two tentative conclusions. The two different kinds of conflicts call for different measures to be undertaken in order to restore consistency. One leading intuition is that in the case of conflicts between tentative conclusions and hard facts, as represented in a background theory T, the hard facts should always prevail.

Another aspect in which the rule-based paradigm differs from Hintikka's original approach is that presuppositions of any kind are allowed, not just disjunctions or generalizations of the possible answers to a given questions. In this sense, the rule-based approach is more general, but of course nothing prevents that in applications only antecedents representing presuppositions to a given question might be allowed. It is worth pointing out that antecedents of defeasible inference rules are not unlike presuppositions, in that they play a role that is intermediate between object-language and meta-language.

We now come to some of the technical details of the proposal. First of all, we assume a background language $\mathscr{L}$ with an associated classical consequence relation $\models$. We notice that other choices are possible, of course, and that in many cases one might want to proceed with a consequence relation that does not satisfy explosion, for instance, and with a relevant or more generally para-consistent consequence relation. We do not explore such options here, as the approach we pursue is modular, and it does not depend on the details of the consequence relation. A para-consistent consequence relation can always be adopted as a drop-in replacement for $\models$.

Recall the basic intuition that Nature provides the inquirer with a stock of *defeasible rules*, allowing the inference of a conclusion whenever the presupposition is met. This leads us to the following definition.

Definition 3.1. A defeasible inference rule has the form $A \rightsquigarrow B$ where A, B are formulas of $\mathscr{L}$ (so $\rightsquigarrow$is not nested). We use $\Gamma, \Delta, \ldots$ for sets of defeasible rules.

Formally, we frame the problem of defeasible interrogative inquiry so conceived as the problem of characterizing the class of defeasible consequences of a given theory. Since the set of defeasible conclusions of a theory might contain conflitcs, solving the problem of defeasible interrogative inquiry requires a *principled* way of settling such conflicts. In other words, what is needed is a way to flesh out the (incomplete) definition below.

Definition 3.2. Given an $\mathscr{L}$-theory T, a (finite) set Δ of rules of the form $A \rightsquigarrow B$ and a formula C, we write $T : \Delta \Vdash C$ to mean that C follows from T in conjunction with Δ.

This leads us to identify the *problem of defeasible inquiry* as the problem requiring us to: (*i*) identify the desirable properties of the relation $T : \Delta \Vdash C$; and (*ii*) provide a precise implementation of the relation $T : \Delta \Vdash C$ satisfying those properties. We take up each of these two tasks in turn.

Fortunately, the desirable formal properties of defeasible consequence relations were already identified in the mid-1980s by Gabbay (1985), who promoted the following three:

- **Reflexivity**: If $A \in T$ then $T : \Delta \Vdash A$.
- **Cut**: If $T : \Delta \Vdash A$ and $T + A : \Delta \Vdash B$ then $T : \Delta \Vdash B$
- **Cautious Monotony**: If $T : \Delta \Vdash A$ and $T : \Delta \Vdash B$ then $T + A : \Delta \Vdash B$.

In particular, the import of the last two properties is a sort of *cumulativity*: Augmenting the theory with the adjunction of a "theorem" does not lead to any *increase* (Cut) or *decrease* (Cautious Mononotony) in inferential power. The process of inquiry is thus, in a sense, *stable*.

It is sometimes argued that the requirement of Cautious Monotony is too restrictive, and that it should be replaced by the more liberal requirement of "rational" monotony below.

- **Rational Monotony**: If $T : \Delta \Vdash A$ and $T : \Delta \nVdash \neg B$ then $T + B : \Delta \Vdash A$.

But a convincing counter-example, due to Stalnaker (1994), can be adapted to the case at hand. The counter-example involves three composers, Verdi, Bizet, and Satie. Suppose we are originally told, by a reliable, but still defeasible source that Verdi is Italian, while Bizet and Satie are French. This defeasible information can be represented by means of defeasible inference rules whose antecedent is tautologous. So let Δ comprise $\top \rightsquigarrow I(v)$, $\top \rightsquigarrow F(b)$ and $\top \rightsquigarrow F(s)$. Our background knowledge, which provides us with strict, non-defeasible information is in turn embodied in a theory T, stating that the relation "x is a compatriot of y," $C(x, y)$, is a congruence with respect to the two incompatible properties I and F and also that Verdi and Bizet are compatriots: $C(v, b)$ (the fact that strict information is false is irrelevant; all that matters is that in the presence of conflicts between defeasible conclusions and strict information it is the former that are retracted). The information at hand does not license the inference that Verdi is Italian, because of the competing inference that he could have been French: $T : \Delta \not\Vdash I(v)$. Similarly, the information does not license the information that Bizet is French, because (symmetrically) he could have been Italian: $T : \Delta \not\Vdash F(b)$. However, there is no reason not to infer that Satie is, in fact, French: $T : \Delta \Vdash F(s)$. The crucial observation is that these two facts (i.e., $T : \Delta \not\Vdash I(v)$ and $T : \Delta \not\Vdash F(b)$) do not allow us to reject the conclusion that Verdi and Satie might be compatriots: $T : \Delta \not\Vdash \neg C(v, s)$. However, if we were to add this un-refuted hypothesis to our background knowledge, we would lose the conclusion that Satie is French

$$T + C(v, s) : \Delta \not\Vdash F(s),$$

since now all three composers must be of the same nationality, either Italian or French. So rational Monotony fails.

We saw that the basic problem in defeasible inquiry with defeasible rules is the principled adjudication of conflicts, either between defeasible conclusions or between defeasible conclusions and facts entailed by the background theory. A particular example concerns rules that are, directly or indirectly, *self-defeating*. In fact, having relaxed the role of presuppositions, it might be that a rule's conclusion defeats thay rule's presupposition: $A \rightsquigarrow \neg A$. Similarly, one can have a pair of rules such as:

$$A \rightsquigarrow B, \qquad\qquad B \rightsquigarrow \neg A.$$

Obviously complex patterns of defeating rules are possible, which are not easily detected. One way to deal with such internal conflicts is by adopting a *Minimal constraint on inference*:

> The presupposition of the rule must be met both *before* and *after* the rule is applied.

The minimal constraint points us in the right direction: when trying to identify the conclusion sets that can be derived from a theory $T : \Delta$, we should characterize them as *minimal fixed points*.

Definition 3.3. It is convenient to use the notations:

- $\mathsf{cons}(\Delta) = \{B \mid A \rightsquigarrow B \in \Delta\}$;
- $S \models_T A$ iff $S \cup T \models A$.

Definition 3.4. A *Conclusion set* (or simply a *C-set*) for a theory $T : \Delta$ is a minimal solution to a fix-point equation, i.e., a set $\mathscr{C} \subseteq \Delta$ of rules s.t.:

(*i*) $\mathscr{C} = \{A \rightsquigarrow B \in \Delta \mid \mathsf{cons}(\mathscr{C}) \models_T A \;\&\; \mathsf{cons}(\mathscr{C}) \not\models_T \neg B\}$;
(*ii*) $\mathscr{C}$ is *minimal* in the sense that if: $\mathscr{D} = \{A \rightsquigarrow B \in \Delta \mid \mathsf{cons}(\mathscr{D}) \models_T A \;\&\; \mathsf{cons}(\mathscr{C}) \not\models_T \neg B\}$, then $\mathscr{C} \subseteq \mathscr{D}$.

Notice the occurrence of $\mathscr{C}$ in (*ii*).

We pause to remark that this is not an *explicit* definition, but indeed it is a fixpoint condition: $\mathscr{C}$ is the set of rules whose presuppositions are met in $\mathscr{C}$ and whose conclusions are not defeated in $\mathscr{C}$, and it is *minimal* among the sets $\mathscr{D}$ of conclusions that meet their own presuppositions and that are not conflicted in $\mathscr{C}$. The first result that we prove is that C-sets exist.

Theorem 3.1. *Every theory $T : \Delta$ has a C-set.*

Proof. A C-set $\mathscr{C}$ for $T : \Delta$ can be obtained by means of a *non-deterministic* inductive construction as the limit of the chain $C_0 \subseteq C_1 \subseteq \cdots$ as follows:

- Put $C_0 = \varnothing$.
- For C_{n+1}, select a maximal subset $\Delta_0 \subseteq \Delta$ of rules s.t.:

  1. $\mathsf{cons}(C_n) \models_T A$ for each $A \rightsquigarrow B$ in Δ_0;
  2. $\mathsf{cons}(C_n \cup \Delta_0)$ is consistent with T.

  Put $C_{n+1} = \Delta_0$.

Define $\mathscr{C} = \bigcup_{n \geq 0} C_n$; then $\mathscr{C}$ is a C-set for $T : \Delta$.

By induction on n we show first that the sequence is increasing, i.e., $C_n \subseteq C_{n+1}$. The case for $n = 0$ is obvious, since $C_0 = \varnothing \subseteq C_1$. Assume $C_n \subseteq C_{n+1}$ to show $C_{n+1} \subseteq C_{n+2}$. Let $A \rightsquigarrow B \in C_{n+1}$; then $\mathsf{cons}(C_n) \models_T A$ and by inductive hypothesis also $\mathsf{cons}(C_{n+1}) \models_T A$. Moreover, if $\mathsf{cons}(C_{n+1} \cup C_{n+2}) \models_T \neg B$, then $\mathsf{cons}(C_{n+1} \cup C_{n+2})$ is inconsistent, against the choice of C_{n+2}. So by maximality $A \rightsquigarrow B \in C_{n+2}$.

Having shown that the C_n sequence is increasing, we put $\mathscr{C} = \bigcup_{0 \leq n} C_n$. We need to show that $\mathscr{C}$ is a C-set. First we notice that $\mathsf{cons}(\mathscr{C})$ is consistent (provided T itself is; if T is inconsistent then $\varnothing$ is the unique C-set for $T : \Delta$). Next we need to show that $\mathscr{C}$ satisfies the fix-point equation from Definition 3.4:

$$\mathscr{C} = \{A \rightsquigarrow B \mid \mathsf{cons}(\mathscr{C}) \models_T A \;\;\&\;\; \mathsf{cons}(\mathscr{C}) \not\models_T \neg B\}.$$

We take up the two inclusions in turn. If $\mathsf{cons}(\mathscr{C}) \models_T A$ and $\mathsf{cons}(\mathscr{C}) \not\models_T \neg B$ then there is $n \geq 0$ such that $\mathsf{cons}(C_n) \models_T A$, and moreover B must be T-consistent with $\mathsf{cons}(C_n \cup C_{n+1})$, otherwise $\mathsf{cons}(C_{n+1}) \models_T \neg B$ whence also $\mathsf{cons}(\mathscr{C}) \models_T \neg B$ since $C_{n+1} \subseteq \mathscr{C}$. By maximality, $A \rightsquigarrow B \in C_{n+1} \subseteq \mathscr{C}$.

If, conversely, $A \rightsquigarrow B \in \mathscr{C}$, then for some $n \geq 0$ we have $A \rightsquigarrow B \in C_{n+1}$, so that $\mathsf{cons}(C_n) \models_T A$, from which also $\mathsf{cons}(\mathscr{C}) \models_T A$. It remains to show that $\mathsf{cons}(\mathscr{C}) \not\models_T \neg B$. If, by reductio, $\mathsf{cons}(\mathscr{C}) \models_T \neg B$, then there is $m \geq 0$ such that $\mathsf{cons}(C_m) \models_T \neg B$. Now let $p = \max(n+1, m)$, so that $\mathsf{cons}(C_p) \models_T B \wedge \neg B$, against the consistency of $\mathscr{C}$.

It remains to establish the minimality condition from the second part of Definition 3.4. Suppose that $\mathscr{D}$ satisfies:

$$\mathscr{D} = \{A \rightsquigarrow B \mid \mathsf{cons}(\mathscr{D}) \models_T A \;\;\&\;\; \mathsf{cons}(\mathscr{C}) \not\models_T \neg B\}.$$

In order to establish that $\mathscr{C} \subseteq \mathscr{D}$ it suffices to shows $C_n \subseteq \mathscr{D}$ by induction on n. Obviously $C_0 = \varnothing \subseteq \mathscr{D}$. Assume $C_n \subseteq \mathscr{D}$ and let $A \rightsquigarrow B \in C_{n+1}$. Then $\mathsf{cons}(C_n) \models_T A$, whence by inductive hypothesis also $\mathsf{cons}(\mathscr{D}) \models_T A$. Moreover $\mathsf{cons}(\mathscr{C}) \not\models_T \neg B$ (since $A \rightsquigarrow B \in C_{n+1} \subseteq \mathscr{C}$ and $\mathscr{C}$ satisfies the fix-point condition, as already shown). Hence $A \rightsquigarrow B \in \mathscr{D}$ as desired. □

We now consider some examples of theories $T : \Delta$ and their C-sets. We beging with the case of self-defeating rules, which is handled quite well.

Example 3.1. Let Δ contain $A \rightsquigarrow \neg A$ as its only member. Then for any T, the theory $T : \Delta$ has a unique C-set $\mathscr{C} = \varnothing$.

This is because if $\mathscr{C}$ is a non-empty C-set then it must contain the rule $A \rightsquigarrow \neg A$ as its only member. If $\mathscr{C}$ is a C-set, then it must satisfy the two conjuncts of the fix-point equation, so that $\mathsf{cons}(\mathscr{C}) \models_T A$, i.e., $\neg A \models_T A$, whence by contraposition in classical logic $\neg A \models_T \neg\neg A$, i.e., $\mathsf{cons}(\mathscr{C}) \models_T \neg(\neg A)$, and the second conjunct fails. Similarly, if the second conjunct holds, the first one must fail. Hence, $\mathscr{C} = \varnothing$.

Example 3.2. If Δ contains $A \rightsquigarrow B$ and $T = \{\neg B\}$ Then $\varnothing$ is the only C-set, and so in particular $\mathsf{cons}(\mathscr{C}) \cup \{\neg B\} \not\models_T \neg A$. So *modus tollens* fails.

Example 3.3. If $T = \{A\}$ and Δ contains $A \rightsquigarrow B$ and $C \rightsquigarrow \neg A$, then $T : \Delta$ has one C-set, $\{A \rightsquigarrow B\}$.

This holds because the only rule potentially defeating $A \rightsquigarrow B$ is $C \rightsquigarrow \neg A$, which is never triggered, as the consequent is not T-consistent.

One important feature of C-sets is that they need not be unique. It is indeed easy to find theories that have multiple C-sets. This is potentially problematic if we are interested in identifying the sentences that are warranted by a theory $T : \Delta$ on the basis of that theory's C-sets.

Proposition 3.1. *C-sets need not be unique.*

Proof. We exhibit an example. Let $T = \{A\}$ and Δ contain the rules $A \rightsquigarrow B$ and $A \rightsquigarrow \neg B$. It is easy to check that any C-set for $T : \Delta$ must trigger exactly one of the two rules; obviously they cannot both be triggered, as the consequents are conflicting; and at least one must be triggered if a C-set is to satisfy the fix-point equation. Consequently $T : \Delta$ has exactly two C-sets:

- $\mathscr{C}_1 = \{A \rightsquigarrow B\}$;
- $\mathscr{C}_2 = \{A \rightsquigarrow \neg B\}$. □

Notice that $\mathscr{C}_1 \cap \mathscr{C}_2 = \varnothing$. If Δ contained also $A \rightsquigarrow C$ then $\mathscr{C}_1 \cap \mathscr{C}_2 = \{A \rightsquigarrow C\}$.

An important tool in the analysis of C-sets is the following theorem, which shows that any C-set can be written as the result of a pseudo-inductive process, i.e., it can be decomposed in stages. In particular, the theorem allows us to "stratify" a C-set into layers. As we will see, Minimality plays a crucial role in the proof.

Theorem 3.2 (C-set Decomposition). *Suppose $\mathscr{C} \subseteq \Delta$ and $C_0, C_1, \ldots$ are sets such that:*

- $C_0 = \varnothing$;
- $C_{n+1} = \{A \rightsquigarrow B \mid \mathsf{cons}(C_n) \models_T A \,\&\, \mathsf{cons}(\mathscr{C}) \not\models_T \neg B\}$.

Then $\mathscr{C}$ is a C-set iff $\mathscr{C} = \bigcup_{n \geq 0} C_n$.

Proof. For the "if" direction, suppose $\mathscr{C} = \bigcup_{n \geq 0} C_n$, to show that $\mathscr{C}$ is a C-set. First we show that $\mathscr{C}$ satisfies the fix-point equation:

$$\begin{aligned} A \rightsquigarrow B \in \mathscr{C} \quad & \Leftrightarrow \quad A \rightsquigarrow B \in \textstyle\bigcup_{n\geq 0} C_n \\ & \Leftrightarrow \quad \exists n \geq 0 : \; A \rightsquigarrow B \in C_n \\ & \Leftrightarrow \quad \exists n \geq 0 : \; \mathsf{cons}(C_n) \models_T A \;\;\&\;\; \mathsf{cons}(C) \not\models_T \neg B \\ & \Leftrightarrow \quad \mathsf{cons}(\mathscr{C}) \models_T A \;\;\&\;\; \mathsf{cons}(\mathscr{C}) \not\models_T \neg B. \end{aligned}$$

Next we show that the minimality condition is met. Suppose

$$\mathscr{D} = \{A \rightsquigarrow B \mid \mathsf{cons}(\mathscr{D}) \models_T a \;\;\&\;\; \mathsf{cons}(\mathscr{C}) \not\models_T \neg B\}.$$

To show that $\mathscr{C} \subseteq \mathscr{D}$ it suffices to prove $\bigcup_{n \geq 0} C_n \subseteq \mathscr{D}$ by induction on n. Obviously $C_0 = \varnothing \subseteq \mathscr{D}$. If $C_n \subseteq \mathscr{D}$ (by the inductive hypothesis) and $A \rightsquigarrow B \in C_{n+1}$, then $\mathsf{cons}(C_n) \models_T A$ and $\mathsf{cons}(C) \not\models_T \neg B$. Then $\mathsf{cons}(\mathscr{D}) \models_T A$, whence $A \rightsquigarrow B \in \mathscr{D}$ as required.

For the "only if" part, suppose $\mathscr{C}$ is a C-set for $T : \Delta$. We need to show $\mathscr{C} = \bigcup_{n+1} C_n$. First we argue as follows:

$$\begin{aligned} A \rightsquigarrow B \in \textstyle\bigcup_{n\geq 0} C_n \quad & \Leftrightarrow \quad \exists n \geq 0 : A \rightsquigarrow B \in C_n \\ & \Leftrightarrow \quad \exists n \geq 0 : \mathsf{cons}(C_n) \models_T A \;\;\&\;\; \mathsf{cons}(\mathscr{C}) \not\models_T \neg B \\ & \Leftrightarrow \quad \mathsf{cons}(\textstyle\bigcup_{n\geq 0} C_n) \models_T A \;\;\&\;\; \mathsf{cons}(\mathscr{C}) \not\models_T \neg B. \end{aligned}$$

It follows that $\bigcup_{n \geq 0} C_n = \{A \rightsquigarrow B \mid \mathsf{cons}(\bigcup_{n \geq 0} C_n) \;\;\&\;\; \mathsf{cons}(\mathscr{C}) \not\models_T \neg B\}$ and by the minimality of $\mathscr{C}$ we have $\mathscr{C} \subseteq \bigcup_{n \geq 0} C_n$. For the converse inclusion it suffices to show $C_n \subseteq \mathscr{C}$ by induction on n. The case for $n = 0$ is obvious as $C_0 = \varnothing$. Assume $C_n \subseteq \mathscr{C}$ and let $A \rightsquigarrow B \in C_{n+1}$. Then $\mathsf{cons}(C_n) \models_T A$ and $\mathsf{cons}(\mathscr{C}) \not\models_T \neg B$, so that $\mathsf{cons}(\mathscr{C}) \models_T A$ and finally $A \rightsquigarrow B \in \mathscr{C}$. □

The theory as developed so far is essentially a "normal" version of Reiter's Default logic (1987).

We now come to main task of the theory, that of identifying the set of conclusions that are warranted by $T : \Delta$. This gives us a notion of C-consequence $\Vdash$, which can then be assessed with respect to the three properties of Reflexivity, Cut, and Cautious Monotony.

Definition 3.5. $T : \Delta \Vdash A$ if and only if $\mathsf{cons}(\mathscr{C}) \models_T A$ for every C-set $\mathscr{C}$ for $T : \Delta$.

The following is obvious, but we enter it into the record nonetheless.

Proposition 3.2 (Reflexivity). *If* $A \in T$ *then* $\mathsf{cons}(\mathscr{C}) \models_T A$ *for every C-set for* $T : \Delta$.

Proposition 3.3 (Cut). *If* $T : \Delta \Vdash A$ *and* $T + A : \Delta \Vdash B$ *then* $T : \Delta \Vdash B$.

Proof. We use Decomposition to show that (under the hypotheses) every C-set for $T : \Delta$ is also a C-set for $T + A : \Delta$. Assume $T : \Delta \Vdash A$ and $T + A : \Delta \Vdash B$. Let $\mathscr{C}$ be a C-set for $T : \Delta$, so that, in particular, $\mathsf{cons}(\mathscr{C}) \models_T A$. We want to show $\mathsf{cons}(\mathscr{C}) \models_T B$, and in turn it suffices to show that $\mathscr{C}$ is a C-set for $T+A : \Delta$ as well, for then $\mathsf{cons}(\mathscr{C}) \models_{T+A} B$, and Cut in classical logic delivers that $\mathsf{cons}(\mathscr{C}) \models_T B$. Observe that:

$$
\begin{aligned}
E \rightsquigarrow F \in \mathscr{C} \quad &\Leftrightarrow \quad \mathsf{cons}(\mathscr{C}) \models_T E \,\&\, \mathsf{cons}(\mathscr{C}) \not\models_T \neg F \\
&\Leftrightarrow \quad \mathsf{cons}(\mathscr{C}) \models_{T+A} E \,\&\, \mathsf{cons}(\mathscr{C}) \not\models_{T+A} \neg F,
\end{aligned}
$$

where the first equivalence obtains because $\mathscr{C}$ is a C-set for $T : \Delta$, and the second equivalence is justified as follows: since $\mathsf{cons}(\mathscr{C}) \models_T A$, we have $\mathsf{cons}(\mathscr{C}) \models_{T+A} E$ if and only if $\mathsf{cons}(\mathscr{C}) \models_T E$ (by Cut and Monotonicity on classical logic) and similarly $\mathsf{cons}(\mathscr{C}) \not\models_{T+A} \neg F$ if and only if $\mathsf{cons}(\mathscr{C}) \not\models_T \neg F$. We conclude that $\mathscr{C}$ satisfies the fix point equation for C-sets for $T + A : \Delta$:

$$\mathscr{C} = \{E \rightsquigarrow F \mid \mathsf{cons}(\mathscr{C}) \models_{T+A} E \,\&\, \mathsf{cons}(\mathscr{C}) \not\models_{T+A} \neg F\}.$$

To show that $\mathscr{C}$ is a C-set for $T + A : \Delta$ we need to show that it is minimal, i.e., that if

$$\mathscr{D} = \{E \rightsquigarrow F \mid \mathsf{cons}(\mathscr{D}) \models_{T+A} E \,\&\, \mathsf{cons}(\mathscr{C}) \not\models_{T+A} \neg F\},$$

then $\mathscr{C} \subseteq \mathscr{D}$. Since $\mathscr{C}$ is a C-set for $T : \Delta$, by the Decomposition theorem, let $\mathscr{C} = \bigcup_{n \geq 0} C_n$, where $C_0 = \varnothing$ and $C_{n+1} = \{E \rightsquigarrow F \mid \mathsf{cons}(C_n) \models_T A \,\&\, \mathsf{cons}(\mathscr{C}) \not\models_T$

$\neg F\}$. So it suffices to prove $C_n \subseteq \mathscr{D}$ by induction on n. The case for $n = 0$ is trivial, so suppose $C_n \subseteq \mathscr{D}$ and let $E \rightsquigarrow F \in C_{n+1}$. Then:

1. $\mathsf{cons}(C_n) \models_T E$, and since $C_n \subseteq \mathscr{D}$, also $\mathsf{cons}(\mathscr{D}) \models_{T+A} E$, by monotony of classical logic;
2. since $\mathsf{cons}(\mathscr{C}) \not\models_T \neg F$ but $\mathsf{cons}(\mathscr{C}) \models_T A$ by hypothesis, also $\mathsf{cons}(\mathscr{C}) \not\models_{T+A} \neg F$, by Cut in classical logic.

We conclude that $E \rightsquigarrow F \in \mathscr{D}$, as desired. □

Proposition 3.4. *Cautious Monotony fails for* $\Vdash$.

Proof. We use a classic counter-example due to Makinson (1994): Consider $T = \varnothing$ and Δ comprising $\top \rightsquigarrow A$ and $A \vee B \rightsquigarrow \neg A$ (where $\top$ is a propositional constant for truth). Then $T : \Delta \Vdash A$ since the unique C-set for $T : \Delta$ contains the first rule. Further, also $T : \Delta \Vdash A \vee B$, but $T + A \vee B \ : \Delta \not\Vdash A$ because now $\varnothing$ is a C-set for the theory. □

4 Defeasible Inquiry, II

The failure of Cautious Monotony for the notion of consequence based on C-sets prompts us to seek a more general notion, which we refer to as *General C-sets.*

Definition 4.1. A general C-set for $T : \Delta$ is a pair $(\mathscr{C}^+, \mathscr{C}^-)$, where:

(i) $\mathscr{C}^+, \mathscr{C}^- \subseteq \Delta$ and $\mathscr{C}^+ \cap \mathscr{C}^- = \varnothing$;
(ii) $\mathscr{C}^+ = \{A \rightsquigarrow B \mid \mathsf{cons}(\mathscr{C}^+) \models_T A \ \& \ \mathsf{cons}(\Delta - \mathscr{C}^-) \not\models_T \neg B\}$;
(iii) $\mathscr{C}^- = \{A \rightsquigarrow B \mid \mathsf{cons}(\mathscr{C}^+) \models_T \neg B\}$.

Just like C-sets are solutions to fixpoint equations, general C-sets are simultaneous solutions to systems (in fact, pairs) of fixpoint equations.

Definition 4.2. Given pairs of sets of rules, the relation $(\mathscr{C}^+, \mathscr{C}^-) \leq (\mathscr{D}^+, \mathscr{D}^-)$ denotes point-wise inclusion $\mathscr{C}^+ \subseteq \mathscr{D}^+$ and $\mathscr{C}^- \subseteq \mathscr{D}^-$.

We now proceed to establish *existence* and *uniqueness* results for general C-sets. The comparison is to the existence of multiple C-sets for the same theory which was established din the previous section.

Theorem 4.1. *Every $T : \Delta$ has a $\leq$-least (i.e., unique minimal in the $\leq$ ordering) general C-set.*

Proof. An inductive construction gives the desired general C-set. Put:

- $C_0^+ = C_0^- = \varnothing$;
- $C_{n+1}^+ = \{A \rightsquigarrow B \mid \mathsf{cons}(C_n^+) \models_T A \ \& \ \mathsf{cons}(\Delta - C_n^-) \not\models_T \neg B\}$;
- $C_{n+1}^- = \{A \rightsquigarrow B \mid \mathsf{cons}(C_{n+1}^+) \models_T \neg B\}$.

We first establish that:

(a) The sequence (C_n^+, C_n^-) is $\leq$-increasing.

Proof. by induction on n. Obviously $C_0^\pm = \varnothing \subseteq C_1^\pm$. So assume $C_n^+ \subseteq C_{n+1}^+$ and similarly $C_n^- \subseteq C_{n+1}^-$. To show $C_{n+1}^+ \subseteq C_{n+2}^+$ assume $A \rightsquigarrow B \in C_{n+1}^+$; then by definition $\mathsf{cons}(C_n^+) \models_T A$ and $\mathsf{cons}(\Delta - C_n^-) \not\models_T \neg B$. By inductive hypothesis, $\mathsf{cons}(C_{n+1}^+) \models_T A$ and since $C_n^- \subseteq C_{n+1}^-$, also $\mathsf{cons}(\Delta - C_{n+1}^-) \not\models_T \neg B$. It follows that $A \rightsquigarrow B \in C_{n+2}^+$. And since $C_{n+1}^+ \subseteq C_{n+2}^+$ (as just shown), also $C_{n+1}^- \subseteq C_{n+2}^-$.

(b) $(\mathscr{C}^+, \mathscr{C}^-) = (\bigcup_n C_n^+, \bigcup_n C_n^-)$ is a general C-set for $T : \Delta$.

Proof. We first show that at each stage $n > 0$ the members of the sequence are disjoint (this is obvious for $n = 0$). Given the definition of C_{n+1}^-, it suffices to show that if $A \rightsquigarrow B \in C_{n+1}^+$ then $\mathsf{cons}(C_{n+1}^+) \not\models_T \neg B$, for then $C_{n+1}^+ \subseteq \Delta - C_{n+1}^-$ follows, i.e., C_{n+1}^+ and C_{n+1}^- are disjoint. But given (a), just proved, we have that $A \rightsquigarrow B \in C_{n+1}^+$ implies $\mathsf{cons}(C_n^+) \not\models_T \neg B$, and since $C_n^- \subseteq C_{n+1}^-$, also $\mathsf{cons}(C_{n+1}^+) \not\models_T \neg B$, as desired.

Next we show $\mathscr{C}^+ = \{A \rightsquigarrow B \mid \mathsf{cons}(\mathscr{C}^+) \models_T A \ \&\ \mathsf{cons}(\Delta - \mathscr{C}^-) \not\models_T \neg B\}$. So suppose $A \rightsquigarrow B$ is such that $\mathsf{cons}(\mathscr{C}^+) \models_T A$ and $\mathsf{cons}(\Delta - \mathscr{C}^-) \not\models_T \neg B$. From the latter, since the sequence is increasing, there is a greatest m such that $\mathsf{cons}(\Delta - C_m^-) \models_T \neg B$ (put $m = 0$ if $\mathsf{cons}(\Delta) \not\models_T \neg B$). So for all $m' > m$ we have $\mathsf{cons}(\Delta - C_{m'}^-) \not\models_T \neg B$. On the other hand, since $\mathsf{cons}(\mathscr{C}^+) \models_T A$, there is $n \geq 0$ such that $\mathsf{cons}(C_n^+) \models_t A$. Put $k = \max(m, n) + 1$. Then $\mathsf{cons}(C_k^+) \models_T A$ and $\mathsf{cons}(\Delta - C_k^-) \not\models_T \neg B$, so that $A \rightsquigarrow B \in C_{k+1}^+ \subseteq \mathscr{C}^+$.

Conversely, if $A \rightsquigarrow B \in \mathscr{C}^+$ then for some n we have $A \rightsquigarrow B \in C_{n+1}^+$ so that $\mathsf{cons}(C_n^+) \models_T A$ and $\mathsf{cons}(\Delta - C_n^-) \not\models_T \neg B$. From the former, $\mathsf{cons}(\mathscr{C}^+) \models_T A$. From the latter, since $C_n^- \subseteq \mathscr{C}^-$, also $\mathsf{cons}(\Delta - \mathscr{C}^-) \not\models_T \neg B$.

And finally we show $\mathscr{C}^- = \{A \rightsquigarrow B \mid \mathsf{cons}(\mathscr{C}^+) \models_T \neg B\}$. This follows from the following equivalences, for $A \rightsquigarrow B \in \Delta$:

$$\begin{aligned} \mathsf{cons}(\mathscr{C}^+) \models_T \neg B &\Leftrightarrow \exists n : \mathsf{cons}(C_n^+) \models_T \neg B \\ &\Leftrightarrow \exists n : A \rightsquigarrow B \in C_n^- \\ &\Leftrightarrow A \rightsquigarrow B \in \mathscr{C}^-. \end{aligned}$$

And finally, the last item:

(c) $(\mathscr{C}^+, \mathscr{C}^-)$ is $\leq$-least among general C-sets for $T : \Delta$.

Suppose $(\mathscr{D}^+, \mathscr{D}^-)$ also satisfies (i), (ii), and (iii) from Definition 4.1. It suffices to show $(C_n^+, C_n^-) \leq (\mathscr{D}^+, \mathscr{D}^-)$ for then $(\mathscr{C}^+, \mathscr{C}^-) \leq (\mathscr{D}^+, \mathscr{D}^-)$ follows. We proceed by induction on n, with the case for $n = 0$ being obvious. To show $C_{n+1}^+ \subseteq \mathscr{D}^+$, let $A \rightsquigarrow B \in C_{n+1}^+$. Then $\mathsf{cons}(C_n^+) \models_T A$ and $\mathsf{cons}(\Delta - C_n^-) \not\models_T \neg B$. By inductive hypothesis $\mathsf{cons}(\mathscr{D}^+) \models_T A$ and $\mathsf{cons}(\Delta - \mathscr{D}^-) \not\models_T \neg B$, so $A \rightsquigarrow B \in \mathscr{D}^+$.

To show $C^-_{n+1} \subseteq \mathscr{D}^-$, let $A \rightsquigarrow B \in \Delta$ and $\mathsf{cons}(C^+_{n+1}) \models_T \neg B$; then $\mathsf{cons}(\mathscr{D}^+) \models_T \neg B$ by the inclusion just established, and $A \rightsquigarrow B \in \mathscr{D}^-$. Obviously $(\mathscr{C}^+, \mathscr{C}^-)$ is also unique, for if $(\mathscr{D}^+, \mathscr{D}^+)$ where also a minimal C-set, then $(\mathscr{C}^+, \mathscr{C}^-) \leq (\mathscr{D}^+, \mathscr{D}^-)$, and viceversa, whence $(\mathscr{C}^+, \mathscr{C}^-) = (\mathscr{D}^+, \mathscr{D}^-)$. This concludes the proof of the theorem. □

As a corollary to this existence and uniqueness theorem we obtain a Decomposition result which will be useful later on.

Corollary 4.1 (Decomposition). *If $(\mathscr{C}^+, \mathscr{C}^-)$ is the least general C-set for $T : \Delta$ then $(\mathscr{C}^+, \mathscr{C}^-) = (\bigcup_n C^+_n, \bigcup_n C^-_n)$ as in the proof of Theorem 4.1 above.*

We are now ready to define the corresponding notion of defeasible consequence.

Definition 4.3. $T : \Delta \Vdash_G A$ iff $\mathsf{cons}(\mathscr{C}^+) \models_T A$ where $(\mathscr{C}^+, \mathscr{C}^-)$ is the least general C-set for $T : \Delta$.

We now show that $\Vdash_G$, so defined, satisfies all three properties of Reflexivity, Cut, and Cautious Monotony. The first is immediate, while the others will follow from a conservativity result.

Proposition 4.1 (Reflexivity). *If $A \in T$ then $T : \Delta \Vdash_G A$.*

Proof. Immediate, since if $A \in T$ then $\mathsf{cons}(\mathscr{C}^+) \models_T A$ for every general C-set for $T : \Delta$. □

The following result gives us a *conservativity result*, whose two halves give us the validity of Cut and Cautious Monotony.

Theorem 4.2 (Conservativity). *If $(\mathscr{C}^+, \mathscr{C}^-)$ is the least general C-set for $T : \Delta$, and $(\mathscr{D}^+, \mathscr{D}^-)$ is the least general C-set for $T + A : \Delta$, and moreover $\mathsf{cons}(\mathscr{C}^+) \models_T A$, then:*

1. $(\mathscr{D}^+, \mathscr{D}^-) \leq (\mathscr{C}^+, \mathscr{C}^-)$;
2. $(\mathscr{C}^+, \mathscr{C}^-) \leq (\mathscr{D}^+, \mathscr{D}^-)$.

So in particular $(\mathscr{C}^+, \mathscr{C}^-) = (\mathscr{D}^+, \mathscr{D}^-)$ and $T : \Delta$ and $T + A : \Delta$ have the same least general C-set.

Proof. We deal with each part in turn. For (1), using decomposition (Corollary 4.1), we let $\mathscr{C}^+ = \bigcup_n C^+_n$ and $\mathscr{C}^- = \bigcup_n C^-_n$. Similarly, let $\mathscr{D}^+ = \bigcup_n D^+_n$ and $\mathscr{D}^- = \bigcup_n D^-_n$. Further, since $\mathsf{cons}(\mathscr{C}^+) \models_T A$, pick $k \geq 0$ such that $\mathsf{cons}(C^+_m) \models_T A$ for all $m \geq k$. It suffices to show:

$$(D^+_n, D^-_n) \leq (C^+_{k+n}, C^-_{k+n}),$$

by induction on n. The basis for $n = 0$ is trivial, since $D^+_0 = \varnothing \subseteq C^+_k$ and likewise $D^-_0 = \varnothing \subseteq C^-_k$. For the inductive step, assume the results holds for n, in order to show:

$$(D^+_{n+1}, D^-_{n+1}) \leq (C^+_{k+n+1}, C^-_{k+n+1}).$$

Let $E \rightsquigarrow F \in D^+_{n+1}$; then we have both:

(*a*) $\mathsf{cons}(D^+_n) \models_{T+A} E$; and (*b*) $\mathsf{cons}(\Delta - D^-_n) \not\models_{T+A} \neg F$.

From the former, $\mathsf{cons}(C^+_{k+n}) \models_{T+A} E$, and since $\mathsf{cons}(C^+_{k+n}) \models_T A$, also $\mathsf{cons}(C^+_{k+n}) \models_T E$. From the latter: since $D^-_n \subseteq C^-_{n+k}$ by the inductive hypothesis, also $\mathsf{cons}(\Delta - C^-_{n+k}) \not\models_{T+A} \neg F$, by monotony of classical logic, and even $\mathsf{cons}(\Delta - C^-_{n+k}) \not\models_T \neg F$. So $E \rightsquigarrow F \in C^+_{n+k+1}$ as desired, and $D^+_{n+1} \subseteq C^+_{n+k+1}$.

For $D^-_{n+1} \subseteq C^-_{n+k+1}$, let $E \rightsquigarrow F \in D^-_{n+1}$. Then $\mathsf{cons}(D^+_{n+1}) \models_{T+A} \neg F$; but $D^+_{n+1} \subseteq C^+_{n+k+1}$ (as just shown), so $\mathsf{cons}(C^+_{n+k+1}) \models_{T+A} \neg F$. And since $\mathsf{cons}(C^+_{n+k+1}) \models_T A$, also $\mathsf{cons}(C^+_{n+k+1}) \models_T \neg F$ by Cut in classical logic. Therefore, $E \rightsquigarrow F \in C^-_{k+n+1}$ as desired. This proves part (1).

For part (2) we need to show $(\mathscr{C}^+, \mathscr{C}^-) \leq (\mathscr{D}^+, \mathscr{D}^-)$, and we proceed by induction to show that $(C^+_n, C^-_n) \leq (\mathscr{D}^+, \mathscr{D}^-)$ for each n. The basis for $n = 0$ holds trivially as before. For the inductive step, assume $(C^+_n, C^-_n) \leq (\mathscr{D}^+, \mathscr{D}^-)$ to show $(C^+_{n+1}, C^-_{n+1}) \leq (\mathscr{D}^+, \mathscr{D}^-)$. If $E \rightsquigarrow F \in C^+_{n+1}$, then:

(*a*) $\mathsf{cons}(C^+_n) \models_T E$; and (*b*) $\mathsf{cons}(\Delta - C^-_n) \not\models_T \neg F$.

From the former and the inductive hypothesis, $\mathsf{cons}(\mathscr{D}^+) \models_T E$, whence by monotonicity of classical logic also $\mathsf{cons}(\mathscr{D}^+) \models_{T+A} E$. If now for reduction $E \rightsquigarrow F \notin \mathscr{D}^+$ it must be that $\mathsf{cons}(\Delta - \mathscr{D}^-) \models_{T+A} \neg F$. By inductive hypothesis $C^-_n \subseteq \mathscr{D}^-$ so also $\mathsf{cons}(\Delta - C^-_n) \models_{T+A} \neg F$.

But $\mathscr{C}^+ \cap \mathscr{C}^- = \varnothing$ by definition, and $C^-_n \subseteq \mathscr{C}^-$, so also $\mathscr{C}^+ \cap C^-_n = \varnothing$, i.e., $\mathscr{C}^+ \subseteq \Delta - C^-_n$. By hypothesis, $\mathsf{cons}(\mathscr{C}^+) \models_T A$ so that $\mathsf{cons}(\Delta - C^-_n) \models_T A$, and by Cut for classical logic the last line of the previous paragraph gives $\mathsf{cons}(\Delta - C^-_n) \models_T \neg F$, against (*b*). We conclude that $E \rightsquigarrow F \in \mathscr{D}^+$, i.e., $C^+_{n+1} \subseteq \mathscr{D}^+$.

Finally, to prove $C^-_{n+1} \subseteq \mathscr{D}^-$:

$$
\begin{array}{llll}
E \rightsquigarrow F \in C^-_{n+1} & \text{only if} & \mathsf{cons}(C^+_{n+1}) \models_T \neg F & \\
& \text{only if} & \mathsf{cons}(\mathscr{D}^+) \models_T \neg F & \text{since } C^+_{n+1} \subseteq \mathscr{D}^+ \\
& \text{only if} & \mathsf{cons}(\mathscr{D}^+) \models_{T+A} \neg F & \\
& \text{only if} & E \rightsquigarrow F \in \mathscr{D}^- & \square
\end{array}
$$

Theorem 4.3 (Cut). *If $T : \Delta \Vdash_G A$ and $T + A : \Delta \Vdash_G B$ then $T : \Delta \Vdash_G B$.*

Proof. Suppose $T : \Delta \Vdash_G A$ and $T + A : \Delta \Vdash_G B$; let $(\mathscr{C}^+, \mathscr{C}^-)$ be the least general C-set for $T : \Delta$. Since $T : \Delta \Vdash_G A$, by hypothesis $\mathsf{cons}(\mathscr{C}^+) \models_T A$, and we want to show $\mathsf{cons}(\mathscr{C}^+) \models_T B$.

If we now let $(\mathscr{D}^+, \mathscr{D}^-)$ be the least general C-set for $T + A : \Delta$, then by hypothesis $\mathsf{cons}(\mathscr{D}^+) \models_{T+A} B$. By Conservativity (Theorem 4.2, part (1)), $\mathscr{D}^+ \subseteq \mathscr{C}^+$, so that also $\mathsf{cons}(\mathscr{C}^+) \models_{T+A} B$. But since $\mathsf{cons}(\mathscr{C}^+) \models_T A$, by Cut in classical logic $\mathsf{cons}(\mathscr{C}^+) \models_T B$. This shows $T : \Delta \Vdash_G B$. $\square$

Theorem 4.4 (Cautious Monotony). *If* $T : \Delta \Vdash_G A$ *and* $T : \Delta \Vdash_G B$ *then* $T + A : \Delta \Vdash_G B$.

Proof. Assume $T : \Delta \Vdash_G A$ and $T : \Delta \Vdash_G B$, and let $(\mathscr{D}^+, \mathscr{D}^-)$ be the least general C-set for $T{+}A : \Delta$. We need to show $\mathsf{cons}(\mathscr{D}^+) \models_{T+A} B$. Let $(\mathscr{C}^+, \mathscr{C}^-)$ be the least general C-set for $T : \Delta$. Then $\mathsf{cons}(\mathscr{C}^+) \models_T B$. By Conservativity (Theorem 4.2, part (2)), $\mathscr{C}^+ \subseteq \mathscr{D}^+$, so by Monotony in classical logic $\mathsf{cons}(\mathscr{D}^+) \models_T B$, and also $\mathsf{cons}(\mathscr{D}^+) \models_{T+A} B$, as required. □

General C-consequence embodies a *cautious* or *skeptical* approach. While conflicts between defeasible rules and hard facts are always resolved in favor of the latter, in the presence of conflicting rules, General C-consequence withholds commitment. It is precisely this feature that allows for the crucial property of Cautious Monotony to hold. Consider the following examples.

Example 4.1. Consider $T = \{A\}$ and $\Delta = \{A \rightsquigarrow B, A \rightsquigarrow \neg B\}$. Then $T : \Delta \nVdash_G B$ and $T : \Delta \nVdash_G \neg B$ since both defeasible rules are potentially conflicted. The least general C-set is $\varnothing$.

Example 4.2. Consider $T = \varnothing$ and $\Delta = \{\top \rightsquigarrow B, A \rightsquigarrow \neg B\}$. Then $T : \Delta \nVdash_G B$, since (again) both rules are potentially conflicted. But notice, in comparison, that on the account of consequence for the original notion of a C-set, $T : \Delta \Vdash B$.

One could make the case that in this case the original notion of C-consequence delivers intuitively preferable results, since the only way to trigger the second rule is if the first is triggered as well, but in such a case the second rule would be conflicted; by contrast, the first rule is always triggered and therefore does not depend on the second rule.

5 Conclusions

Based on the construal of defeasible interrogative inquiry as defeasible inference rule, we have provided two frameworks, broadly inspired by Antonelli (2005), giving rise to two distinct notion of consequence: C-consequence and general C-consequence. In defeasible inference rules of the form $A \rightsquigarrow B$, the antecedent A plays a meta-theoretic role similar to that played, in Hintikka's framework, by the *presupposition* of a question. But our proposal differs from Hintikka's in that the resulting notion of consequence is *supra-classical* thereby allowing the inquirer to use the full power of classical logic. In contrast, Hintikka's notion, as pointed out, has to be *subclassical*, since the presupposition $A \vee \neg A$ of a yes/no question of the form A? need not be satisfied in each case.

But the most distinctive feature of our notion of consequence lies in its formal properties. After identifying the appropriate version of Gabbay's three desiderata of Refleixvity, Cut, and Cautious Monotony, we have shown that the last one fails for C-consequence, and that it is only the general version that meets all three. Cautious

Monotony is crucial because it allows the interrogative process to proceed in a cumulative manner, by the progressive accumulation of intermediate results that can be later employed in order to establish new ones.

References

Antonelli, G. A. (2005). *Grounded consequence for defeasible logic*. Cambridge/New York: Cambridge University Press.

Gabbay, D. (1985). Theoretical foundations for non-monotonic reasoning in expert systems. In K. R. Apt (Ed.), *Logics and models of concurrent systems* (pp. 439–457). New York: Springer. ISBN 0-387-15181-8, http://dl.acm.org/citation.cfm?id=101969.101988.

Hintikka, J. (1984). The logic of science as a model-oriented logic. In *PSA: Proceedings of the Biennial meeting of the philosophy of science association* (pp. 177–185). ISSN 02708647, http://www.jstor.org/stable/192338.

Hintikka, J. (1988). What is the logic of experimental inquiry? *Synthése, 74*, 173–190.

Hintikka, J., Halonen, I., & Mutanen, A. (2002). Interrogative logic as a general theory of reasoning. In R. H. Johnson & J. Woods (Eds.), *Handbook of practical reasoning*. Dordrecht: Kluwer Academic.

Makinson, D. (1994). General patterns in nonmonotonic reasoning. In D. M. Gabbay, C. J. Hogger, & J. A. Robinson (Eds.), *Handbook of logic in artificial intelligence and logic programming*, (Vol. 3, pp. 35–110). New York: Oxford University Press. ISBN 0-19-853747-6, http://dl.acm.org/citation.cfm?id=186124.186126.

Reiter, R. (1987). A logic for default reasoning. In M. L. Ginsberg (Ed.), *Readings in nonmonotonic reasoning* (pp. 68–93). San Francisco: Morgan Kaufmann. ISBN 0-934613-45-1, http://dl.acm.org/citation.cfm?id=42641.42646.

Stalnaker, R. (1994). What is a nonmonotonic consequence relation? *Fundamenta Informaticae, 21*(1, 2), 7–21. ISSN 0169-2968, http://dl.acm.org/citation.cfm?id=2383424.2383425.

On Search for Law-Like Statements as Abductive Hypotheses by Socratic Transformations

Mariusz Urbański and Andrzej Wiśniewski

Abstract We define a mechanism by which abductive hypotheses having the form of law-like statements are generated. We use the Socratic transformations approach as the underlying proof method.

Keywords Erotetic logic • Socratic proofs • Abduction • Law-like statements

1 Aims

If, as Jaakko Hintikka (2007, p. 38) claims, abduction constitutes the central problem in contemporary epistemology, then designing an adequate logic of abduction is one of the most important challenges faced by contemporary logic. The logical structure of the well-known Peircean scheme of abductive reasoning is this: from an observation that A (an abductive goal), and from the known rule that if H, then A, infer H (an abductive hypothesis, or an abducible; cf. Peirce (1958, 5.189)). However, this schema may be elaborated in detail in different ways, which lead to different models of abduction (see Urbański (2016)).

Slightly expanding the Peircean scheme, we may claim that the aim of abductive reasoning is to fill, by means of a hypothesis H, a certain gap between some dataset X (a database, a belief set, a body of knowledge) and a goal A, unattainable from X. Let us stress that both abductive hypotheses and goals may be, depending on the type of abductive reasoning, propositions, laws, rules, or even theories (cf. Gabbay and Woods (2005) and Magnani (2004, 2009)). One important issue in research on abduction is whether filling this gap is intrinsically of explanatory character or not. If so, then abduction is, as a matter of fact, a version of the Inference to the Best

Work on this paper was supported by funds of the National Science Centre, Poland (DEC-2012/04/A/HS1/00715).

M. Urbański (✉) • A. Wiśniewski
Department of Logic and Cognitive Science, Institute of Psychology, Adam Mickiewicz University, Poznań, Poland
e-mail: Mariusz.Urbanski@amu.edu.pl; Andrzej.Wisniewski@amu.edu.pl

C. Başkent (ed.), *Perspectives on Interrogative Models of Inquiry*, Logic, Argumentation & Reasoning 8, DOI 10.1007/978-3-319-20762-9_7

Explanation (IBE), understood in the sense of Harman (1965) or Lipton (2004), or according to some refined accounts of IBE, for example Kuipers' (2004) Inference to the Best Theory. If not, then abduction may serve explanatory as well as predictive or purely deductive, or in fact any other purposes. An example of this second stance is the algorithmic perspective, proposed by Gabbay and Woods, according to which an abductive hypothesis H "is legitimately dischargeable to the extent to which it makes it possible to prove (or compute) from a database a formula not provable (or computable) from it as it is currently structured" (Gabbay and Woods 2005, p. 88).

We shall follow the latter point of view and focus on computational issues, however with substantial explanatory flavour. Our purpose is to find a mechanism by which one can arrive at abductive hypotheses having the form of law-like statements (LLSs for short). We shall use the Socratic transformations (ST) approach (Wiśniewski 2004c) as a proof method on which hypotheses generation mechanism will be based.

Our aim is not trivial. On the one hand, approaches to abduction based on different proof methods do not produce LLSs as outcomes; examples include Analytic Tableaux method (Aliseda 1997, 2006), sequent calculi (Mayer and Pirri 1993), dynamic proof method of adaptive logics (Meheus et al. (2002) and Meheus and Batens (2006); it should be noted that Gauderis and Van de Putte (2012) offer account on abduction of generalizations within the adaptive logic framework). The same holds for the approaches based on the ST method proposed so far (see Urbański (2003), and Wiśniewski (2004b)). On the other hand, even though we agree that there is more to abduction than just IBE (cf. Hintikka (2007, pp. 41–44)), there are also close affinities between abduction and search for an explanation (see Thagard (1995, 2007)). As a result, a mechanism which enables a "computation" of explanatory abductive hypotheses in the form of LLSs seems highly attractive.

In this paper we shall not consider the problem of evaluation of abductive hypotheses. This is a somewhat different issue which can be satisfactorily dealt with by computer science rather than logical means. A convincing example is offered in papers by Komosinski et al. (2012, 2014), where multi-criteria dominance relation approach is employed.

2 Socratic Transformations

The ST approach offers a formal explication of the idea of solving logical problems of entailment or derivability by pure questioning, that is, by transforming the relevant initial question into consecutive questions without making any use of answers to the questions just transformed. Such *Socratic transformations* may be either successful or unsuccessful. Roughly, a successful transformation ends with a question of a specified final form, which can be answered in only one rational way. A successful transformation is a *Socratic proof*. Socratic transformations are guided by *erotetic rules*[1] which have only questions as premises and conclusions. These rules form the core of *erotetic calculi*.

We appeal here to the interrogative idea for a reason. We share Hintikka's conviction that "the interrogative approach can be argued to be a general theory of reasoning" (Hintikka et al. 1999, p. 47). Questions play far more important role in problem solving than it is typically recognized. Moreover, when explicit operations on questions, in the roles of premises or conclusions, are allowed in formal modeling of such processes, the payoff is a substantially more robust insight both into their real structure and into their computational properties. In order to justify these claims by some case-study examples we refer the reader to, int. al., Wiśniewski (2004a), Bolotov et al. (2006), Leszczyńska (2007), and Urbański and Łupkowski (2010). However, although Jaakko Hintikka is nowadays one of the best-known advocates of the interrogative idea, we rely here on different assumptions and on a different approach to the logic of questions.

We shall show how the ST approach works on the example of the E^{PQ} calculus, on which our abductive mechanism will be based (see Sect. 3). E^{PQ} is an erotetic counterpart of Pure Calculus of Quantifiers (PQ). Our presentation of this calculus will be based on the one given in Leszczyńska-Jasion et al. (2013). Detailed account on ST can be found, e.g., in Wiśniewski (2004c) and Wiśniewski and Shangin (2006). For elaboration of an erotetic background of ST, which is Inferential Erotetic Logic, see Wiśniewski (1995, 2013).

2.1 Language

Let us start with a language $\mathcal{L}$ of PQ with $\neg$ (negation), $\rightarrow$ (implication), $\wedge$ (conjunction) and $\vee$ (disjunction) as primitive connectives, and both $\forall$ (general quantifier) and $\exists$ (existential quantifier). The language $\mathcal{L}$ contains individual parameters, but it does not contain function symbols or identity. By a *term* of $\mathcal{L}$ we mean an individual variable or a parameter. We assume the usual notions of well-formed formula (wff) and sentence of $\mathcal{L}$. Now, let us extend $\mathcal{L}$ with a question-forming operator ? and the sign $\vdash$. The resulting language $\mathcal{L}^*$ has two disjoint categories of meaningful expressions: *declarative well-formed formulas* (hereafter: d-wffs), and *questions*. Questions of $\mathcal{L}^*$ are based on sequences of *atomic d-wffs* of $\mathcal{L}^*$, that is, expressions of the form:

$$S \vdash A$$

where S is a finite sequence (possibly empty) of sentences of $\mathcal{L}$, and A is a sentence of $\mathcal{L}$. A *pure sentence* is a sentence of $\mathcal{L}$ with no individual parameters. Note that

[1]"Erotetic" comes from Greek "erotema" which means "question".

atomic d-wffs of $\mathcal{L}^*$ are (single-conclusioned) sequents. A *sequent* is called *pure* if it contains only pure sentences.

In what follows we will refer to atomic d-wffs of $\mathcal{L}^*$ simply as to *sequents*, yet always having in mind that only sequents with single sentences of $\mathcal{L}$ in the succedent are taken into consideration. We use Greek lower case letters ϕ, ψ, χ, ω (possibly with subscripts) as metavariables for sequents, and Greek upper case letters Φ, Ψ, Γ as variables for sequences of sequents.

A *question* of the language $\mathcal{L}^*$ is an expression of the form:

$$?\,(\Phi)$$

where Φ is a non-empty finite sequence of sequents; the terms of this sequence are called *constituents* of the question, and we say that the question is *based on* the sequence.

Some notational conventions will be useful. The following:

$$S\,'\,T$$

stands for the *concatenation* of sequences S and T of PQ-formulas. By

$$S\,'\,A$$

we refer to the concatenation of S and the one-term sequence $\langle A \rangle$, where A is a PQ-wff. The concatenation of sequences Φ and Ψ of sequents is referred to as:

$$\Phi; \Psi$$

whereas the inscription:

$$\Phi; \phi$$

denotes the concatenation of a sequence of sequents Φ and the one-term sequence $\langle \phi \rangle$, where ϕ is a sequent. Of course, the inscription:

$$\Phi; \phi; \Psi$$

refers to the concatenation of $\Phi; \phi$ and a sequence of sequents Ψ. Any of S, T, Φ, and Ψ can be empty.

Thus when $\Phi = \langle \phi_1, \ldots, \phi_n \rangle$, the corresponding question can be written as:

$$?\,(\phi_1; \ldots; \phi_n)$$

and we will proceed that way. If $\Phi = \langle \phi \rangle$, then we write the question as:

$$?\,(\phi)$$

and we say that the question is based on a single-conclusioned sequent.

A question of the form: $?\ (S_1 \vdash A_1; \ldots; S_n \vdash A_n)$ can read: "Is it the case that: A_1 is PQ-entailed by S_1 and ... and A_n is PQ-entailed by S_n?"; due to the completeness of PQ, "PQ-entailed by" can be replaced by "PQ-derivable from." (By entailment by/derivability from a sequence we mean entailment by/derivability from the set of all the terms of the sequence.) When $n = 1$, the question pertains to the claim of a single sequent.

2.2 The Calculus E^{PQ}

In a Socratic transformation one transforms a question into another question. Here is the list of erotetic rules that govern the relevant transformations of questions of $\mathcal{L}^*$:

$$\mathbf{L}_\alpha: \frac{?\ (\Phi; S\,'\,\alpha\,'\,T \vdash C; \Psi)}{?\ (\Phi; S\,'\,\alpha_1\,'\,\alpha_2\,'\,T \vdash C; \Psi)} \qquad \mathbf{R}_\alpha: \frac{?\ (\Phi; S \vdash \alpha; \Psi)}{?\ (\Phi; S \vdash \alpha_1; S \vdash \alpha_2; \Psi)}$$

$$\mathbf{L}_\beta: \frac{?\ (\Phi; S\,'\,\beta\,'\,T \vdash C; \Psi)}{?\ (\Phi; S\,'\,\beta_1\,'\,T \vdash C; S\,'\,\beta_2\,'\,T \vdash C; \Psi)} \qquad \mathbf{R}_\beta: \frac{?\ (\Phi; S \vdash \beta; \Psi)}{?\ (\Phi; S\,'\,\beta_1^* \vdash \beta_2; \Psi)}$$

$$\mathbf{L}_{\neg\neg}: \frac{?\ (\Phi; S\,'\,\neg\neg A\,'\,T \vdash C; \Psi)}{?\ (\Phi; S\,'\,A\,'\,T \vdash C; \Psi)} \qquad \mathbf{R}_{\neg\neg}: \frac{?\ (\Phi; S \vdash \neg\neg A; \Psi)}{?\ (\Phi; S \vdash A; \Psi)}$$

$$\mathbf{L}_\forall: \frac{?(\Phi; S\,'\,\forall x_i A\,'\,T \vdash B; \Psi)}{?(\Phi; S\,'\,\forall x_i A\,'\,A(x_i/\tau)\,'\,T \vdash B; \Psi)} \qquad \mathbf{R}_\forall: \frac{?(\Phi; S \vdash \forall x_i A; \Psi)}{?(\Phi; S \vdash A(x_i/\tau); \Psi)}$$

$\mathbf{L}_\forall$: provided that x_i is free in A, τ is any parameter

$\mathbf{R}_\forall$: provided that x_i is free in A, and τ is a parameter which does not occur in S nor in A

$$\mathbf{L}_\exists: \frac{?(\Phi; S\,'\,\exists x_i A\,'\,T \vdash B; \Psi)}{?(\Phi; S\,'\,A(x_i/\tau)\,'\,T \vdash B; \Psi)} \qquad \mathbf{R}_\exists: \frac{?(\Phi; S \vdash \exists x_i A; \Psi)}{?(\Phi; S\,'\,\forall x_i \neg A \vdash A(x_i/\tau); \Psi)}$$

$\mathbf{L}_\exists$: provided that x_i is free in A, and τ is a parameter which does not occur in S, A, T, B

$\mathbf{R}_\exists$: provided that x_i is free in A, τ is any parameter

$$\mathbf{L}_\kappa: \frac{?(\Phi; S\,'\,\kappa\,'\,T \vdash C; \Psi)}{?(\Phi; S\,'\,\kappa^*\,'\,T \vdash C; \Psi)} \qquad \mathbf{R}_\kappa: \frac{?(\Phi; S \vdash \kappa; \Psi)}{?(\Phi; S \vdash \kappa^*; \Psi)}$$

We shall call rules $\mathbf{R}_\alpha$ and $\mathbf{L}_\beta$ *branching rules*, as the resulting "question-conclusion" has more constituents than the "question-premise". Consequently, we will call the remaining erotetic rules *non-branching rules* (in particular, the quantificational rules of E^{PQ} are non-branching). The letters "**L**" and "**R**" indicate that the appropriate rule "operates" on the left or right side of the turnstile $\vdash$. For brevity, we have used the α, β–notation. This is explained in the following table (see Smullyan (1995)):

α	α_1	α_2	β	β_1	β_2	β_1^*
$A \wedge B$	A	B	$\neg(A \vee B)$	$\neg A$	$\neg B$	A
$\neg(A \vee B)$	$\neg A$	$\neg B$	$A \vee B$	A	B	$\neg A$
$\neg(A \rightarrow B)$	A	$\neg B$	$A \rightarrow B$	$\neg A$	B	A

β_1^* may be called the *complement* of β_1.

Rules $\mathbf{L}_\kappa$ and $\mathbf{R}_\kappa$ cover the cases of quantifiers in the scope of negation and dummy quantification according to the following table:

κ	κ^*
$\neg\forall x_i A$	$\exists x_i \neg A$
$\neg\exists x_i A$	$\forall x_i \neg A$
$\forall x_i A$, where x_i is not free in A	A
$\exists x_i A$, where x_i is not free in A	A

It is easily visible that the rules of E^{PQ} are designed in such a way that each constituent of the "question-conclusion" is PQ-valid if and only if each constituent of the "question-premise" is PQ-valid. On the other hand, it can be shown that each application of a rule of E^{PQ} retains validity (in the sense of Inferential Erotetic Logic) of the corresponding erotetic inference. For a justification of the above claims see Wiśniewski (2004c) and Wiśniewski and Shangin (2006).

The concept of Socratic transformation is given by the following definition:

Definition 1. A sequence $\langle s_1, s_2, \ldots \rangle$ of questions is a *Socratic transformation of a question* ? $(S \vdash A)$ *via the rules of an erotetic calculus* E^{PQ} iff the following conditions hold:

(i) $s_1 = ?(S \vdash A)$;
(ii) s_i, where $i > 1$, results from s_{i-1} by an application of an erotetic rule of E^{PQ}.

Consider the following example (Leszczyńska-Jasion et al. 2013, p. 977) of a Socratic transformation of sequent $\vdash \exists x P(x) \vee \exists x Q(x) \rightarrow \exists x(P(x) \vee Q(x))$:

Example 1.

1.$?(\vdash \exists xP(x) \vee \exists xQ(x) \rightarrow \exists x(P(x) \vee Q(x))$ $\mathbf{R}_\beta$
2.$?(\exists xP(x) \vee \exists xQ(x) \vdash \exists x(P(x) \vee Q(x)))$ $\mathbf{R}_\beta$
3.$?(\exists xP(x) \vdash \exists x(P(x) \vee Q(x))\ ;\ \exists xQ(x) \vdash \exists x(P(x) \vee Q(x)))$ $\mathbf{L}_\exists$
4.$?(P(a) \vdash \exists x(P(x) \vee Q(x))\ ;\ \exists xQ(x) \vdash \exists x(P(x) \vee Q(x)))$ $\mathbf{R}_\exists$
5.$?(P(a), \forall x\neg(P(x) \vee Q(x)) \vdash P(a) \vee Q(a)\ ;\ \exists xQ(x) \vdash \exists x(P(x) \vee Q(x)))$ $\mathbf{R}_\beta$
6.$?(P(a), \forall x\neg(P(x) \vee Q(x)), \neg P(a) \vdash Q(a)\ ;\ \exists xQ(x) \vdash \exists x(P(x) \vee Q(x)))$ $\mathbf{L}_\exists$
7.$?(P(a), \forall x\neg(P(x) \vee Q(x)), \neg P(a) \vdash Q(a)\ ;\ Q(a) \vdash \exists x(P(x) \vee Q(x)))$ $\mathbf{R}_\exists$
8.$?(P(a), \forall x\neg(P(x) \vee Q(x)), \neg P(a) \vdash Q(a)\ ;\ Q(a), \forall x\neg(P(x) \vee Q(x)) \vdash P(a) \vee Q(a))$ $\mathbf{R}_\beta$
9.$?(P(a), \forall x\neg(P(x) \vee Q(x)), \neg P(a) \vdash Q(a)\ ;\ Q(a), \forall x\neg(P(x) \vee Q(x)), \neg P(a) \vdash Q(a))$

The last question of the above sequence has an interesting property: the affirmative answer to it is, in a sense, evident, as all the constituents of this question express some basic facts about (PQ) entailment. Thus, the answer to the first question of the sequence is also affirmative: it is true that $\exists xP(x) \vee \exists xQ(x) \rightarrow \exists x(P(x) \vee Q(x))$ is entailed by the empty set, and the sequence of Example 1 is not just a transformation: it is a successful transformation, that is, a proof.

Definition 2. Let $S \vdash A$ be a pure sequent. A finite Socratic transformation $\langle Q_1, \ldots, Q_n \rangle$ of question $?(S \vdash A)$ via the rules of E^{PQ} is a *Socratic proof of sequent* $S \vdash A$ *in the calculus* E^{PQ} iff for each constituent ϕ of Q_n:

(a) ϕ is of the form $T \,'\, B \,'\, U \vdash B$, or
(b) ϕ is of the form $T \,'\, B \,'\, U \,'\, \neg B \,'\, W \vdash C$, or
(c) ϕ is of the form $T \,'\, \neg B \,'\, U \,'\, B \,'\, W \vdash C$.

Constituents/sequents of the form (a), (b) and (c) are called *successful.*

In what follows by a successful (unsuccessful) Socratic transformation we will mean a Socratic transformation which is (which is not) a Socratic proof.

Calculus E^{PQ} pertains to the Pure Calculus of Quantifiers in the following sense:

Theorem 1. *Let* $S \vdash A$ *be a pure sequent.* $S \vdash A$ *is provable in* E^{PQ} *iff* $S \vdash A$ *is PQ-valid.*

The reader will find the proof in Wiśniewski and Shangin (2006).

3 A View from E^{PQ}

Now we are in a position to define an abductive mechanism which makes use of E^{PQ}. We assume that the initial question of a Socratic transformation is based on a pure sequent (i.e. a sequent which involves only parameter-free sentences). This is not required by E^{PQ} (only Socratic proofs are supposed to start that way), but we impose this restriction for a reason.

A law-like statement (LLS) is a first-order sentence of the form:

$$\forall x_{i_1} \ldots \forall x_{i_n} (A(x_{i_1}, \ldots, x_{i_n}) \rightarrow B(x_{i_1}, \ldots, x_{i_n}))$$

where $A(x_{i_1}, \ldots, x_{i_n})$ and $B(x_{i_1}, \ldots, x_{i_n})$ are parameter-free sentential functions which involve $x_{i_1}, \ldots, x_{i_n}$ as the only free variables. We consider LLSs which are expressions of $\mathcal{L}$. Let $A(x_i/\tau)$ designate a sentence which results from a sentential function Ax_i (x_i is here the only free variable of A) by the replacement of (each occurrence of) variable x_i by parameter τ. According to the rules of E^{PQ}, a wff of the form $A(x_i/\tau)$ occurs in a constituent of a question of a Socratic transformation of the considered kind due to an application of any of the rules: $\mathbf{L}_\forall$, $\mathbf{R}_\forall$, $\mathbf{L}_\exists$, $\mathbf{R}_\exists$, and is always a sentence. Moreover, such a formula never occurs in an initial question (sequent) of a Socratic proof (because the initial question has to be based on a pure sequent).

We introduce the following rule of abduction:

(abd)

$$\frac{?(\Phi; S'A(x_i/\tau)'T \vdash B(x_i/\tau); \Psi)}{?(\Phi; S'A(x_i/\tau)'T'\forall x_i(Ax_i \to Bx_i) \vdash B(x_i/\tau); \Psi)}$$

Observe that we require that τ must replace x_i both in Ax_i and in Bx_i; in other words, it is required that the appropriate sentential functions (recall that each of them occurs in a sequent in the scope of a quantifier) must share a free variable and that this variable has been replaced by τ in both cases. In general, this is not univocal, but since we are going to extend a given Socratic transformation which starts with a question based on a pure sequent, univocality is retained.

Rule **(abd)** is supposed to be applied when we have an unsuccessful constituent in the last question of a completed Socratic transformation. Of course, it is not the case that **(abd)** is always applicable; for example, **(abd)** is not applicable to the last term of the following unsuccessful Socratic transformation (in order to improve readability, from now on we highlight a formula which the rule indicated to the right operates on):

1. $?(\exists x_1 Px_1 \vdash \forall x_1 Px_1)$ $\mathbf{L}_\exists$
2. $?(P\tau_1 \vdash \forall x_1 Px_1)$ $\mathbf{R}_\forall$
3. $?(P\tau_1 \vdash P\tau_2)$

Observe that rule **(abd)**, if applicable, enables us to "compute" a LLS given that τ is the only parameter of $A(x_i/\tau)$ and $B(x_i/\tau)$ (recall that a LLS must be parameter-free). If there are more parameters involved, the situation is more complicated (see below). Of course, unlike other rules, **(abd)** does not preserve joint validity from top to bottom.

Definition 3. By an *abductive extension* of an unsuccessful finite Socratic transformation $\mathbf{s} = Q_1, \ldots, Q_n$ of $?(S \vdash A)$ via E^{PQ} we mean a finite sequence of questions $Q_1^*, \ldots, Q_n^*, Q_{n+1}^*, \ldots, Q_u^*$ such that:

1. $Q_i = Q_i^*$ for $i = 1, \ldots, n$,
2. Q_{m+1}^* results from Q_m^* by **(abd)** for $m = n, n+1, \ldots, u-1$,
3. rule **(abd)** is applied only with respect to unsuccessful constituents,
4. if rule **(abd)** has been applied with respect to k-th constituent of m-th ($n \leq m < u$) question, then rule **(abd)** is not applied with respect to k-th constituent of any question with an index greater than m.

By a *proto-abducible* of an abductive extension of **s** we mean any wff introduced to a constituent of a question of **s** by means of an application of rule **(abd)**. We say that an abductive extension is *completed* if each constituent of the last question of it is either successful or involves a proto-abducible left of the turnstile.

Clause 4 of Definition 3 amounts to the requirement that **(abd)** is applied only once with respect to a given unsuccessful constituent of the last question of

s (observe that **(abd)** is not a branching rule). In the case of a completed abductive extension of **s** rule **(abd)** has been applied to each unsuccessful constituent of the last question of **s** (these constituents are rewritten to consecutive questions and are dealt with step by step).

Example 2 (space between lines indicates where the analysed unsuccessful ST ends; the proto-abducible is underlined).

1. $?(\forall x_1 Px_1 \vdash \forall x_1 Rx_1)$ **R**$_\forall$
2. $?(\forall x_1 Px_1 \vdash R\tau_1)$ **L**$_\forall$
3. $?(\forall x_1 Px_1, P\tau_1 \vdash R\tau_1)$ **(abd)**

4. $?(\forall x_1 Px_1, P\tau_1, \underline{\forall x_1(Px_1 \rightarrow Rx_1)} \vdash R\tau_1)$

Observe that $\forall x_1 Px_1 \not\models \forall x_1 Rx_1$, but $\{\forall x_1 Px_1, \forall x_1(Px_1 \rightarrow Rx_1)\} \models \forall x_1 Rx_1$.

Example 3.

1. $?(\forall x_1(Px_1 \rightarrow Rx_1) \vdash \forall x_1(Px_1 \rightarrow Gx_1))$ **R**$_\forall$
2. $?(\forall x_1(Px_1 \rightarrow Rx_1) \vdash P\tau_1 \rightarrow G\tau_1)$ **R**$_\rightarrow$
3. $?(\forall x_1(Px_1 \rightarrow Rx_1), P\tau_1 \vdash G\tau_1)$ **L**$_\forall$
4. $?(\forall x_1(Px_1 \rightarrow Rx_1), P\tau_1 \rightarrow R\tau_1, P\tau_1 \vdash G\tau_1)$ **R**$_\rightarrow$
5. $?(\forall x_1(Px_1 \rightarrow Rx_1), \neg P\tau_1, P\tau_1 \vdash G\tau_1;$ ***(abd)***
   $\forall x_1(Px_1 \rightarrow Rx_1), R\tau_1, P\tau_1 \vdash G\tau_1)$

6. $?(\forall x_1(Px_1 \rightarrow Rx_1), \neg P\tau_1, P\tau_1 \vdash G\tau_1;$
   $\forall x_1(Px_1 \rightarrow Rx_1), R\tau_1, P\tau_1, \underline{\forall x_1(Rx_1 \rightarrow Gx_1)} \vdash G\tau_1)$

Again, we have $\{\forall x_1(Px_1 \rightarrow Rx_1), \forall x_1(Rx_1 \rightarrow Gx_1)\} \models \forall x_1(Px_1 \rightarrow Gx_1)$.

The above unsuccessful transformation 1–5 of Example 3 can also be extended to:

6'. $?(\forall x_1(Px_1 \rightarrow Rx_1), \neg P\tau_1, P\tau_1 \vdash G\tau_1;$
   $\forall x_1(Px_1 \rightarrow Rx_1), R\tau_1, P\tau_1, \underline{\forall x_1(Px_1 \rightarrow Gx_1)} \vdash G\tau_1)$

In this case, however, the proto-abducible is trivial, that is, it is identical with the sentence which stays right to the turnstile in the initial question (sequent).

Now, observe that in both cases we can "add" the proto-abducible to the "premises" of the initial sequent and we receive a successful Socratic transformation of the question obtained in this way (see Examples 4 and 5).

Example 4.

1. $?(\forall x_1 Px_1, \forall x_1(Px_1 \to Rx_1) \vdash \forall x_1 Rx_1)$ **R**$_\forall$
2. $?(\forall x_1 Px_1, \forall x_1(Px_1 \to Rx_1) \vdash R\tau_1)$ **L**$_\forall$
3. $?(\forall x_1 Px_1, P\tau_1, \forall x_1(Px_1 \to Rx_1) \vdash R\tau_1)$ **L**$_\forall$
4. $?(\forall x_1 Px_1, P\tau_1, \forall x_1(Px_1 \to Rx_1), P\tau_1 \to R\tau_1 \vdash R\tau_1)$ **L**$_\to$
5. $?(\forall x_1 Px_1, P\tau_1, \forall x_1(Px_1 \to Rx_1), \neg P\tau_1 \vdash R\tau_1;$
   $\forall x_1 Px_1, P\tau_1, \forall x_1(Px_1 \to Rx_1), R\tau_1 \vdash R\tau_1)$

Example 5.

1. $?(\forall x_1(Px_1 \to Rx_1), \forall x_1(Rx_1 \to Gx_1) \vdash \forall x_1(Px_1 \to Gx_1))$ **R**$_\forall$
2. $?(\forall x_1(Px_1 \to Rx_1), \forall x_1(Rx_1 \to Gx_1) \vdash P\tau_1 \to G\tau_1)$ **R**$_\to$
3. $?(\forall x_1(Px_1 \to Rx_1), \forall x_1(Rx_1 \to Gx_1), P\tau_1 \vdash G\tau_1)$ **L**$_\forall$
4. $?(\forall x_1(Px_1 \to Rx_1), P\tau_1 \to R\tau_1\ \forall x_1(Rx_1 \to Gx_1), P\tau_1 \vdash G\tau_1)$ **L**$_\to$
5. $?(\forall x_1(Px_1 \to Rx_1), \neg P\tau_1, \forall x_1(Rx_1 \to Gx_1), P\tau_1 \vdash G\tau_1;$ **L**$_\forall$
   $\forall x_1(Px_1 \to Rx_1), R\tau_1, \forall x_1(Rx_1 \to Gx_1), P\tau_1 \vdash G\tau_1)$
6. $?(\forall x_1(Px_1 \to Rx_1), \neg P\tau_1, \forall x_1(Rx_1 \to Gx_1), P\tau_1 \vdash G\tau_1;$ **L**$_\to$
   $\forall x_1(Px_1 \to Rx_1), R\tau_1, \forall x_1(Rx_1 \to Gx_1), R\tau_1 \to G\tau_1, P\tau_1 \vdash G\tau_1)$
7. $?(\forall x_1(Px_1 \to Rx_1), \neg P\tau_1, \forall x_1(Rx_1 \to Gx_1), P\tau_1 \vdash G\tau_1;$
   $\forall x_1(Px_1 \to Rx_1), R\tau_1, \forall x_1(Rx_1 \to Gx_1), \neg R\tau_1, P\tau_1 \vdash G\tau_1;$
   $\forall x_1(Px_1 \to Rx_1), R\tau_1, \forall x_1(Rx_1 \to Gx_1), G\tau_1, P\tau_1 \vdash G\tau_1)$

The above observation can be generalized. The following holds:

Theorem 2. *Let $S \vdash A$ be a pure sequent,* **s** *be a finite unsuccessful Socratic transformation of $?(S \vdash A)$ via the rules of E^{PQ}, and* $\mathbf{s}^*$ *be a completed abductive extension of* **s** *such that all the proto-abducibles of* $\mathbf{s}^*$ *are parameter-free. Let S^* be a sequence of all the proto-abducibles of* $\mathbf{s}^*$. *The sequent $S'S^* \vdash A$ is provable in E^{PQ} and thus A is CL-entailed by the set made up of all the terms of the sequence $S'S^*$.*

Proof. Let us observe that we can assign to each unsuccessful constituent of the last question of **s** exactly one proto-abducible, namely that one which is introduced when rule **(abd)** is applied with respect to this constituent. To put it differently: if i-th constituent of the last question of **s** is unsuccessful, then there exists a proto-abducible which was introduced in $\mathbf{s}^*$ when rule **(abd)** was applied with respect to i-th constituent of a question of $\mathbf{s}^*$ of an index equal or greater to the index of the last question of **s** (recall that **(abd)** is a non-branching rule, and, since $\mathbf{s}^*$ is completed, each unsuccessful constituent of the last question is "dealt with" in some question of $\mathbf{s}^*$).

We take **s** and modify it as follows:

(a) we replace each sequent, $T \vdash C$, which is a constituent of a question of **s**, with the sequent $T'S^* \vdash C$; note that $S \vdash A$ transforms into a *pure* sequent $S'S^* \vdash A$. Then we proceed analogously as in **s**;
(b) we take the leftmost unsuccessful constituent of the last question of the transformation received from **s** in the above manner. Since S^* always occurs left of the turnstile, this constituent is a sequent of the form:

$$U'A(x_i/\tau)'W'\forall x_i(Ax_i \rightarrow Bx_i)'Z \vdash B(x_i/\tau)$$

Now we apply rule $L_\forall$ with respect to the above constituent and we obtain the following constituent (of the same index) in the next question:

$$(\$) \quad U'A(x_i/\tau)'W' < \forall x_i(Ax_i \rightarrow Bx_i), A(x_i/\tau) \rightarrow B(x_i/\tau) >' Z \vdash B(x_i/\tau)$$

In the next step we apply rule $L_\rightarrow$ with respect to ($) and we obtain two "new" successful sequents at the place where ($) has occurred;
(c) we repeat the procedure described in (b) with regard to the leftmost unsuccessful constituent of the question obtained at the previous step.

It is clear that the above procedure terminates in a finite number of steps and thus produces a finite Socratic transformation of $?(S'S^* \vdash A)$. Since unsuccessful constituents are eliminated step by step, we end with a Socratic proof of $S'S^* \vdash A$. Therefore, by soundness of E^{PQ}, A is PQ-entailed by the set made up of all the terms of $S'S^*$. This completes the proof. □

In order to obtain a general scheme we need a method of extraction of LLSs from proto-abducibles which involve parameters.

Since, by definition, both parts of an LLS must share variables, for our purposes we consider the case in which all the proto-abducibles introduced by **(abd)** are of the form:

$$(\#) \quad \forall x_i(A(x_i, x_{i_1}/\tau_1, \ldots, x_{i_n}/\tau_n) \rightarrow B(x_i, x_{i_1}/\tau'_1, \ldots, x_{i_n}/\tau'_n))$$

where $x_i, x_{i_1}, \ldots, x_{i_n}$ are distinct variables, τ_i need not be distinct from τ'_i (although can be), and $\tau_1, \ldots, \tau_n$, as well as $\tau'_1, \ldots, \tau'_n$, need not be pairwise distinct. Again, (#) is univocal due to the fact that a given unsuccessful Socratic transformation is the starting point. If (#) is a proto-abducible of the considered kind and $\tau_i = \tau'_i$ for $1 \leq i \leq n$, then the following

$$\forall x_{i_1} \ldots \forall x_{i_n} \forall x_i(A(x_i, x_{i_1}, \ldots, x_{i_n}) \rightarrow B(x_i, x_{i_1}, \ldots, x_{i_n})) \tag{1}$$

is *the abducible corresponding* to (#). If, however, $\tau_i \neq \tau'_i$ for some (but not all) i, where $1 \leq i \leq n$, then the abducible corresponding to (#) falls under the schema:

$$\forall x_{j_1} \ldots \forall x_{j_k} \forall x_i (\exists x_{j_{k+1}} \ldots \exists x_{j_n} A(x_i, x_{j_1}, \ldots, x_{j_n}) \\ \rightarrow \forall x_{j_{k+1}} \ldots \forall x_{j_n} B(x_i, x_{j_1}, \ldots, x_{j_n})) \tag{2}$$

where $x_{j_1} \ldots x_{j_k}$ are all the variables among $x_{i_1}, \ldots, x_{i_n}$ which are replaced in (#) by the same parameters in the antecedent and the consequent, and $x_{j_{k+1}} \ldots x_{j_n}$ are all the variables among $x_{i_1}, \ldots, x_{i_n}$ which are replaced in (#) by distinct parameters in the antecedent and the consequent. Finally, if $\tau_i \neq \tau_i'$ for all i, where $1 \leq i \leq n$, then the abducible has the form:

$$\forall x_i (\exists x_{i_1} \ldots \exists x_{i_n} A(x_i, x_{i_1}, \ldots, x_{i_n}) \rightarrow \forall x_{i_1} \ldots \forall x_{i_n} B(x_i, x_{i_1}, \ldots, x_{i_n})) \tag{3}$$

Note that in either case the abducible involves the "original" variables which were replaced by parameters during the initial Socratic transformation. Note also that in each case the abducible constitutes an LLS.

Example 6 (for brevity, we use x for x_1, and y for x_2).

1. $?(\forall x \exists y Pxy \vdash \exists y \forall x Pxy)$ **$R_\exists$**
2. $?(\forall x \exists y Pxy, \forall y \neg \forall x Pxy \vdash \forall x Px\tau_1)$ **$L_\forall$**
3. $?(\forall x \exists y Pxy, \forall y \neg \forall x Pxy, \neg \forall x Px\tau_1 \vdash \forall x Px\tau_1)$ **$R_\forall$**
4. $?(\forall x \exists y Pxy, \forall y \neg \forall x Pxy, \neg \forall x Px\tau_1 \vdash P\tau_2\tau_1)$ **$L_{\neg\forall}$**
5. $?(\forall x \exists y Pxy, \forall y \neg \forall x Pxy, \exists x \neg Px\tau_1 \vdash P\tau_2\tau_1)$ **$L_\exists$**
6. $?(\forall x \exists y Pxy, \forall y \neg \forall x Pxy, \neg P\tau_3\tau_1 \vdash P\tau_2\tau_1)$ ***(abd)***

7. $?(\forall x \exists y Pxy, \forall y \neg \forall x Pxy, \neg P\tau_3\tau_1, \underline{\forall y(\neg P\tau_3 y \rightarrow P\tau_2 y)} \vdash P\tau_2\tau_1)$

The abducible is $\forall y(\exists x \neg Pxy \rightarrow \forall x Pxy)$. Observe that the abducible is CL-equivalent to $\forall x \forall y Pxy$.

In order to obtain a Socratic proof of

$$\forall x \exists y Pxy, \forall y(\exists x \neg Pxy \rightarrow \forall x Pxy) \vdash \exists y \forall x Pxy$$

it is sufficient to add the abducible left of the turnstile in the initial sequent of Example 6, proceed as above, apply rule $L_\forall$ to the abducible w.r.t. τ_1, apply rule $L_\rightarrow$, apply rule $L_{\neg\exists}$ to $\neg\exists x \neg Px\tau_1$ just obtained, apply rule $L_\forall$ to $\forall x \neg\neg Px\tau_1$ w.r.t. τ_3, and apply rule $L_\forall$ to $\forall x Px\tau_1$ w.r.t. τ_2.

One can prove the following:

Theorem 3. *Let $S \vdash A$ be a pure sequent. Let* **s** *be a finite unsuccessful Socratic transformation of $?(S \vdash A)$ via the rules of E^{PQ}, and let* $\mathbf{s}^*$ *be a completed abductive extension of* **s** *such that all the proto-abducibles of* $\mathbf{s}^*$ *are of the form (#) specified above. Let S^{**} be a sequence of all the abducibles which correspond to the proto-abducibles of* $\mathbf{s}^*$. *Then the sequent $S'S^{**} \vdash A$ is provable in E^{PQ} and thus A is CL-entailed by the set made up of all the terms of the sequence $S'S^{**}$.*

Proof. If an abducible falls under the schema (1), we proceed similarly as in the proof of Theorem 2. Suppose that an abducible is of the form (2) or of the form (3). One can get from it $\neg A(x_i/\tau, x_{i_1}/\tau_1, \ldots, x_{i_n}/\tau_n)$ as well as $B(x_i/\tau, x_{i_1}/\tau_1', \ldots, x_{i_n}/\tau_n')$.

An unsuccessful Socratic transformation can be abductively extended if only rule **(abd)** is applicable to the unsuccessful constituents of the transformation, regardless of whether entailment/derivability holds in the initial sequent. Hence a practical problem arises: at which point one should give up in applying the rules of E^{PQ} and apply rule **(abd)**? There is no general solution to this problem. A practical advice might be: if you end with a question whose unsuccessful constituents involve only atomic sentences right of the turnstile, and atomic sentences as well as compound formulas of the form $\forall x_i D$ (where x_i is free in D) left of the turnstile, try to apply rule **(abd)**. When you end with a completed abductive extension, the relevant abducibles either describe prospective goals of further deductions from accessible premises/databases (if these deductions are successfully completed, a positive solution to the main problem is arrived at) or are hypotheses to be tested (if tested with a success, you know that your problem can be resolved by means of new data).

By the way, the mechanism sketched above can be applied in proof-heuristics.

4 A View from E^{APQ}

The calculus E^{APQ} ('*A*' stands for 'applied') differs from E^{PQ} in language: now individual constants may occur in sequents, including the sequents to be (Socratically) proven. Moreover, instead of rules $\mathbf{L}_\forall$ and $\mathbf{R}_\exists$ of E^{PQ}, we now have:

$\mathbf{L}_\forall^A$

$$\frac{?(\Phi; S'\forall x_i A'T \vdash B; \Psi)}{?(\Phi; S'\forall x_i A' A(x_i/\xi)'T \vdash B; \Psi)}$$

provided that x_i is free in A; ξ is a parameter or an individual constant

$\mathbf{R}_\exists^A$

$$\frac{?(\Phi; S \vdash \exists x_i A; \Psi)}{?(\Phi; S'\forall x_i \neg A \vdash A(x_i/\xi); \Psi)}$$

provided that x_i is free in A; ξ is a parameter or an individual constant

The remaining rules of E^{APQ} are those of E^{PQ}.

The practical difference is that we are now able to consider abduction of LLSs on the basis of premises in which individual constants occur (and thus we touch the problem of explanation of facts by laws). The formal mechanism of abduction is the same as in the case of E^{PQ}, however. The rule **(abd)** is not modified, so these are only the shared parameters that count.

A weakening of the rule **(abd)** in the following way:

(abd′)

$$\frac{?(\Phi; S'A(x_i/\xi)'T \vdash B(x_i/\xi); \Psi)}{?(\Phi; S'A(x_i/\xi)'T'\forall x_i(Ax_i \rightarrow Bx_i) \vdash B(x_i/\xi); \Psi)}$$

where ξ is a parameter or an individual constant

raises a formal problem, since $A(x_i/\xi)$ and $B(x_i/\xi)$ are not univocal with respect to initial premises in which individual constants occur. Moreover, philosophical generality connected with the use of parameters is lost. On the other hand, some examples are appealing (see Examples 7 and 8).

Example 7.

1. $?(Pa \vdash Ra)$ *(abd′)*
2. $?(Pa, \underline{\forall x_1(Px_1 \rightarrow Rx_1)} \vdash Ra)$

Example 8.

1. $?(Pa \rightarrow Ra \vdash Pa \rightarrow Ga)$ $\mathbf{R}_{\rightarrow}$
2. $?(Pa \rightarrow Ra, Pa \vdash Ga)$ $\mathbf{L}_{\rightarrow}$
3. $?(\neg Pa, Pa \vdash Ga;\ Ra, Pa \vdash Ga)$ *(abd′)*
4. $?(\neg Pa, Pa \vdash Ga; Ra, Pa, \underline{\forall x_1(Rx_1 \rightarrow Gx_1)} \vdash Ga)$

A possible solution is to restrict **(abd′)** to atomic sentences which share an individual constant and are parameter-free. Now $A(\gamma)$ stands for a parameter-free atomic sentence in which individual constant γ occurs, and similarly for $B(\gamma)$. We would have **(abd)** and the following:

(abd″)

$$\frac{?(\Phi; S'A(\gamma)'T \vdash B(\gamma); \Psi)}{?(\Phi; S'A(\gamma)'T'\forall x_i(Ax_i \rightarrow Bx_i) \vdash B(\gamma); \Psi)}$$

Example 9.

1. $?(Pa \vee Ra \vdash Ga)$ $\mathbf{L}_{\vee}$
2. $?(Pa \vdash Ga; Ra \vdash Ga)$ *(abd″)*
3. $?(Pa, \underline{\forall x_1(Px_1 \rightarrow Gx_1)} \vdash Ga;\ Ra \vdash Ga)$ *(abd″)*
4. $?(Pa, \forall x_1(Px_1 \rightarrow Gx_1) \vdash Ga; Ra, \underline{\forall x_1(Rx_1 \rightarrow Gx_1)} \vdash Ga)$

Observe that is *not* required that the “shared” individual constant occupies the same position in *A* and in *B* (see Example 10).

Example 10.

1. $Pab \vdash Rca$ **(abd″)**
2. $Pab, \underline{\forall x_1(Px_1b \rightarrow Rcx_1)} \vdash Rca$

A generalization of **(abd″)** to the case when there are more shared individual constants is obvious. It is unclear, however, how to define abductive extensions of unsuccessful Socratic transformations, because a "mixed" case (shared parameters and shared individual constants) may arise.

5 Concluding Remarks

The algorithmic perspective offers a very broad account on abductive reasoning. One may even claim that it is too generous, and this claim can be expressed in Hintikka's (2007, p. 45) terms of distinction between definitory and strategic rules of inference as follows. In the algorithmic perspective focus on effective computability of a solution to an abductive problem may lead to overrating move-by-move correctness of a reasoning, determined by the definitory rules. This, in turn, results in underestimating the role of strategic rules, constituting the essence of abduction as an ampliative reasoning (Hintikka 2007, pp. 45–52). Thus procedures defined within the algorithmic perspective may fail to meet the criteria for full-fledged abduction. In our opinion there are two possible ways of responding to such a claim. The first one would involve conceptual considerations on the very nature of abduction, which we do not pursue in this paper. The second one is of slightly functional but still legitimate character. Our purpose here was to find a mechanism by which abductive hypotheses in the form of law-like statements can be generated. Bearing in mind the distinction between abductive process and product (Aliseda 2006, p. 32) we do not claim that this mechanism is itself abductive, that is, that we described some kind of mental logic of abduction. What we did is this: psychological adequacy apart, we characterized an effective way of computing formulas of well-defined form of law-like statements, which may play the role of abducibles in certain contexts.

References

Aliseda, A. (1997). *Seeking explanations: Abduction in logic, philosophy of science and artificial intelligence*. Amsterdam: Institute for Logic, Language and Computation.

Aliseda, A. (2006). *Abductive reasoning. Logical investigations into discovery and explanation*. Dordrecht: Springer.

Bolotov, A., Łupkowski, P., & Urbański, M. (2006). Search and check. Problem solving by problem reduction. In A. Cader, L. Rutkowski, R. Tadeusiewicz, & J. Zurada (Eds.), *Artificial intelligence and soft computing* (pp. 505–510). Warszawa: Academic Publishing House EXIT.

Gabbay, D. M., & Woods, J. (2005). *The reach of abduction. Insight and trial.* Amsterdam: Elsevier.

Gauderis, T., & Van de Putte, F. (2012). Abduction of generalizations. *Theoria, 27*(3), 345–363.

Harman, G. (1965). Inference to the best explanation. *Philosophical Review, 74*(1), 88–95.

Hintikka, J. (2007). Abduction – inference, conjecture, or an answer to a question? In *Socratic epistemology. Explorations of knowledge-seeking by questioning* (pp. 38–60). Cambridge: Cambridge University Press.

Hintikka, J., Halonen, I., & Mutanen, A. (1999). Interrogative logic as a general theory of reasoning. In *Inquiry as inquiry: A logic of scientific discovery* (Volume 5 of Jaakko Hintikka selected papers, pp. 47–90). Dordrecht/Boston/London: Kluwer Academic.

Komosinski, M., Kups, A., & Urbański, M. (2012). Multi-criteria evaluation of abductive hypotheses: Towards efficient optimization in proof theory. In *Proceedings of the 18th International Conference on Soft Computing* (pp. 320–325). Brno: Czech Republic.

Komosinski, M., Kups, A., Leszczyńska-Jasion, D., & Urbański, M. (2014). Identifying efficient abductive hypotheses using multi-criteria dominance relation. *ACM Journal on Computational Logic, 15*(4), 28:1–28:20.

Kuipers, T. A. F. (2004). Inference to the best theory, rather than inference to the best explanation. Kinds of abduction and induction. In F. Stadler (Ed.), *Induction and deduction in the sciences* (pp. 25–51). Dordrecht/Boston/London: Kluwer Academic.

Leszczyńska, D. (2007). *The method of socratic proofs for normal modal propositional logics.* Poznań: Adam Mickiewicz University Press.

Leszczyńska-Jasion, D., Urbański, M., & Wiśniewski, A. (2013). Socratic trees. *Studia Logica, 101*, 959–986.

Lipton, P. (2004). *Inference to the best explanation.* London: Routledge.

Magnani, L. (2004). Reasoning through doing. Epistemic mediators in scientific discovery. *Journal of Applied Logic, 2*, 439–450.

Magnani, L. (2009). Abducing chances in hybrid humans as decision makers. *Information Sciences, 179*(11), 1628–1638.

Mayer, M. C., & Pirri, F. (1993). First order abduction via tableau and sequent calculi. *Bulletin of the IGPL, 1*, 99–117.

Meheus, J., & Batens, D. (2006). A formal logic of abductive reasoning. *Logic Journal of the IGPL, 14*, 221–236.

Meheus, J., Verhoeven, L., Van Dyck, M., & Provijn, D. (2002). Ampliative adaptive logics and the foundation of logic-based approaches to abduction. In L. Magnani, N. J. Nersessian, & C. Pizzi (Eds.), *Logical and computational aspects of model-based reasoning* (pp. 39–71). Dordrecht: Kluwer Academic.

Peirce, C. S. (1931–1958). *Collected works.* Cambridge: Harvard University Press.

Smullyan, R. (1995). *First-order logic.* New York: Dover.

Thagard, P. (1995). *Abductive reasoning: Logic, visual thinking and coherence.* Cambridge: MIT.

Thagard, P. (2007). Abductive inference: From philosophical analysis to neural mechanisms. In A. Feeney & E. Heit (Eds.), *Inductive reasoning: Cognitive, mathematical, and neuroscientific approaches* (pp. 226–247). Cambridge: Cambridge University Press.

Urbański, M. (2003). Computing abduction with Socratic proofs. In *International workshop "Problem Solving in the Sciences: Adaptive and Interrogative Perspectives"*, Brussels, 8–10 May 2003.

Urbański, M. (2016). *Models of abductive reasoning.* LiT Verlag (To appear). Berlin.

Urbański, M., & Łupkowski, P. (2010). Erotetic search scenarios: Revealing interrogator's hidden agenda. In P. Łupkowski & M. Purver (Eds.), *Semantics and pragmatics of dialogue* (pp. 67–74). Poznań: Polskie Towarzystwo Kognitywistyczne.

Wiśniewski, A. (1995). *The posing of questions: Logical foundations of erotetic inferences.* Dordrecht/Boston/London: Kluwer Academic.

Wiśniewski, A. (2004a). Erotetic search scenarios, problem-solving, and deduction. *Logique et Analyse, 185–188*, 139–166.
Wiśniewski, A. (2004b). *A note on abduction and consistency checks by Socratic transformations.* Research report. Poznań: Institute of Psychology, Adam Mickiewicz University.
Wiśniewski, A. (2004c). Socratic proofs. *Journal of Philosophical Logic, 33*(3), 299–326.
Wiśniewski, A. (2013). *Questions, inferences, and scenarios.* London: College Publications.
Wiśniewski, A., & Shangin, V. (2006). Socratic proofs for quantifiers. *Journal of Philosophical Logic, 35*(2), 147–178.

A Dynamic Logic of Interrogative Inquiry

Yacin Hamami

Abstract We propose a dynamic-epistemic analysis of the different epistemic operations constitutive of the process of interrogative inquiry, as described by Hintikka's Interrogative Model of Inquiry (IMI). We develop a dynamic logic of questions for representing interrogative steps, based on Hintikka's treatment of questions in the IMI, along with a dynamic logic of inferences for representing deductive steps, based on the tableau method. We then merge these two systems into a dynamic logic of interrogative inquiry which articulates a joint treatment of questions and inferences, providing thereby a unified framework representing the informational dynamics of interrogative inquiry. We provide sound and complete axiomatic systems for the three dynamic logics that we introduce, we compare our framework with existing approaches, and we finally propose several directions for further work.

Keywords Interrogative model of inquiry • Dynamic epistemic logic • Question • Inference

1 Introduction and Motivation

The process of *inquiry* is one of the major topics of investigation in the formal and philosophical studies of rational agency. Notable approaches to the formal modelling of inquiry comprise the learning theory of Kelly (1996), the game-theoretic account of Hintikka (1999), the abductive perspective of Aliseda (2006), and the approach from belief revision theory of Genot (2009). Undoubtedly, questions play a crucial role in the human activity of inquiry as a means to obtain information, as exemplified in the contexts of conversation or communication. Some authors have even argued that any form of inquiry can be seen as a questioning procedure (Collingwood 1940; Hintikka 2007). The process of *information-seeking by questioning* has been commonly referred to as *interrogative inquiry*.

Y. Hamami (✉)
Centre for Logic and Philosophy of Science, Vrije Universiteit Brussel, Pleinlaan 2, B-1050 Brussels, Belgium
e-mail: yacin.hamami@vub.ac.be

C. Başkent (ed.), *Perspectives on Interrogative Models of Inquiry*, Logic, Argumentation & Reasoning 8, DOI 10.1007/978-3-319-20762-9_8

The key figure associated to the logical and philosophical investigations of interrogative inquiry is Jaakko Hintikka. His approach has been organized around the development of the so-called *Interrogative Model of Inquiry (IMI)* (Hintikka 1988, 1999, 2007) which represents interrogative inquiry as a *game* between two players called the *Inquirer* and *Nature*. The game is played on a fixed model M and the role of the Inquirer is to answer a given question, or to establish a given conclusion, from a background theory T. To this end, the Inquirer can make *interrogative moves*, which consist in putting questions to Nature and registering the answers as additional premises, or *deductive moves*, which consist in drawing logical inferences from the information already obtained by the Inquirer. Thus, according to the IMI, an interrogative inquiry is a sequence of interrogative and deductive steps, which respectively consist in *asking questions* and *drawing inferences*.

The background assumption of this paper is that the development of a theory of interrogative inquiry, and a formalization of the IMI, can be carried out in the program of *logical dynamics of information and interaction* (van Benthem 2011). This assumption is supported by (i) the recent developments on dynamic logics of questions and inferences, (ii) the possibility to represent interrogative inquiry as a temporal process via the notion of protocol, and (iii) the capacity to account for the social dimension of interrogative inquiry using multi-agent systems, logics for interaction, and game-theoretic frameworks. However, such an enterprise must start by understanding the informational dynamics of interrogative inquiry.

This is precisely the aim of this paper: to develop a dynamic-epistemic analysis of the different operations of information acquisition constitutive of the process of interrogative inquiry. Our ambition is to inscribe our investigation both in the program of logical dynamics and in the line of Hintikka's approach to interrogative inquiry. This is motivated by the fact that (i) the IMI offers a framework for investigating interrogative inquiry in the program of logical dynamics and (ii) the framework of Dynamic-Epistemic Logics (DEL) offers the necessary tools and methodology to develop a formally precise account of the informational dynamics of interrogative inquiry.

This paper is organized as follows. In Sect. 2, we develop a logical modelling of interrogative steps under the form of a dynamic logic of questions based on Hintikka's representation of questions. In Sect. 3, we develop a dynamic logic of inferences which represents deductive steps as tableau construction steps following Hintikka's representation of inferences in the IMI. In Sect. 4, we represent the combination of interrogative and deductive steps in a dynamic logic of interrogative inquiry which articulates a joint treatment of questions and inferences, and which aims thereby to capture the informational dynamics of interrogative inquiry as described by the IMI. Our main technical results are sound and complete axiomatizations for these three logics, describing precisely the epistemic effects of the different epistemic operations constitutive of the process of interrogative inquiry. Section 5 is a brief comparison of our dynamic-epistemic analysis of interrogative inquiry with other approaches. Section 6 ends this paper with some concluding remarks and suggestions for further work.

2 Modelling Interrogative Steps: A Dynamic Logic of Questions

For representing *interrogative steps* as *questions* in the IMI, Hintikka adopts a representation of questions based on his own work on the semantics and pragmatics of questions (Hintikka 1976). The aim of this section is to develop a dynamic-epistemic modelling of interrogative steps based on this representation. Thus, after a brief presentation of Hintikka's approach to the representation of questions, we will show how the methodology of dynamic-epistemic logics can fruitfully be adopted to make explicit the informational dynamics of interrogative steps in interrogative inquiry according to the conceptual description of the IMI. Our approach will consist in the development of a suitable dynamic logic of questions for which we will provide a sound and complete axiomatic system.

2.1 Hintikka on Questions: Propositional Question, Presupposition and Oracle

The treatment of questions and answers which underlines the IMI is based on what we will call *Hintikka's theory of questions*, which originated in Hintikka (1976) and has been developed further in Hintikka (1999, 2007). This theory is the basis for the definition of the definitory rule for questioning of *Interrogative Logic*[1] (henceforth, IL) which aims to govern the possible interrogative steps that the inquirer can make in an interrogative inquiry. In the perspective of developing a dynamic logic of questions based on Hintikka's theory of questions, it will be useful to present this theory at work in the interrogative rule of IL in order to understand how, according to the IMI, the notions of *propositional question*, *presupposition*, and *oracle* operate in the mechanics of interrogative steps.[2]

IL was designed to capture the reasoning of an inquirer aiming to find out unknown aspects of a given model M, representing the actual world. In this reasoning process, the inquirer can make *requests for information* about the model M. According to the IMI, these requests for information are conceived as *questions* to a particular source called the *oracle*. Thus, the IMI must incorporate a representation

[1] 'Interrogative Logic' refers to the logical system developed by Hintikka et al. (1999) which provides a logical theory of interrogative reasoning as an extension of first-order logic with a rule for questioning.

[2] Hintikka's theory of questions involves an additional important notion: the *desideratum* of a question which specifies "the epistemic state that the questioner wants to be brought about (in the normal use of questions)" (Hintikka 2007, p. 25). This notion plays a limited role in the propositional case since, as soon as the oracle picks an answer among the set of possible answers of a propositional question and delivers it to the inquiring agent, the agent is automatically brought in an epistemic state that satisfies the desideratum of the propositional question. For this reason, we do not consider the notion of desideratum in this paper.

of questions and answers. The role of Hintikka's theory of questions is precisely to fill this task. According to this theory, a question is identified by its set of possible answers. In the propositional case, a *propositional question* Q is simply identified with a finite set of formulas that we denote by $Q = (\gamma_1, \ldots, \gamma_k)$ where $\gamma_1, \ldots, \gamma_k$ are propositional formulas, and is read as "which one of the following holds: $\gamma_1, \ldots, \gamma_k$?". Among propositional questions, *yes-no questions* are questions of the form $(\gamma, \neg\gamma)$.

The notion of question comes with the important notion of *presupposition*. According to Hintikka, a question can be *meaningfully* asked only if its presupposition has been established by the inquirer.[3] In the case of propositional questions, the presupposition of a question $Q = (\gamma_1, \ldots, \gamma_k)$ is simply the disjunction of all its possible answers.

Finally, the *oracle* is formalized, in IL, via an answer set Φ, containing all the available answers from the oracle, and satisfying the following hypotheses (Hintikka et al. 1999, p. 48): (1) there is only one oracle, (2) the set of answers the oracle will provide remains constant throughout the inquiry, (3) all of the oracle's answers are true, and known by the inquirer to be true. We now have all the ingredients to state the definitory rule for questioning of IL:

> If the presupposition of a question occurs on the left side of a *subtableau*, the inquirer may address the corresponding question to the oracle. If the oracle answers, the answer is added to the left side of the *subtableau*. (Hintikka 1999, p. 51)

In IL, the left side of the initial tableau contains all the initial premises. Then, during the inquiry, the left side records all that has been established by the inquirer, either through logical inferences or by questioning. Thus, what the definitory rule for questioning says is the following: as soon as the inquirer has established the presupposition of a question Q, she has the possibility to address the corresponding question to the oracle, and if she chooses to do so, the obtained answer will depend on the information available to the oracle. The definitory rule for questioning of IL has then a strong dynamic-epistemic flavor: the left side of the tableau represents the epistemic situation of the inquirer, the action of questioning having for effect to modify this epistemic situation. We will now show how this dynamics can be made explicit in the logical framework of a dynamic logic of questions.

2.2 A Dynamic Logic of Questions

Our task is now to develop a dynamic logic of questions which (i) accounts for the dynamic and epistemic aspects of interrogative steps in interrogative inquiry and (ii) adopts the representation of questions provided by Hintikka's theory of questions.

---

[3]Notice that the notion of presupposition plays a crucial role in the limitations of the inquiry process: "[T]he limits of inquiry are obviously determined to a large extent by the available presuppositions of questions and answers. [...] It follows that all doctrines concerning the limitations of scientific or other kinds of knowledge-seeking will have to be discussed by reference to the presuppositions of questions and questioning". (Hintikka 2007, p. 84).

2.2.1 The Static Component

We have seen in the previous section that a question is identified with its set of possible answers. Our first step is to define what we mean by a possible answer. To this end, we define an *inquiry language* $\mathscr{I}$ which delimits the scope of the formulas that can be the answers to some questions. Since we focus on the propositional case, we will only consider *propositional questions*, i.e., questions for which a possible answer is simply a propositional formula. In this case, the inquiry language $\mathscr{I}$ is the propositional language:

Definition 1 (Inquiry language $\mathscr{I}$). Let P be a countable set of atomic propositions. The *inquiry language* $\mathscr{I}$ is given by

$$\gamma ::= p \mid \neg\gamma \mid (\gamma \wedge \gamma)$$

where $p \in \mathsf{P}$.

The static language that we consider is the language of *epistemic logic*[4] to which we add an *oracle operator*:

Definition 2 (Epistemic language $\mathscr{E}_O$). Let P be a set of atomic propositions. The epistemic inquiry language $\mathscr{E}_O$ is given by

$$\varphi ::= p \mid \neg\varphi \mid (\varphi \wedge \varphi) \mid K\varphi \mid \Phi\gamma$$

where $p \in \mathsf{P}$ and $\gamma \in \mathscr{I}$.

In $\mathscr{E}_O$, formulas of the form $K\varphi$ are read as "the agent knows that φ" and formulas of the form $\Phi\gamma$ are read as "γ is in the answer set of the oracle".

In epistemic logic, the knowledge of the agent is encoded into an epistemic model $M = \langle W, \sim, V\rangle$. How can we represent the oracle in this case? We shall first recall that the oracle refers to the source of information about the actual world. Usually, the actual world is represented by a designated world in a given epistemic model. Since all the worlds of an epistemic model $M = \langle W, \sim, V\rangle$ can be potentially designated to be the actual world, we will need to associate an oracle answer set to each world w in W. Thus, we will define the oracle as a function:

$$\Phi : w \in W \mapsto \Phi(w) \in \mathscr{P}(\mathscr{I}).$$

Following Hintikka, we will make the following assumptions on the oracle: for each world $w \in W$, (1) there is only one oracle associated to w (represented by the answer set $\Phi(w)$), (2) the answer set $\Phi(w)$ remains constant throughout the inquiry, (3) the oracle's answers are true. We then define the notion of *epistemic inquiry model* as follows[5]:

---

[4]See Appendix A for a brief presentation of epistemic logic.

[5]We provide here a general definition for epistemic inquiry models. We will then restrict it with additional requirements when we will define our intended class of models.

Definition 3 (Epistemic inquiry model). An epistemic inquiry model is a tuple $M = \langle W, \sim, V, \Phi\rangle$ where:

- $\langle W, \sim, V\rangle$ is an epistemic model,[6]
- $\Phi : W \to \mathscr{P}(\mathscr{I})$ is a function representing the oracle which associates to each world $w \in W$ a set of formulas $\Phi(w) \subseteq \mathscr{I}$.

In the definition of epistemic inquiry models, we already integrate the hypothesis (1) on the oracle. We will integrate hypothesis (3) when we will define our intended class of models, and hypothesis (2) in the next section. We now define the semantics for the language $\mathscr{E}_O$:

Definition 4 (Semantics for $\mathscr{E}_O$). Let $M = \langle W, \sim, V, \Phi\rangle$ be an epistemic inquiry model. The semantics for $\mathscr{E}_O$ is given by the semantics for the epistemic language[7] $\mathscr{E}$ plus the following semantic definition for the oracle operator Φ

$$M, w \models \Phi\gamma \ \text{ iff } \ \gamma \in \Phi(w).$$

In this work, we will impose the following restrictions on epistemic inquiry models: let $M = \langle W, \sim, V, \Phi\rangle$ be an epistemic inquiry model,

Veridicality for the oracle: we will require that the oracle is always *truthful*, i.e., for all $w \in W$, if $\gamma \in \Phi(w)$, then $M, w \models \gamma$.

Coherence property for the oracle: we will require a *coherence property* for the oracle, i.e., for all $w \in W$, if $\gamma \in \Phi(w)$, then $\gamma \in \Phi(u)$ for all $u \in W$ such that $u \sim w$ and $M, u \models \gamma$.

The veridicality property corresponds to the hypothesis (3) on the oracle. The intuitive meaning of the coherence property is the following: if in the world w the oracle is able to provide the information γ about w, then it is able to provide the information γ in all the worlds epistemically indistinguishable from w by the agent in which γ is true. This aims to reflect the idea that the informative power of the oracle is *uniform* on the epistemic range of the agent.

Thus, our intended class of models $\mathbf{E_I}$, which is a subclass of the class of epistemic inquiry models, is defined as follows[8]:

Definition 5 (Class of models $\mathbf{E_I}$). Let $M = \langle W, \sim, V, \Phi\rangle$ be an epistemic inquiry model. $M \in \mathbf{E_I}$ if and only if M satisfies the veridicality and coherence properties for the oracle.

[6]As defined in Appendix A. In all this paper, we make the common assumption that the indistinguishability relation $\sim$ is an *equivalence relation.*

[7]The semantics for the epistemic language $\mathscr{E}$ is defined in Appendix A.

[8]In the following, by 'epistemic inquiry models' we will mean models of this class.

2.2.2 The Dynamic Component

In the dynamic component, we aim to provide a semantic definition for a dynamic operator which would represent the *action* of making an *interrogative step*. To this end, we first need to extend our previous language into an *epistemic inquiry language* $\mathscr{E}_{\mathscr{I}}$ by adding a *dynamic 'question to the oracle' operator* (henceforth, *question operator*):

Definition 6 (Epistemic inquiry language $\mathscr{E}_{\mathscr{I}}$). Let P be a set of atomic propositions. The epistemic inquiry language $\mathscr{E}_{\mathscr{I}}$ is given by

$$\varphi ::= p \mid \neg\varphi \mid (\varphi \wedge \varphi) \mid K\varphi \mid \Phi\gamma \mid [(\gamma_1, \ldots, \gamma_k)?]\varphi$$

where $p \in \mathsf{P}$, $\gamma, \gamma_1, \ldots, \gamma_k \in \mathscr{I}$ and $k \geq 2$.

In this language, formulas of the form $[(\gamma_1, \ldots, \gamma_k)?]\varphi$ are read as "φ is the case after the inquiring agent has addressed the question 'which one of the following holds: $\gamma_1,\ldots,\gamma_k$?' to the oracle".

The semantic definition for the question operator will be built from two components: the first one is the definition of the *question operation* on epistemic inquiry models, the second one is the definition of the *precondition* to this operation. In order to define the question operation, we first have to recall how an epistemic model is modified after an incoming of *hard information*[9]:

Definition 7 (Hard information update). Let $M = \langle W, \sim, V, \Phi\rangle$ be an epistemic inquiry model and let $\gamma \in \mathscr{I}$. The epistemic inquiry model $M|\gamma = \langle W', \sim', V', \Phi'\rangle$ is given by

- $W' := \{w' \in W \mid M, w' \models \gamma\}$,
- $\sim' := \sim \cap (W' \times W')$,
- $V' := V \upharpoonright W'$,
- $\Phi' := \Phi \upharpoonright W'$.

We then represent the effect of *asking* a question to the oracle under the form of a *conditional incoming of hard information*: if the answer to the question is available to the oracle, then the action of asking a question will lead to a hard information update with the answer.[10] Formally, this *'question to the oracle' operation* (henceforth, *question operation*) is defined as follows:

[9]For a presentation of the notion of hard information update, along with a general presentation of Dynamic Epistemic Logic (DEL) and Public Announcement Logic (PAL), we refer the reader to the textbook (van Ditmarsch et al. 2007) and the monograph (van Benthem 2011). PAL has been developed by Plaza (1989) and independently by Gerbrandy and Groeneveld (1997). A more general approach is the one of Baltag et al. (1998) which provides a general account of multi-agent updates through epistemic events.

[10]This presupposes that there is at most a unique answer to a given question. This assumption will be introduced shortly, when we will model the precondition for the agent to be able to address a question to the oracle.

Definition 8 (Question operation). Let (M, w) be a pointed epistemic inquiry model where $M = \langle W, \sim, V, \Phi \rangle$, let $Q = (\gamma_1, \ldots, \gamma_k)$ be a propositional question and let $A = \{\gamma_1, \ldots, \gamma_k\} \cap \Phi(w)$. The model $M_{(\gamma_1,\ldots,\gamma_k)?}(w)$ is obtained as follows

- if $A = \emptyset$, then $M_{(\gamma_1,\ldots,\gamma_k)?}(w) := M$,
- if $A \neq \emptyset$, then $M_{(\gamma_1,\ldots,\gamma_k)?}(w) := M | \bigwedge A$ where $\bigwedge A$ denotes the conjunction of all the formulas in A.

Notice that, after a question operation, the answer sets associated to the remaining worlds of the considered epistemic inquiry model are left unchanged by the operation. This feature corresponds to the hypothesis (2) on the oracle. Notice also that one can easily check that the result of applying a question operation to an epistemic inquiry model yields an epistemic inquiry model, i.e., the veridicality and coherence properties for the oracle are preserved in the resulting model.

The second component of the definition of the question operator is the *precondition* to the question operation. It is through the notion of precondition that we will introduce the last element of Hintikka's theory of questions that we need to integrate in our framework: the notion of *presupposition*.

As we have seen in the questioning rule of IL, the agent *must* have established the presupposition of a question in order to be able to address it to the oracle. In our epistemic framework, this can be translated as follows: the agent must *know* the presupposition of a question in order to be able to address it to the oracle. Formally, if $M = \langle W, \sim, V, \Phi \rangle$ is an epistemic inquiry model, $w \in W$ represents the actual world and $Q = (\gamma_1, \ldots, \gamma_k)$ is a propositional question, then the following condition must be satisfied in order for the inquiring agent to ask the question Q:

$$M, w \models K(\gamma_1 \vee \cdots \vee \gamma_k).$$

In this paper, we will adopt a stronger notion of presupposition for propositional questions. If $Q = (\gamma_1, \ldots, \gamma_k)$ is a propositional question, instead of requiring that the agent knows that *at least one* of the possible answers to Q is the case, we will require that the agent knows that *one and only one* of the possible answers to Q is the case.[11] Our proposal can then formally be stated as follows: if $M = \langle W, \sim, V, \Phi \rangle$ is an epistemic inquiry model, $w \in W$ represents the actual world and $Q = (\gamma_1, \ldots, \gamma_k)$ is a propositional question, the following condition must be satisfied in order for the inquiring agent to address the question to the oracle:

[11] This is arguably a strong idealization of the questioning process since it limits substantially the questions that the agent can address to the oracle. The interest of the idealization is to simplify the dynamics of questioning insofar as there is only one choice available to the oracle when it comes to answer a given question. However, the idealization can be withdrawn by introducing in the framework an explicit representation of the way the oracle chooses its answer to a question when several alternative answers are available. We leave aside such refinements of the questioning process, as this would make heavier the formal presentation of our dynamic logic of questions. We choose to focus instead in this paper on the interaction between the informational dynamics of questions and inferences.

$M, w \models K\mathsf{presup}(Q)$ where

$$\mathsf{presup}(Q) := (\gamma_1 \vee \cdots \vee \gamma_k) \wedge \bigwedge_{j_1 \neq j_2 \text{ and } j_1, j_2 \in [\![1,k]\!]} \neg(\gamma_{j_1} \wedge \gamma_{j_2}).$$

We thereby get the precondition to the question operation with respect to the pointed model (M, w) and the question Q. Thus, we integrate the notion of presupposition under the form of a *precondition* to the question operation on the model, the precondition being that the agent knows the presupposition to the question. We now have all the ingredients to provide the semantic definition of the dynamic *question operator*:

Definition 9 (Semantics for $\mathscr{E}_{\mathscr{I}}$). Let $M = \langle W, \sim, V, \Phi \rangle$ be an epistemic inquiry model. The semantics for the epistemic inquiry language $\mathscr{E}_{\mathscr{I}}$ is given by the semantics for the epistemic language $\mathscr{E}_O$ plus the following semantic definition for the question operator

$$M, w \models [(\gamma_1, \ldots, \gamma_k)?]\varphi \text{ iff } M, w \models \mathsf{pre}(Q) \text{ implies } M_{(\gamma_1, \ldots, \gamma_k)?}(w), w \models \varphi,$$

where $\mathsf{pre}(Q) := K\mathsf{presup}(Q)$ and $Q = (\gamma_1, \ldots, \gamma_k)$.

2.3 Soundness and Completeness

First of all, we define the logic $\mathsf{E_I}$ aiming to characterize syntactically the formulas of $\mathscr{E}_{\mathscr{I}}$ that are valid on the class of models $\mathbf{E_I}$:

Definition 10 (Logic $\mathsf{E_I}$). The logic $\mathsf{E_I}$ is built from the static epistemic logic EL[12] plus the following axioms

1. $\Phi\gamma \rightarrow \gamma$ (veridicality for the oracle)
2. $\Phi\gamma \rightarrow K(\gamma \rightarrow \Phi\gamma)$ (coherence property for the oracle)

and the reduction axioms for the question operator of Table 1.

Table 1 Reduction axioms for the question operator

$[(\gamma_1, \ldots, \gamma_k)?]p$	$\leftrightarrow$	$\mathsf{pre}(Q) \rightarrow$	p
$[(\gamma_1, \ldots, \gamma_k)?]\neg\varphi$	$\leftrightarrow$	$\mathsf{pre}(Q) \rightarrow$	$\neg[(\gamma_1, \ldots, \gamma_k)?]\varphi$
$[(\gamma_1, \ldots, \gamma_k)?]\varphi \wedge \psi$	$\leftrightarrow$	$\mathsf{pre}(Q) \rightarrow$	$[(\gamma_1, \ldots, \gamma_k)?]\varphi \wedge [(\gamma_1, \ldots, \gamma_k)?]\psi$
$[(\gamma_1, \ldots, \gamma_k)?]\Phi\gamma$	$\leftrightarrow$	$\mathsf{pre}(Q) \rightarrow$	$\Phi\gamma$
$[(\gamma_1, \ldots, \gamma_k)?]K\varphi$	$\leftrightarrow$	$\mathsf{pre}(Q) \rightarrow$	$(\bigwedge_{1 \leq i \leq k} \neg\Phi\gamma_i \wedge K\varphi) \vee$ $(\bigvee_{1 \leq i \leq k} (\Phi\gamma_i \wedge K(\gamma_i \rightarrow [(\gamma_1, \ldots, \gamma_k)?]\varphi))$

[12]The axioms for EL are provided in Appendix A.

The first four axioms of Table 1 express the usual relationship between a dynamic-epistemic operator and boolean connectives. The fifth axiom describes the precise epistemic effect of asking a question on the informational state of the inquiring agent: if the agent knows φ after having asked the question $Q = (\gamma_1, \ldots, \gamma_k)$, this means that *either* the answer to Q is not available to the oracle and the agent knew φ before asking the question, *or* the answer γ_i to Q is available to the oracle and the agent happens to know φ as the result of receiving the answer γ_i, i.e., as the result of a hard information update with γ_i.[13] The following theorem says that the logic $\mathsf{E_I}$ is sound and complete with respect to the class of models $\mathbf{E_I}$:

Theorem 1 (Soundness and completeness of $\mathsf{E_I}$). *For every formula $\varphi \in \mathscr{E}_{\mathscr{I}}$:*

$$\models_{\mathbf{E_I}} \varphi \quad \textit{if and only if} \quad \vdash_{\mathsf{E_I}} \varphi.$$

Proof. The soundness and the completeness of the static part is proved by a standard completeness-via-canonicity argument (see chapter 4 of Blackburn et al. (2002)). We start by proving the soundness of the reduction axioms of $\mathsf{E_I}$. Consider the first axiom: $[(\gamma_1, \ldots, \gamma_k)?]p \leftrightarrow \mathsf{pre}(\gamma_1, \ldots, \gamma_k) \rightarrow p$.

Let (M, w) be a pointed epistemic inquiry model. Assume that $M, w \models [(\gamma_1, \ldots, \gamma_k)?]p$ and $M, w \models \mathsf{pre}(\gamma_1, \ldots, \gamma_k)$. By the semantic definition of the question operator, we have that $M_{(\gamma_1,\ldots,\gamma_k)?}(w), w \models p$. Then, we have to consider two different cases:

- For all $i \in [\![1, k]\!]$, $\gamma_i \notin \Phi(w)$: in this case $M_{(\gamma_1,\ldots,\gamma_k)?}(w) := M$ and we thereby have that $M, w \models p$.
- There exists $i \in [\![1, k]\!]$ s.t. $\gamma_i \in \Phi(w)$: in this case $M_{(\gamma_1,\ldots,\gamma_k)?}(w) := M|\gamma_i$ so we get that $M|\gamma_i, w \models p$ and thereby that $M, w \models p$.[14]

In the other way around, assume that $M, w \models \mathsf{pre}(\gamma_1, \ldots, \gamma_k) \rightarrow p$ and assume also that $M, w \models \mathsf{pre}(\gamma_1, \ldots, \gamma_k)$. Then, we have that $M, w \models p$ and we can directly see that, in all cases, $M_{(\gamma_1,\ldots,\gamma_k)?}(w), w \models p$.

The soundness of the other reduction axioms can be proved in a similar way.[15] Finally, the completeness part is proved by a standard DEL-style translation argument: by working inside out, the reduction axioms translate the dynamic formulas into corresponding static ones. Then, we appeal to completeness for the static base logic. □

[13] Of course, it might also be possible, in this second case, that the agent knew φ before asking the question Q.

[14] Since we have by hypothesis $M, w \models \mathsf{pre}(\gamma_1, \ldots, \gamma_k)$, we know that if there exists $i \in [\![1, k]\!]$ such that $\gamma_i \in \Phi(w)$, this γ_i is unique, i.e., there is no $j \in [\![1, k]\!]$ with $j \neq i$ such that $\gamma_j \in \Phi(w)$. This is the reason why we can write in this case that $M_{(\gamma_1,\ldots,\gamma_k)?}(w) := M|\gamma_i$.

[15] The proof of the soundness of the fifth axiom appeals to the coherence property for the oracle.

3 Modelling Deductive Steps: A Dynamic Logic of Inferences

According to the IMI, the second key epistemic operation constitutive of interrogative inquiry is *logical inference*. Hintikka's favorite way for representing inferences is based on the tableau method, seeing inferences as *tableau construction steps*. Following Hintikka, our objective will be to show how this view on inferences can be put in a dynamic-epistemic perspective in order to achieve an explicit representation of the informational dynamics of deductive steps in the process of interrogative inquiry. To this end, after a brief presentation of the tableau method, we will develop a *tableau-based dynamic logic of inferences* for which we will provide a sound and complete axiomatic system.

3.1 Inferences as Tableau Construction Steps

Deductive steps in the IMI, and in IL, are represented as *tableau construction steps* according to the usual rules of tableau construction. We now provide some background on the tableau method in the propositional case. The presentation that we adopt is based on the notion of *unsigned semantic tree* from Smullyan (1968) (henceforth referred to as *semantic tree* or *tableau*), which is defined as follows:

Definition 11 (Semantic tree). A semantic tree for $\gamma \in \mathscr{I}$ is a binary tree whose nodes are labelled with formulas of the inquiry language $\mathscr{I}$, which has for root γ and which is generated by the following tableau construction rules:

$$\begin{array}{c}\gamma_1 \wedge \gamma_2\\ | \\ \gamma_1 \\ | \\ \gamma_2\end{array} \qquad\qquad \begin{array}{c}\neg(\gamma_1 \wedge \gamma_2)\\ \diagup \quad \diagdown \\ \neg\gamma_1 \quad\; \neg\gamma_2\end{array} \qquad\qquad \begin{array}{c}\neg\neg\gamma\\ | \\ \gamma\end{array}$$

In this work we will represent semantic trees as indexed sets of branches, where branches are sets of formulas. Thus, if $\mathscr{T}$ is a semantic tree with root $\gamma \in \mathscr{I}$, we identify $\mathscr{T}$ with the indexed set $\{\mathscr{R}, \mathscr{B}_i\}_{i \in \mathbb{N}}$, where $\mathscr{R} = \{\gamma\}$ and $\mathscr{B}_i \in \mathscr{P}(\mathscr{I})$ for all $i \in \mathbb{N}$, such that

- $\mathscr{B}_0, \ldots, \mathscr{B}_n$ are the non-empty sets of formulas corresponding to the $n+1$ branches of $\mathscr{T}$,
- $\mathscr{B}_i = \emptyset$ for all $i > n$.

We will denote by $\mathsf{STrees}(\mathscr{I}) \subseteq \mathscr{P}(\mathscr{I})^{\mathbb{N}}$ the class of all semantic trees on the inquiry language $\mathscr{I}$. For convenience reasons, we sometimes abuse notation and just write $\mathscr{T} = \{\mathscr{R}, \mathscr{B}_0, \ldots, \mathscr{B}_n\}$. Closure rules for branches and semantic trees are defined as follows:

Definition 12 (Closure rules). Let $\mathscr{T} \in \mathsf{STrees}(\mathscr{I})$. We say that a branch $\mathscr{B}_i$ of $\mathscr{T}$ is closed if there exists a formula $\varphi \in \mathscr{I}$ such that $\varphi \in \mathscr{B}_i$ and $\neg\varphi \in \mathscr{B}_i$. We say that $\mathscr{T}$ is closed if all its branches are closed.

In the IMI, the tableau method is used to make logical deduction from previously acquired knowledge. The following theorem says that this method is sound and complete[16]:

Theorem 2 (Soundness and completeness of the tableau method). *Let Γ be a finite subset of $\mathscr{I}$ and let $\gamma \in \mathscr{I}$. Γ logically entails γ if and only if there exists a closed tableau with root $\bigwedge \Gamma \wedge \neg\gamma$.*

Proof. See D'Agostino (1999). □

3.2 A Tableau-Based Dynamic Logic of Inferences

In order to develop a tableau-based dynamic logic of inferences, we will adopt the same methodology as in the previous section, i.e., we will go from the static to the dynamic: in the *static component*, we will introduce the suitable static structures necessary (i) to represent the notions of explicit and implicit knowledge and (ii) to deal with semantic trees in a modal framework; in the *dynamic component*, we capture the informational dynamics associated to inferences by representing the different stages of an inferential process according to the tableau method.

3.2.1 The Static Component

First, we shall define the notions of *implicit* and *explicit knowledge*. To this end, we will adopt the same approach as the one of dynamic logics of inferences (Velázquez-Quesada 2009; van Benthem and Velázquez-Quesada 2010), i.e., we will use the two-level semantic-syntactic format proposed in van Benthem (2008). According to this approach, *implicit knowledge* is represented in the same way knowledge is usually represented in epistemic logic using possible world semantics, and *explicit knowledge* is represented syntactically via a set of formulas associated to each world in the model. We introduce the following terminology: we refer to sets of (true) formulas associated to each world in the model, representing the explicit information that the agent has about each of these worlds, as *local* explicit knowledge; we say that a formula γ is *global* explicit knowledge if γ is local explicit knowledge in all the worlds present in the agent's epistemic range.

Then, we also want to represent the *ongoing inferential process* that the agent is engaged in in order to acquire explicit knowledge. To this end, we will associate a semantic tree to each world in an epistemic model. We refer to the semantic trees associated to each world in the model as *local* inferential processes, and we say

[16]Since we are working in the propositional case, the tableau method constitutes here a decision procedure for checking that a formula γ is logically entailed by a finite set of premises Γ (D'Agostino 1999).

that a semantic tree represents a *global* inferential process when it is present in the different worlds of the agent's epistemic range.[17]

We now define the *tableau epistemic language* $\mathscr{T}\mathscr{E}_0$ by adding to the language of epistemic logic a modal operator E to express explicit knowledge, along with two operators R and Br_i to express the basic properties of semantics trees:

Definition 13 (Tableau epistemic language $\mathscr{T}\mathscr{E}_0$). Let P be a set of atomic propositions. The tableau epistemic language $\mathscr{T}\mathscr{E}_0$ is given by

$$\varphi ::= p \mid \neg\varphi \mid (\varphi \wedge \varphi) \mid K\varphi \mid E\gamma \mid R\gamma \mid Br_i\gamma$$

where $p \in \mathsf{P}$, $\gamma \in \mathscr{I}$ and $i \in \mathbb{N}$.

In this language, $K\varphi$ is read as "the agent implicitly knows that φ", $E\gamma$ is read as "the agent explicitly knows locally that γ", $KE\gamma$ is read as "the agent explicitly knows globally that γ", $R\gamma$ is read as "γ is the root of the semantic tree entertained by the agent", and $Br_i\gamma$ is read as "the formula γ is present on the ith branch of the semantic tree entertained by the agent".

Local explicit knowledge will be represented by sets of formulas associated to each world in the epistemic model, and the ongoing inferential processes will be represented by semantic trees also associated to each world in the model, leading to the following definition of *tableau epistemic models*:

Definition 14 (Tableau epistemic model). A tableau epistemic model is a tuple $M = \langle W, \sim, V, \mathsf{E}, \mathsf{T}\rangle$ where:

- $M = \langle W, \sim, V\rangle$ is an epistemic model,[18]
- $\mathsf{E} : W \rightarrow \mathscr{P}(\mathscr{I})$ is a function which associates to each world $w \in W$ a set of formulas of the inquiry language $\mathscr{I}$,
- $\mathsf{T} : W \rightarrow \mathscr{P}(\mathscr{I})^{\mathbb{N}}$, is a function which associates to each world $w \in W$ a set $\mathsf{T}(w) = \{\mathscr{R}(w), \mathscr{B}_i(w)\}_{i \in \mathbb{N}} \in \mathscr{P}(\mathscr{I})^{\mathbb{N}}$.

The tableau epistemic language $\mathscr{T}\mathscr{E}_0$ is interpreted on tableau epistemic models as follows:

Definition 15 (Semantics for the tableau epistemic language $\mathscr{T}\mathscr{E}_0$). Let (M, w) be a pointed tableau epistemic model where $M = \langle W, \sim, V, \mathsf{E}, \mathsf{T}\rangle$. The semantics for the tableau epistemic language $\mathscr{T}\mathscr{E}_0$ is given by the semantics for the epistemic language $\mathscr{E}$ plus the semantic definitions for the operators E, R and Br_i

$$M, w \models E\gamma \;\text{ iff }\; \gamma \in \mathsf{E}(w)$$

[17] The hypotheses that we will adopt in this section will turn out to make the notions of local and global explicit knowledge collapse into one unique notion of *explicit knowledge*, which will be the counterpart of the notion of *implicit knowledge*. It will also have for effect to make collapse the notions of local and global inferential processes into one unique notion of *inferential process*.

[18] Here again, we assume that the indistinguishability relation is an *equivalence relation*.

$$M, w \models R\gamma \text{ iff } \gamma \in \mathscr{R}(w)$$

$$M, w \models Br_i\gamma \text{ iff } \gamma \in \mathscr{B}_i(w)$$

In this work, we will impose the following restrictions on tableau epistemic models: let $M = \langle M, \sim, V, \mathsf{E}, \mathsf{T}\rangle$ be a tableau epistemic model,

Veridicality for local explicit knowledge: for all $w \in W$, if $\gamma \in \mathsf{E}(w)$, then $M, w \models \gamma$.

Coherence property for local explicit knowledge: for all $w \in W$, if $\gamma \in \mathsf{E}(w)$ and $u \sim w$ with $u \in W$, then $\gamma \in \mathsf{E}(u)$.

Structural property for semantic trees: for all $w \in W$, if $\gamma \in \mathscr{R}(w)$, then (i) there is no $\gamma' \neq \gamma$ such that $\gamma' \in \mathscr{R}(w)$ and (ii) $\mathsf{T}(w) = \{\mathscr{R}(w), \mathscr{B}_i(w)\}_{i\in\mathbb{N}}$ is a semantic tree with root γ.

Coherence property for semantic trees: for all $w \in W$, (i) if $\gamma \in \mathscr{R}(w)$ and $u \sim w$ with $u \in W$, then $\gamma \in \mathscr{R}(u)$, and (ii) if $\gamma \in \mathscr{B}_i(w)$ and $u \sim w$ with $u \in W$, then $\gamma \in \mathscr{B}_i(u)$.

The intuitive idea behind the coherence property for local explicit knowledge is to ask for local explicit knowledge at a world w to be preserved in all the worlds epistemically indistinguishable from w by the agent. This assumption is also made in the recent literature on dynamic logics of inferences (Velázquez-Quesada 2009; van Benthem and Velázquez-Quesada 2010). The structural property for semantic trees makes sure that $\mathsf{T}(w) \in \mathsf{STrees}(\mathscr{I})$ for all $w \in W$, which means that $\mathsf{T}(w)$ has indeed the structure of a semantic tree. The coherence property for semantic trees intervenes in our framework consistently with the coherence property that we imposed on local explicit knowledge. It then follows from this requirement that the same semantic tree is associated to the different worlds present in the epistemic range of the agent. Our intended class of models **TE** is then defined as follows[19]:

Definition 16 (Class of models TE). let $M = \langle W, \sim, V, \mathsf{E}, \mathsf{T}\rangle$ be a tableau epistemic model. $M \in$ **TE** if and only if M satisfies the veridicality and coherence properties for local explicit knowledge and the structural and coherence properties for semantic trees.

It is important to notice that, since we require local explicit knowledge to be true, all global explicit knowledge is also implicit knowledge, i.e., the following principle is valid on our intended class of models: $KE\gamma \to K\gamma$. Besides, due to the coherence property and the fact that we consider the epistemic indistinguishability relation to be an equivalence relation, we have that local and global epistemic knowledge coincide, i.e., the following principle is valid on our intended class of models: $KE\gamma \leftrightarrow E\gamma$. We obtain thereby a unique notion of *explicit knowledge*, equivalently represented by the operators E or KE, which is the counterpart of the notion of *implicit knowledge* represented by the operator K. In the same way, by assuming the coherence property for semantic trees and by considering the

[19] In the following, by 'tableau epistemic models' we will mean models of this class.

epistemic indistinguishability relation to be an equivalence relation, we necessarily have that local and global inferential processes coincide, yielding a unique notion of *inferential process* whose function is to transform implicit knowledge into explicit knowledge.

Expressing the Closure of Semantic Trees in the Language $\mathscr{T}\mathscr{E}_0$

The tableau epistemic language $\mathscr{T}\mathscr{E}_0$ allows us to express the closure of the semantic tree entertained by the agent. To see this, assume that the agent entertains a semantic tree with root $\bigwedge \Gamma \wedge \neg\gamma$. We first consider the finite set $\mathbf{T}(\Gamma,\gamma)$ of all the formulas in $\mathscr{I}$ that can occur as a node of a semantic tree with root $\bigwedge \Gamma \wedge \neg\gamma$:

$$\mathbf{T}(\Gamma,\gamma) := \left\{\gamma' \in \mathscr{I} \mid \gamma' \text{ occurs as a node of some } \mathscr{T} \in \mathsf{STrees}(\mathscr{I})_{\Gamma,\gamma}\right\}.$$

We denote by $\mathsf{STrees}(\mathscr{I})_{\Gamma,\gamma}$ the set of all semantic trees with root $\bigwedge \Gamma \wedge \neg\gamma$. The closure of the ith branch of a semantic tree with root $\bigwedge \Gamma \wedge \neg\gamma$ can then be expressed by: $\mathsf{closed}(\mathscr{B}_i)_{\Gamma,\gamma} := \bigvee_{\gamma' \in \mathbf{T}(\Gamma,\gamma)} (Br_i\gamma' \wedge Br_i\neg\gamma')$, and its emptiness can be expressed by: $\mathsf{empty}(\mathscr{B}_i)_{\Gamma,\gamma} := \bigwedge_{\gamma' \in \mathbf{T}(\Gamma,\gamma)} \neg Br_i\gamma'$. Finally, since a semantic tree with root $\bigwedge \Gamma \wedge \neg\gamma$ has a maximum number of branches that we denote by $n_{\Gamma,\gamma} + 1$, we can form the following formula: $\mathsf{closed}(\Gamma,\gamma) := \bigwedge_{0 \leq i \leq n_{\Gamma,\gamma}} \left(\mathsf{closed}(\mathscr{B}_i)_{\Gamma,\gamma} \vee \mathsf{empty}(\mathscr{B}_i)_{\Gamma,\gamma}\right)$. The following proposition shows that this formula expresses the closure of semantic trees in our framework:

Proposition 1. *Let M be a tableau epistemic model with $M = \langle W, \sim, V, \mathsf{E}, \mathsf{T}\rangle$. For all $w \in W$, $M, w \models R(\bigwedge \Gamma \wedge \neg\gamma) \wedge \mathsf{closed}(\Gamma,\gamma)$ if and only if $\mathsf{T}(w) \in \mathsf{STrees}(\mathscr{I})_{\Gamma,\gamma}$ and $\mathsf{T}(w)$ is closed.*

Proof. See Appendix B. □

Expressing the Structural Properties of Semantic Trees in the Language $\mathscr{T}\mathscr{E}_0$

The main issue regarding completeness for the static fragment of our tableau-based dynamic logic of inferences will be to express, in the axioms, the structural property for semantic trees. It turns out that this can be done in the language $\mathscr{T}\mathscr{E}_0$. To this end, we need to introduce the notion of a *γ-tree impossible configuration*:

Definition 17 (γ-tree impossible configuration). Let X be a finite subset of $\mathbf{Br} := \{Br_i\gamma \mid i \in \mathbb{N} \text{ and } \gamma \in \mathscr{I}\} \cup \{\neg Br_i\gamma \mid i \in \mathbb{N} \text{ and } \gamma \in \mathscr{I}\}$. We say that X is a γ-tree impossible configuration if for any $\mathscr{T} = \{\mathscr{R}, \mathscr{B}_i\}_{i\in\mathbb{N}} \in \mathsf{STrees}(\mathscr{I})$ with root γ there exist $\gamma' \in \mathscr{I}$ and $i \in \mathbb{N}$ such that (i) $\gamma' \in \mathscr{B}_i$ and $\neg Br_i\gamma' \in X$ or (ii) $\gamma' \notin \mathscr{B}_i$ and $Br_i\gamma' \in X$. The set $\mathbf{ImpConf}(\gamma) \subseteq \mathscr{T}\mathscr{E}_0$ is defined as follows:

$$\mathbf{ImpConf}(\gamma) := \left\{\bigwedge X \,\middle|\, X \text{ is a } \gamma\text{-tree impossible configuration}\right\}.$$

Intuitively, a finite subset of **Br** can be seen as a (partial) description of an element $\mathscr{T} \in \mathscr{P}(\mathscr{I})^{\mathbb{N}}$ by stipulating the presence or absence of certain formulas in some branches of $\mathscr{T}$. A γ-tree impossible configuration is then such a description that is 'incompatible' with any semantic tree with root γ. This allows us to express the structural property of semantic trees through the following axiom stating that if γ is the root of the semantic tree entertained by the agent, then this tree cannot be (partially) described by a γ-tree impossible configuration: $R\gamma \rightarrow \neg\chi$ for $\chi \in$ **ImpConf**(γ). The following proposition shows that this axiom is indeed valid on the class of models **TE**:

Proposition 2. *Let M be a tableau epistemic model with $M = \langle W, \sim, V, \mathsf{E}, \mathsf{T}\rangle$. For all $w \in W$, we have $M, w \models R\gamma \rightarrow \neg\chi$ for $\chi \in$* **ImpConf**(γ).

Proof. See Appendix B. □

The following lemma says that given $\mathscr{T} \in \mathscr{P}(\mathscr{I})^{\mathbb{N}}$ such that $\mathscr{T}$ is not a semantic tree with root γ, we can always construct a γ-tree impossible configuration 'compatible' with $\mathscr{T}$. This lemma will play a key role in the completeness proof for the static fragment of our tableau-based dynamic logic of inferences.

Lemma 1. *Let $\mathscr{T} = \{\mathscr{R}, \mathscr{B}_i\}_{i\in\mathbb{N}} \in \mathscr{P}(\mathscr{I})^{\mathbb{N}}$. If $\mathscr{T}$ is not a semantic tree with root γ, then there exists a γ-tree impossible configuration X such that (i) if $\neg Br_i\gamma' \in X$ then $\gamma' \notin \mathscr{B}_i$ and (ii) if $Br_i\gamma' \in X$ then $\gamma' \in \mathscr{B}_i$.*

Proof. See Appendix B. □

3.2.2 The Dynamic Component

In the previous section, we have presented a language able (i) to represent the distinction between explicit and implicit knowledge and (ii) to describe static properties of the semantic tree entertained by the agent. In the dynamic component, we want to extend this language in order to represent *inferential processes* dynamically as model operations. To this end, we need to introduce three kinds of model operations: one dealing with *tableau construction steps*, representing progression steps in inferential processes, one dealing with *tableau creation steps*, representing the creation of a new inferential process, and one dealing with *drawing conclusions*, representing the final step of acquisition of *explicit knowledge* concluding an inferential process.

Operation of Tableau Construction

The *tableau construction operation* aims to represent a unitary step of progression in an inferential process. It consists in expanding a semantic tree, present in all the worlds of the agent's epistemic range, by applying the suitable tableau-constructing rule to a formula present in the tree. Formally, the tableau construction operation takes as input a branch and a formula, and is defined as follows:

Definition 18 (Tableau construction operation). Let (M, w) be a pointed tableau epistemic model with $M = \langle W, \sim, V, \mathsf{E}, \mathsf{T}\rangle$, let $i \in \mathbb{N}$ and let $\alpha \in \mathscr{I}$ such that (i) $\alpha \in \mathscr{B}_i(w)$ and (ii) no construction rule has already been applied to α in the branch $\mathscr{B}_i(w)$. The model $M_{(i,\alpha)}(w) = \langle W', \sim', V', \mathsf{E}', \mathsf{T}'\rangle$ is given by

- $W' := W$, $\sim' := \sim$, $V' := V$, $\mathsf{E}' := \mathsf{E}$, for every $u \in W$ such that $u \nsim w$, $\mathsf{T}'(u) := \mathsf{T}(u)$,
- for every $u \in W$ such that $u \sim w$, $\mathsf{T}'(u)$ is such that $\mathscr{B}_l(u)' := \mathscr{B}_l(u)$ for all $l \neq i$ and $l \neq n+1$,[20] and $\mathscr{B}_i(u)'$ and $\mathscr{B}_{n+1}(u)'$ are obtained in the following way:

  $\wedge$: if $\alpha := \alpha_1 \wedge \alpha_2$, then $\mathscr{B}_i(u)' := \mathscr{B}_i(u) \cup \{\alpha_1, \alpha_2\}$ and $\mathscr{B}_{n+1}(u)' := \mathscr{B}_{n+1}(u)$,
  $\neg\wedge$: if $\alpha := \neg(\alpha_1 \wedge \alpha_2)$, then $\mathscr{B}_i(u)' := \mathscr{B}_i(u) \cup \{\neg\alpha_1\}$ and $\mathscr{B}_{n+1}(u)' := \mathscr{B}_i(u) \cup \{\neg\alpha_2\}$,
  $\neg$: if $\alpha := \neg\neg\alpha_1$, then $\mathscr{B}_i(u)' := \mathscr{B}_i(u) \cup \{\alpha_1\}$ and $\mathscr{B}_{n+1}(u)' := \mathscr{B}_{n+1}(u)$.

Notice that the result of applying a tableau construction operation on a tableau epistemic model is still a tableau epistemic model: this is due to the fact that (i) this operation is done according to the tableau construction rules and (ii) the coherence property for semantic trees is preserved by a tableau construction operation since the modifications on semantic trees are done in a uniform way on the epistemic range of the agent.

Operation of Tableau Creation

The *tableau creation operation* consists in representing the creation of a new inferential process by the agent, in which she aims to show that a given formula logically follows from a finite set of premises. Formally, this operation takes as input a formula $\gamma \in \mathscr{I}$ (the conclusion to be established) and a finite set of formulas $\Gamma \subseteq \mathscr{I}$ (the premises), and is defined as follows:

Definition 19 (Tableau creation operation). Let (M, w) be a pointed tableau epistemic model with $M = \langle W, \sim, V, \mathsf{E}, \mathsf{T}\rangle$, let Γ be a finite subset of $\mathscr{I}$ and let $\gamma \in \mathscr{I}$. The model $M_{+(\Gamma,\gamma)}(w) = \langle W', \sim', V', \mathsf{E}', \mathsf{T}'\rangle$ is given by

- $W' := W$, $\sim' := \sim$, $V' := V$, $\mathsf{E}' := \mathsf{E}$,
- for every $u \in W$ such that $u \nsim w$, $\mathsf{T}'(u) := \mathsf{T}(u)$,
- for every $u \in W$ such that $u \sim w$, $\mathsf{T}'(u) := \{\mathscr{R}(u), \mathscr{B}_0(u)\}$ with $\mathscr{R}(u) := \{\bigwedge \Gamma \wedge \neg\gamma\}$ and $\mathscr{B}_0(u) := \{\bigwedge \Gamma \wedge \neg\gamma\}$.

Thus, the tableau creation operation with input (Γ, γ) consists in replacing the semantic tree entertained by the agent with a new semantic tree with root $\bigwedge \Gamma \wedge \neg\gamma$. In other words, this creation operation represents the starting point of an inferential process which aims to establish that γ logically follows from premises Γ. Such

[20] Here $n+1$ is the index of the first empty branch of $\mathsf{T}(u) = \{\mathscr{B}_0(u), \ldots, \mathscr{B}_n(u)\}$.

an inferential process can lead to the acquisition of γ as explicit knowledge under certain conditions, as described by the next operation of tableau conclusion.

Operation of Tableau Conclusion

The *tableau conclusion operation* consists in modelling the final step of an inferential process by which the agent can acquire explicit knowledge through logical deduction. More precisely, if the agent entertains a semantic tree with root $\bigwedge \Gamma \wedge \neg\gamma$ such that (i) the tree is closed, which means that the agent has established that γ logically follows from Γ, and (ii) premises Γ are explicit knowledge, the agent can *infer* or *conclude* γ from Γ, which we represent by an acquisition of γ as explicit knowledge. Formally, the tableau conclusion operation takes as input a formula $\gamma \in \mathscr{I}$ and a finite set of formulas $\Gamma \subseteq \mathscr{I}$, and is defined as follows:

Definition 20 (Tableau conclusion operation). Let (M, w) be a pointed tableau epistemic model with $M = \langle W, \sim, V, \mathsf{E}, \mathsf{T}\rangle$ such that (i) $\mathsf{T}(w)$ is a closed tableau with root $\bigwedge \Gamma \wedge \neg\gamma$ and (ii) $\Gamma \subseteq \mathsf{E}(w)$, where Γ is a finite subset of $\mathscr{I}$ and $\gamma \in \mathscr{I}$. The model $M_{-(\Gamma,\gamma)}(w) = \langle W', \sim', V', \mathsf{E}', \mathsf{T}'\rangle$ is given by

- $W' := W$, $\sim' := \sim$, $V' := V$,
- for all $u \not\sim w$, $\mathsf{E}'(u) := \mathsf{E}(u)$,
- for all $u \sim w$, $\mathsf{E}'(u) := \mathsf{E}(u) \cup \{\gamma\}$,
- $\mathsf{T}' := \mathsf{T}$.

Notice that applying a tableau conclusion operation to a tableau epistemic model yields a tableau epistemic model: (i) due to the soundness of the tableau method (Theorem 2) and the explicit knowledge of the premises Γ, the formula γ added to the sets of explicit knowledge is true in all the worlds of the agent's epistemic range and (ii) the tableau conclusion operation preserves the coherence property for local explicit knowledge.

Syntax and Semantics for the Tableau Epistemic Language

We now extend our previous tableau epistemic language with three dynamic operators for *tableau construction*, *tableau creation*, and *tableau conclusion*:

Definition 21 (Tableau epistemic language $\mathscr{TE}$). Let P be a set of atomic propositions. The tableau epistemic language $\mathscr{TE}$ is given by the BNF for the language $\mathscr{TE}_0$ plus the following ones

$$[(i,\alpha)_{(\Gamma,\gamma)}]\varphi \mid [+(\Gamma,\gamma)]\varphi \mid [-(\Gamma,\gamma)]\varphi$$

where $i \in \mathbb{N}$, $\alpha, \gamma \in \mathscr{I}$ and Γ is a finite subset of $\mathscr{I}$.

In $\mathscr{TE}$, $[(i,\alpha)_{(\Gamma,\gamma)}]\varphi$ is read as "φ is the case after the application of a tableau construction rule to the formula α in the ith branch of the semantic tree with root $\bigwedge \Gamma \wedge \neg\gamma$ entertained by the agent", $[+(\Gamma,\gamma)]\varphi$ is read as "φ is the case after the creation of a new semantic tree with root $\bigwedge \Gamma \wedge \neg\gamma$", and $[-(\Gamma,\gamma)]\varphi$ is read as "φ is the case after the agent has concluded γ from premises Γ".

The precondition for a tableau construction operation is the following: the formula α to which the operation is applied has to be present on the ith branch of the semantic tree with root $\bigwedge \Gamma \wedge \neg\gamma$ entertained by the agent, and no construction rule has already been applied to α in this branch. This latter condition can be expressed in the language $\mathscr{TE}$. To see this, notice first that we can describe exactly the configuration of a semantic tree with root $\bigwedge \Gamma \wedge \neg\gamma$: since there are finitely many formulas that can occur in such a tree, and a maximal number of branches for such a tree, we can consider the conjunction of formulas in **Br** saying for each formula in $\mathbf{T}(\Gamma,\gamma)$ and each branch whether the formula is present or not in the branch. Then, notice also that there are finitely many configurations for a semantic tree with root $\bigwedge \Gamma \wedge \neg\gamma$. Let $\mathsf{NC}(i,\alpha)_{(\Gamma,\gamma)}$ denote the disjunction of the formulas expressing the exact configurations of the semantic trees with root $\bigwedge \Gamma \wedge \neg\gamma$ in which no construction rule has already been applied to α in the ith branch. Such a formula expresses that the semantic tree entertained by the agent is such that no construction rule has already been applied to α in its ith branch. Formally, the precondition for a tableau construction operation can be expressed in the tableau epistemic language $\mathscr{TE}$ as follows:

$$\mathsf{cons}(i,\alpha)_{(\Gamma,\gamma)} := R\left(\bigwedge \Gamma \wedge \neg\gamma\right) \wedge Br_i\alpha \wedge \mathsf{NC}(i,\alpha)_{(\Gamma,\gamma)}.$$

Since the agent can always create a new semantic tree, there is no precondition for a tableau creation operation. For a tableau conclusion operation with input (Γ,γ), the precondition is threefold: (i) the agent has to entertain a tree with root $\bigwedge \Gamma \wedge \neg\gamma$, (ii) the tree has to be closed, assuring that γ logically follows from Γ, and (iii) the agent must have explicit knowledge of the premises Γ. Formally, the precondition of a tableau conclusion operation can be expressed in $\mathscr{TE}$ as follows:

$$\mathsf{conc}(\Gamma,\gamma) := R\left(\bigwedge \Gamma \wedge \neg\gamma\right) \wedge \mathsf{closed}\,(\Gamma,\gamma) \wedge \bigwedge_{\gamma' \in \Gamma} \mathsf{E}\gamma'.$$

This leads to the following semantics for the dynamic operators of tableau construction, creation, and conclusion:

Definition 22 (Semantics for the language $\mathscr{TE}$). Let (M,w) be a tableau epistemic model where $M = \langle W, \sim, V, \mathsf{E}, \mathsf{T}\rangle$. The semantics for the tableau epistemic language $\mathscr{TE}$ is given by the semantics for the language $\mathscr{TE}_0$ plus the following semantic definitions for the tableau construction, creation, and conclusion operators

$$M,w \models [(i,\alpha)_{(\Gamma,\gamma)}]\varphi \text{ iff } M,w \models \mathsf{cons}(i,\alpha)_{(\Gamma,\gamma)} \text{ implies } M_{(i,\alpha)}(w),w \models \varphi$$
$$M,w \models [+(\Gamma,\gamma)]\varphi \text{ iff } M_{+(\Gamma,\gamma)}(w),w \models \varphi$$
$$M,w \models [-(\Gamma,\gamma)]\varphi \text{ iff } M,w \models \mathsf{conc}(\Gamma,\gamma) \text{ implies } M_{-(\Gamma,\gamma)}(w),w \models \varphi.$$

3.3 Soundness and Completeness

First of all, we define the logic TE_0 aiming to characterize syntactically the formulas of the static language $\mathscr{T}\mathscr{E}_0$ that are valid on the class of models **TE**:

Definition 23 (Logic TE_0). The logic TE_0 is built from the axioms and rules for the static epistemic logic EL plus the following axioms

1. $E\gamma \to \gamma$ (veridicality for local explicit knowledge)
2. $E\gamma \to KE\gamma$ (coherence property for local explicit knowledge)
3. $R\gamma \to KR\gamma$ (coherence property for semantic trees)
4. $Br_i\gamma \to KBr_i\gamma$ (coherence property for semantic trees)
5. $R\gamma \wedge R\gamma' \to \bot$ for $\gamma \neq \gamma'$ (structural property for semantic trees)
6. $R\gamma \to \neg\chi$ for $\chi \in \mathbf{ImpConf}(\gamma)$ (structural property for semantic trees)

We now show that the logic TE_0 is sound and complete with respect to the class of models **TE**:

Theorem 3 (Soundness and completeness of TE_0). *For every formula $\varphi \in \mathscr{T}\mathscr{E}_0$:*

$$\models_{\mathbf{TE}} \varphi \quad \textit{if and only if} \quad \vdash_{\mathsf{TE}_0} \varphi.$$

Proof. The soundness part is obtained directly by checking that the axioms of TE_0 are valid on the class of models **TE**. The completeness part is obtained by a standard completeness-via-canonicity argument (see chapter 4 of Blackburn et al. (2002)). To this end, we define the canonical model of the logic TE_0 as the tuple $M^{\mathsf{TE}_0} = \langle W^{\mathsf{TE}_0}, \sim^{\mathsf{TE}_0}, V^{\mathsf{TE}_0}, \mathsf{E}^{\mathsf{TE}_0}, \mathsf{T}^{\mathsf{TE}_0}\rangle$, where W^{TE_0}, $\sim^{\mathsf{TE}_0}$ and V^{TE_0} are defined as usual, and $\mathsf{E}^{\mathsf{TE}_0}$ and $\mathsf{T}^{\mathsf{TE}_0}$ are defined as follows:

- $\mathsf{E}^{\mathsf{TE}_0}(w) := \{\gamma \in \mathscr{I} \mid E\gamma \in w\}$,
- $\mathsf{T}^{\mathsf{TE}_0}(w) := \{\mathscr{R}(w), \mathscr{B}_i(w)\}_{i \in \mathbb{N}}$ where $\mathscr{R}(w) := \{\gamma \in \mathscr{I} \mid R\gamma \in w\}$ and $\mathscr{B}_i(w) := \{\gamma \in \mathscr{I} \mid Br_i\gamma \in w\}$.

To complete the argument, all we have to do is to check that $M^{\mathsf{TE}_0} \in \mathbf{TE}$. From the axioms 1., 2., 3. and 4., we can easily show that M^{TE_0} satisfies the veridicality and coherence properties for local explicit knowledge and the coherence property for semantic trees. It remains to show that, for every $w \in W^{\mathsf{TE}_0}$, $\mathsf{T}^{\mathsf{TE}_0}(w)$ satisfies the structural property for semantic trees: if $\gamma \in \mathscr{R}(w)$, then (i) there is no $\gamma' \neq \gamma$ such that $\gamma' \in \mathscr{R}(w)$ and (ii) $\mathsf{T}^{\mathsf{TE}_0}(w) := \{\mathscr{R}(w), \mathscr{B}_i(w)\}_{i \in \mathbb{N}}$ is a semantic tree with root γ. Assume that $\gamma \in \mathscr{R}(w)$. By axiom 5., we get that there is no $\gamma' \neq \gamma$ such that $\gamma' \in \mathscr{R}(w)$. Now assume towards a contradiction that $\mathsf{T}^{\mathsf{TE}_0}(w)$ is not a semantic tree with root γ. By Lemma 1, there exists a γ-tree impossible configuration X such that for any $\gamma' \in \mathscr{I}$: (i) if $\neg Br_i\gamma' \in X$ then $\gamma' \notin \mathscr{B}_i(w)$ and (ii) if $Br_i\gamma' \in X$ then $\gamma' \in \mathscr{B}_i(w)$. Clearly $X \subseteq w$, and since w is a maximal TE_0-consistent set of formulas, we get $\bigwedge X \in w$. Let $\chi := \bigwedge X$. Since X is a γ-tree impossible configuration, we have that $\chi \in \mathbf{ImpConf}(\gamma)$ and thereby, from axiom 6., we get that $R\gamma \to \neg\chi \in w$. From $R\gamma \in w$ and $R\gamma \to \neg\chi \in w$ we get that $\neg\chi \in w$. Hence, we have that $\chi \in w$

and $\neg\chi \in w$ which is a contradiction since w is a maximal TE_0-consistent set of formulas. We conclude that for every $w \in W^{\mathsf{TE}_0}$, $\mathsf{T}^{\mathsf{TE}_0}(w)$ is a semantic tree with root γ. □

We then obtain the logic TE by extending the static logic TE_0 with the reduction axioms for the dynamic operators of tableau construction, creation, and conclusion:

Definition 24 (Logic TE). The logic TE is built from the static logic TE_0 plus the reduction axioms for the tableau construction (Table 2),[21] tableau creation (Table 3), and tableau conclusion (Table 4) operators.

We can now show that the logic TE is sound and complete with respect to the class of models **TE**:

Theorem 4 (Soundness and completeness of TE). *For every formula $\varphi \in \mathcal{TE}$:*

$$\models_{\mathbf{TE}} \varphi \quad \textit{if and only if} \quad \vdash_{\mathsf{TE}} \varphi.$$

Table 2 Reduction axioms for the tableau construction operator

$[i,\alpha]p$	$\leftrightarrow$	$\mathsf{cons}(i,\alpha) \to p$	
$[i,\alpha]\neg\varphi$	$\leftrightarrow$	$\mathsf{cons}(i,\alpha) \to \neg[i,\alpha]\varphi$	
$[i,\alpha](\varphi \wedge \psi)$	$\leftrightarrow$	$\mathsf{cons}(i,\alpha) \to [i,\alpha]\varphi \wedge [i,\alpha]\psi$	
$[i,\alpha]K\varphi$	$\leftrightarrow$	$\mathsf{cons}(i,\alpha) \to K[i,\alpha]\varphi$	
$[i,\alpha]E\gamma'$	$\leftrightarrow$	$\mathsf{cons}(i,\alpha) \to E\gamma'$	
$[i,\alpha]R\gamma'$	$\leftrightarrow$	$\mathsf{cons}(i,\alpha) \to R\gamma'$	
$[i,p]Br_{i'}\gamma'$	$\leftrightarrow$	$\mathsf{cons}(i,p) \to Br_{i'}\gamma'$	
$[i,\neg p]Br_{i'}\gamma'$	$\leftrightarrow$	$\mathsf{cons}(i,\neg p) \to Br_{i'}\gamma'$	
$[i,\alpha_1 \wedge \alpha_2]Br_{i'}\gamma'$	$\leftrightarrow$	$\mathsf{cons}(i,\alpha_1 \wedge \alpha_2) \to Br_{i'}\gamma'$	for $i' \neq i$
$[i,\alpha_1 \wedge \alpha_2]Br_{i}\gamma'$	$\leftrightarrow$	$\mathsf{cons}(i,\alpha_1 \wedge \alpha_2) \to Br_{i}\gamma'$	for $\gamma' \neq \alpha_1,\alpha_2$
$[i,\alpha_1 \wedge \alpha_2]Br_{i}\gamma'$	$\leftrightarrow$	$\top$	for $\gamma'=\alpha_1$ or $\gamma'=\alpha_2$
$[i,\neg(\alpha_1 \wedge \alpha_2)]Br_{i'}\gamma'$	$\leftrightarrow$	$\mathsf{cons}(i,\neg(\alpha_1 \wedge \alpha_2)) \to Br_{i'}\gamma' \vee$ $(Br_i\gamma' \wedge \mathsf{empty}(\mathscr{B}_{i'})_{\Gamma,\gamma} \wedge \neg\,\mathsf{empty}(\mathscr{B}_{i'-1})_{\Gamma,\gamma})$	for $\gamma' \neq \neg\alpha_1,\neg\alpha_2$
$[i,\neg(\alpha_1 \wedge \alpha_2)]Br_{i'}\neg\alpha_1$	$\leftrightarrow$	$\mathsf{cons}(i,\neg(\alpha_1 \wedge \alpha_2)) \to Br_{i'}\neg\alpha_1$	for $i' \neq i$
$[i,\neg(\alpha_1 \wedge \alpha_2)]Br_{i}\neg\alpha_1$	$\leftrightarrow$	$\top$	
$[i,\neg(\alpha_1 \wedge \alpha_2)]Br_{0}\neg\alpha_2$	$\leftrightarrow$	$\mathsf{cons}(i,\neg(\alpha_1 \wedge \alpha_2)) \to Br_{0}\neg\alpha_2$	
$[i,\neg(\alpha_1 \wedge \alpha_2)]Br_{i'}\neg\alpha_2$	$\leftrightarrow$	$\mathsf{cons}(i,\neg(\alpha_1 \wedge \alpha_2)) \to Br_{i'}\neg\alpha_2 \vee$ $(\mathsf{empty}(\mathscr{B}_{i'})_{\Gamma,\gamma} \wedge \neg\mathsf{empty}(\mathscr{B}_{i'-1})_{\Gamma,\gamma})$	for $i' > 0$
$[i,\neg\neg\alpha]Br_{i'}\gamma'$	$\leftrightarrow$	$\mathsf{cons}(i,\neg\neg\alpha) \to Br_{i'}\gamma'$	for $i' \neq i$
$[i,\neg\neg\alpha]Br_{i}\gamma'$	$\leftrightarrow$	$\mathsf{cons}(i,\neg\neg\alpha) \to Br_{i}\gamma'$	for $\gamma' \neq \alpha$
$[i,\neg\neg\alpha]Br_{i}\alpha$	$\leftrightarrow$	$\top$	

[21] For readability reasons, the subscripts (Γ,γ) have been omitted in the dynamic operators and in the preconditions of the formulas present in Table 2.

Table 3 Reduction axioms for the tableau creation operator

$[+(\Gamma,\gamma)]\,p$	$\leftrightarrow$	p	
$[+(\Gamma,\gamma)]\,\neg\varphi$	$\leftrightarrow$	$\neg\,[+(\Gamma,\gamma)]\,\varphi$	
$[+(\Gamma,\gamma)]\,(\varphi\wedge\psi)$	$\leftrightarrow$	$[+(\Gamma,\gamma)]\,\varphi\wedge[+(\Gamma,\gamma)]\,\psi$	
$[+(\Gamma,\gamma)]\,K\varphi$	$\leftrightarrow$	$K\,[+(\Gamma,\gamma)]\,\varphi$	
$[+(\Gamma,\gamma)]\,E\gamma'$	$\leftrightarrow$	$E\gamma'$	
$[+(\Gamma,\gamma)]\,R\gamma'$	$\leftrightarrow$	$\bot$	for $\gamma'\neq(\bigwedge\Gamma\wedge\neg\gamma)$
$[+(\Gamma,\gamma)]\,R\,(\bigwedge\Gamma\wedge\neg\gamma)$	$\leftrightarrow$	$\top$	
$[+(\Gamma,\gamma)]\,Br_i\gamma'$	$\leftrightarrow$	$\bot$	for $i>0$
$[+(\Gamma,\gamma)]\,Br_0\gamma'$	$\leftrightarrow$	$\bot$	for $\gamma'\neq(\bigwedge\Gamma\wedge\neg\gamma)$
$[+(\Gamma,\gamma)]\,Br_0\,(\bigwedge\Gamma\wedge\neg\gamma)$	$\leftrightarrow$	$\top$	

Table 4 Reduction axioms for the tableau conclusion operator

$[-(\Gamma,\gamma)]\,p$	$\leftrightarrow$	$\mathsf{conc}(\Gamma,\gamma)\rightarrow p$	
$[-(\Gamma,\gamma)]\,\neg\varphi$	$\leftrightarrow$	$\mathsf{conc}(\Gamma,\gamma)\rightarrow\neg\,[-(\Gamma,\gamma)]\,\varphi$	
$[-(\Gamma,\gamma)]\,(\varphi\wedge\psi)$	$\leftrightarrow$	$\mathsf{conc}(\Gamma,\gamma)\rightarrow[-(\Gamma,\gamma)]\,\varphi\wedge[-(\Gamma,\gamma)]\,\psi$	
$[-(\Gamma,\gamma)]\,K\varphi$	$\leftrightarrow$	$\mathsf{conc}(\Gamma,\gamma)\rightarrow K\,[-(\Gamma,\gamma)]\,\varphi$	
$[-(\Gamma,\gamma)]\,E\gamma'$	$\leftrightarrow$	$\mathsf{conc}(\Gamma,\gamma)\rightarrow E\gamma'$	for $\gamma'\neq\gamma$
$[-(\Gamma,\gamma)]\,E\gamma$	$\leftrightarrow$	$\top$	
$[-(\Gamma,\gamma)]\,R\gamma$	$\leftrightarrow$	$\mathsf{conc}(\Gamma,\gamma)\rightarrow R\gamma$	
$[-(\Gamma,\gamma)]\,Br_i\gamma$	$\leftrightarrow$	$\mathsf{conc}(\Gamma,\gamma)\rightarrow Br_i\gamma$	

Proof. The soundness part is proved by checking that all the reduction axioms are valid on the class of models **TE**. The completeness part is proved by a standard DEL-style translation argument: by working inside out, the reduction axioms translate the dynamic formulas into corresponding static ones. Then, we appeal to completeness for the static base logic TE_0. □

4 Combining Questions and Inferences: A Dynamic Logic of Interrogative Inquiry

Asking questions and *making inferences* are two different, but complementary, ways to obtain information. In daily life, people use a combination of both questions and inferences when they are involved in information-seeking processes. This is also the case in scientific practice which shows a subtle interplay between theoretical and experimental works, taking respectively the form of logical deduction in mathematical frameworks and questions put to Nature, i.e., observations and experiments. According to the IMI, the interaction between questions and inferences lies at the heart of the informational dynamics of interrogative inquiry, as Hintikka puts it:

> Deduction (logic) and interrogation appear as two interacting and mutually reinforcing components of inquiry. Neither is dispensable. Questions are needed to bring in substantially new information, and deductions are needed both for the purpose of spelling out the consequences of such information and, more importantly, for the purpose of paving the way for new questions by establishing their presuppositions. [...]
>
> [...] there is no absolute sense in which one of the two intertwined components of interrogative inquiry, deductions and questioning, is more important or more difficult, absolutely speaking. (Hintikka 1999, p. 35)

Using the terminology introduced in the two previous sections, Hintikka's description of the informational dynamics of interrogative inquiry can be rephrased as follows:

- By *asking questions*, the agent can acquire new explicit knowledge that does not logically follow from previously acquired one. In our framework, asking questions is also the only way for the agent to acquire implicit knowledge, i.e., to eliminate epistemic possibilities.
- By *making inferences*, the agent can potentially acquire any explicit knowledge that logically follows from previously acquired one. In particular, inferences can be used to acquire explicit knowledge of the presuppositions of questions.[22]

From a logical perspective, capturing the informational dynamics of interrogative inquiry requires a joint treatment of questions and inferences. In the two previous sections, we have treated questions and inferences separately by developing on one hand a dynamic logic of questions, and on the other hand a dynamic logic of inferences. We will now merge these two systems into a *dynamic logic of questions and inferences*, which will be the straightforward combination of the two systems developed in the previous sections. We will argue that this system captures all the information acquisition operations constitutive of the process of interrogative inquiry, as described by the IMI, and we thereby refer to it as our *dynamic logic of interrogative inquiry*. We will illustrate the functioning of our framework with a concrete example.

4.1 A Dynamic Logic of Interrogative Inquiry

Combining our previous dynamic logic of questions and dynamic logic of inferences is, for the most part, straightforward. Two points deserve particular attention: one is to define the question operation while working with implicit and explicit knowledge; the other is to introduce explicit knowledge into the precondition to the question operation. We will deal with these two issues when they will appear in the presentation of the system. First of all, we define the *interrogative inquiry language* $\mathscr{TE}_{\mathscr{I}}$ as the combination of the languages $\mathscr{TE}$ and $\mathscr{E}_{\mathscr{I}}$:

[22] In our framework, the precondition for asking a question is to have (explicit) knowledge of its presupposition. Thus, the operation of "paving the way for new questions by establishing their presuppositions" is here represented by the acquisition of explicit knowledge of the presuppositions of questions.

Definition 25 (Interrogative inquiry language $\mathscr{T}\mathscr{E}_{\mathscr{I}}$). Let P be a set of atomic propositions. The interrogative inquiry language $\mathscr{T}\mathscr{E}_{\mathscr{I}}$ is given by the combination of the BNF for the languages $\mathscr{T}\mathscr{E}$ and $\mathscr{E}_{\mathscr{I}}$.

Then, an *interrogative inquiry model* is defined as a tableau epistemic model plus an oracle function:

Definition 26 (Interrogative inquiry model). An interrogative inquiry model is a tuple $M = \langle W, \sim, V, \mathsf{E}, \mathsf{T}, \Phi \rangle$ where:

- $M = \langle W, \sim, V, \mathsf{E}, \mathsf{T} \rangle$ is a tableau epistemic model,
- $\Phi : W \to \mathscr{P}(\mathscr{I})$ is a function representing the oracle which associates to each world $w \in W$ a set of formulas $\Phi(w) \subseteq \mathscr{I}$.

The restrictions that we put on the class of interrogative inquiry models are the same as before, yielding our intended class of models $\mathbf{TE_I}$[23]:

Definition 27 (Class of models $\mathbf{TE_I}$). Let $M = \langle W, \sim, V, \mathsf{E}, \mathsf{T}, \Phi \rangle$ be an interrogative inquiry model. $M \in \mathbf{TE_I}$ if and only if M satisfies the veridicality and coherence properties for the oracle, the veridicality and coherence properties for local explicit knowledge, and the structural and coherence properties for semantic trees.

The model operations of tableau construction, tableau creation, and tableau conclusion are defined in the same way as in the previous section. However, the question operation needs to be adapted to the implicit and explicit knowledge setting. Our proposal to do so is the following: when the answer to a question is available to the oracle, (i) the model undergoes a hard information update with the answer and (ii) the answer becomes explicit knowledge. Formally, this leads to the following definition for the question operation:

Definition 28 (Question operation). Let (M, w) be a pointed interrogative inquiry model where $M = \langle W, \sim, V, \mathsf{E}, \mathsf{T}, \Phi \rangle$, let $Q = (\gamma_1, \ldots, \gamma_k)$ be a propositional question, and let $A = \{\gamma_1, \ldots, \gamma_k\} \cap \Phi(w)$. The model $M_{(\gamma_1,\ldots,\gamma_k)?}(w)$ is obtained as follows

1. if $A = \emptyset$, then $M_{(\gamma_1,\ldots,\gamma_k)?}(w) := M$,
2. if $A \neq \emptyset$, then $M_{(\gamma_1,\ldots,\gamma_k)?}(w) := \langle W', \sim', V', \mathsf{E}', \mathsf{T}', \Phi' \rangle$ where
   - $W' := \{w' \in W \mid M, w' \models \bigwedge A\}$,
   - $\sim' := \sim \cap (W' \times W')$,
   - $V' := V \restriction W'$,
   - $E' : W' \to \mathscr{P}(\mathscr{I})$ with
     - $\mathsf{E}(u)' := \mathsf{E}(u) \cup A$ for all $u \in W'$ s.t. $u \sim w$,
     - $\mathsf{E}(u)' := \mathsf{E}(u)$ for all $u \in W'$ s.t. $u \nsim w$,
   - $\mathsf{T}' := \mathsf{T} \restriction W'$, $\Phi' := \Phi \restriction W'$.[24]

[23]In the following, by 'interrogative inquiry models' we will mean models of the class $\mathbf{TE_I}$.

[24]One can easily check that the question operation preserves the class of models $\mathbf{TE_I}$.

The semantics for the language $\mathcal{TE_I}$ is directly obtained from the semantics for the languages $\mathcal{TE}$ and $\mathcal{E_I}$ except for the question operator since we need to adapt its semantic definition to the implicit and explicit knowledge setting. To this end, it seems natural to say that, in order to ask a question, the agent needs to have *explicit knowledge* of the presupposition of the question. Formally, this amounts to change the operator K into E in the precondition to the question operation:

Definition 29 (Semantics for the language $\mathcal{TE_I}$). Let (M, w) be a pointed interrogative inquiry model where $M = \langle W, \sim, V, \mathsf{E}, \mathsf{T}, \Phi \rangle$. The semantics for the language $\mathcal{TE_I}$ is given by the semantics for $\mathcal{TE}$ and the semantics for $\mathcal{E_I}$ in which the semantic definition of the question operator is replaced by the following one

$$M, w \models [(\gamma_1, \ldots, \gamma_k)?]\varphi \text{ iff } M, w \models \mathsf{pre}(Q) \text{ implies } M_{(\gamma_1,\ldots,\gamma_k)?}(w), w \models \varphi,$$

where $\mathsf{pre}(Q) := E\,\mathsf{presup}(\gamma_1, \ldots, \gamma_k)$ and $Q = (\gamma_1, \ldots, \gamma_k)$.

4.2 Soundness and Completeness

We first define the logic $\mathsf{TE_I}$ from the logics TE and $\mathsf{E_I}$ and additional reduction axioms:

Definition 30 (Logic $\mathsf{TE_I}$). The logic $\mathsf{TE_I}$ is built from the axioms and rules of inference of the logics TE and $\mathsf{E_I}$, along with the additional reduction axioms of Table 5.

We can now show that the logic $\mathsf{TE_I}$ is sound and complete with respect to the class of models $\mathbf{TE_I}$:

Theorem 5 (Soundness and completeness of $\mathsf{TE_I}$). *For every formula $\varphi \in \mathcal{TE_I}$:*

$$\models_{\mathbf{TE_I}} \varphi \quad \textit{if and only if} \quad \vdash_{\mathsf{TE_I}} \varphi.$$

Table 5 Additional reduction axioms for the logic $\mathsf{TE_I}$

Question operator	
$[(\gamma_1, \ldots, \gamma_k)?]\,E\gamma$	$\leftrightarrow\ \mathsf{pre}(Q) \to E\gamma$ where $\gamma \neq \gamma_i$ for all $i \in [\![1, k]\!]$
$[(\gamma_1, \ldots, \gamma_k)?]\,E\gamma$	$\leftrightarrow\ \mathsf{pre}(Q) \to E\gamma \vee \Phi\gamma$ where $\gamma = \gamma_i$ for some $i \in [\![1, k]\!]$
$[(\gamma_1, \ldots, \gamma_k)?]\,R\gamma$	$\leftrightarrow\ \mathsf{pre}(Q) \to R\gamma$
$[(\gamma_1, \ldots, \gamma_k)?]\,Br_i\gamma$	$\leftrightarrow\ \mathsf{pre}(Q) \to Br_i\gamma$
Tableau construction, creation, and conclusion operators	
$[(i, \alpha)_{(\Gamma,\gamma)}]\,\Phi\gamma'$	$\leftrightarrow\ \mathsf{cons}(i, \alpha)_{(\Gamma,\gamma)} \to \Phi\gamma'$
$[+(\Gamma, \gamma)]\,\Phi\gamma'$	$\leftrightarrow\ \Phi\gamma'$
$[-(\Gamma, \gamma)]\,\Phi\gamma'$	$\leftrightarrow\ \mathsf{conc}(\Gamma, \gamma) \to \Phi\gamma'$

Proof. The soundness part is proved by checking that all the reduction axioms are valid on the class of models $\mathbf{TE_I}$. The completeness part is proved by a standard DEL-style translation argument: by working inside out, the reduction axioms translate the dynamic formulas into corresponding static ones. Then, we appeal to completeness for the static base logic. □

4.3 General Remarks

Our dynamic logic of interrogative inquiry inherits the representations of questions and inferences from the two logical systems developed in the previous sections: it represents questions following Hintikka's theory of questions and represents inferences as tableau construction steps. In this way, it is in direct line with Hintikka's treatment of questions and inferences in the IMI.

It also accounts for the informational dynamics of interrogative inquiry as described at the beginning of this section: a question has for effect, when the answer is available to the oracle, (i) to modify the explicit knowledge of the inquiring agent by adding the answer to the sets of explicit knowledge and (ii) to modify her implicit knowledge by eliminating the worlds from the epistemic range of the agent incompatible with the obtained answer. Since the information obtained by questioning comes from the oracle, asking questions can bring in new explicit knowledge that does not logically follow from previously acquired one. Then, inferences can be used to acquire explicit knowledge by spelling out the logical consequences of previously acquired explicit knowledge. Finally, the precondition to the question operation in the semantics for the question operator integrates in our framework the necessity for the inquiring agent to establish the presupposition of a question as explicit knowledge in order to address it to the oracle. The process of establishing presuppositions of questions is itself a mixture of information obtained through questions and inferences.

Thus, our dynamic logic of interrogative inquiry offers a working formal framework representing the operations of information acquisition constitutive of the process of interrogative inquiry, as described by Hintikka's IMI. It also provides a first dynamic-epistemic account of the relation between the epistemic actions of asking questions and drawing inferences. We now illustrate our framework with an example bringing into play the different dynamic operations that we introduced.

4.4 An Illustrative Example

In the following example, the goal of the inquiring agent is to answer the yes-no question $(p \wedge q, \neg(p \wedge q))$, i.e., to acquire explicit knowledge of the conjunction

$p \wedge q$ or its negation. We present below one possible path of actions to achieve this goal, using the different epistemic operations of our dynamic logic of interrogative inquiry:

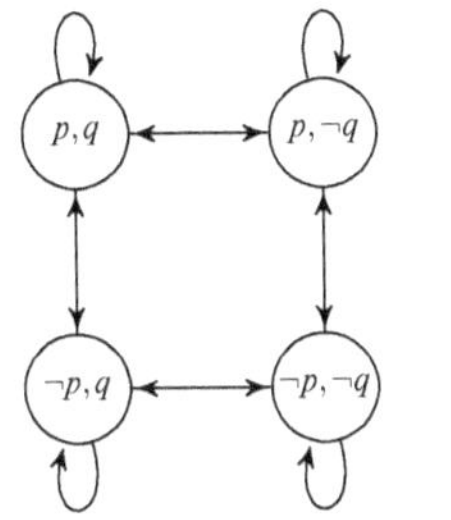

$\Phi(w) = \{p, q\}$
$\mathsf{E}(w) = \{p \oplus \neg p\}$

We consider an initial situation in which the agent has no implicit knowledge and no explicit knowledge about p and q. We let w denote the actual world in which p and q are true (the top-left world in the picture). The answer to the question of the inquirer in the actual world w is then $p \wedge q$. The oracle $\Phi(w)$ at world w has information about p and q, but not about the conjunction $p \wedge q$. Thus, one possible way for the agent to achieve her goal is to first ask if p is the case, then ask if q is the case, and then deduce $p \wedge q$. To this end, the agent first needs to establish the presupposition $p \oplus \neg p$ ('$\oplus$' denotes exclusive disjunction) of the question $(p, \neg p)$?. Since the presupposition is a tautology, the agent does not need any background explicit knowledge as she can create a tree with root $\neg(p \oplus \neg p)$, construct the tree fully, and use the conclusion operation to acquire explicit knowledge of $p \oplus \neg p$. The situation resulting from these operations is depicted on the left.

Having established the presupposition of the question $(p, \neg p)$?, the agent can address the question to the oracle. Since p is in the answer set of the oracle $\Phi(w)$, asking the question $(p, \neg p)$? has for effect (i) to eliminate the worlds in which p is false and (ii) to provide the agent with explicit knowledge of p. The agent can then repeat the same operation as before for establishing the presupposition $q \oplus \neg q$ of the question $(q, \neg q)$?. The resulting situation is depicted on the right.

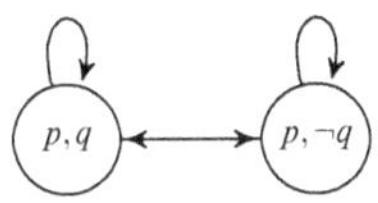

$\Phi(w) = \{p, q\}$
$\mathsf{E}(w) = \{p \oplus \neg p, p, q \oplus \neg q\}$

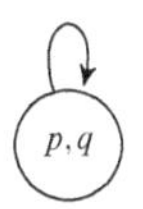

$\Phi(w) = \{p, q\}$
$\mathsf{E}(w) = \{p \oplus \neg\, p,$
$p, q \oplus \neg q, q, p \wedge q\}$

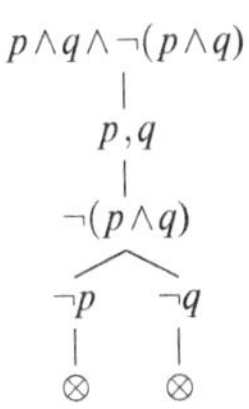

The agent can then ask the question $(q, \neg q)$?, which results in the elimination of the world in which q is false, and in the acquisition of q as explicit knowledge. At this point, the agent has implicit knowledge about $p \wedge q$, but not explicit knowledge. To acquire explicit knowledge, she needs to create a semantic tree with root $p \wedge q \wedge \neg(p \wedge q)$ and construct the tree fully. Then, the agent knows that $p \wedge q$ follows logically from premises p and q, and since she has explicit knowledge about p and q, she can conclude or infer $p \wedge q$. The resulting epistemic situation is depicted on the left. The agent has thus answered the question $(p \wedge q, \neg(p \wedge q))$ and thereby achieved her initial inquiry goal.

5 Comparison with Other Approaches

There exist several approaches in the literature to the logical modelling of questions, inferences, and their relation. In this section, we relate the present work to some of them, emphasizing on the comparison with existing DEL approaches.

Questions. There have been many contributions to the logical studies of questions and answers since the 1970s (see Harrah (1984), Wiśniewski (1995), and Groenendijk and Stokhof (1997)). Our approach to the logical modelling of questions did not consist in developing a new representation of questions. Rather, one of our goals was to inscribe our work in the line of Hintikka (1976) and to show how Hintikka's theory of questions can be put in a dynamic-epistemic perspective. Currently, there exist three main DEL approaches to the representation of questions: the dynamic logic of questions of van Benthem and Minică (2012), the logic of questions and public announcement of Peliš and Majer (2011), and the inquisitive dynamic epistemic logic of Ciardelli and Roelofsen (2015). The present work diverges from these developments with respect to two important points: (i) the representation of questions on which it is based and (ii) the general context in which the role of questions is investigated. Our particular interest in the process of interrogative inquiry leads then to two specific contributions of our approach: (i) an account of the epistemic action of questioning for non-logically omniscient agents and (ii) an analysis of the relation between the epistemic actions of asking questions and drawing inferences.

Inferences. Two recent DEL approaches to the representation of inferences are the dynamic logic of inference and update of Velázquez-Quesada (2009) and the dynamic logic of awareness of van Benthem and Velázquez-Quesada (2010). Our tableau-based dynamic logic of inferences departs from these two frameworks by implementing a specific method for carrying out inferential processes, namely the *tableau method*, providing thereby the inquirer with a *sound* and *complete* method for making logical deduction. In the propositional case, the tableau method has the important advantage to provide the inquirer with a *decision method* for making logical deduction.

Logic of interrogative inquiry. As far as we know, there does not exist any DEL approach neither to the representation of the action of questioning for non-logically omniscient agents, nor to the joint treatment of questions and inferences. Consequently, the closest system to our dynamic logic of interrogative inquiry is the Interrogative Logic (IL) of Hintikka et al. (1999). Although IL has been a source of inspiration for the development of our dynamic logic of interrogative inquiry, the two systems differ in scope: IL is designed as a proof system for a general theory of reasoning with rules for deduction and questioning, while our dynamic logic of interrogative inquiry aims to analyze and formalize the informational dynamics of the process of interrogative inquiry. Thus, our system accounts for a number of features left asides, or left implicit, by IL, in particular (i) the explicit dynamics of the epistemic actions of asking questions and drawing inferences, (ii) the distinction between explicit and implicit knowledge in the representation of interrogative and deductive steps, and (iii) the behavior of the epistemic action of questioning in the absence of logical omniscience.

6 Conclusion and Further Work

In this work, we have proposed a logical analysis of the informational dynamics of the process of interrogative inquiry, as described by the IMI. This has resulted in the development of a dynamic logic of interrogative inquiry which represents interrogative and deductive steps as *epistemic actions* modifying the informational state of the agent.

As mentioned in the introduction, this work is only a first, but necessary, step towards the development of a theory of interrogative inquiry in the program of logical dynamics of information and interaction. We then see two main research directions for further work: (i) to overcome the limitations of the present framework and (ii) to work towards a full-fledged theory of interrogative inquiry.

One of the main limitations of our approach concerns the assumptions we made on the oracle, in particular regarding our choice of inquiry language. Thus, one straightforward way to extend our system is to enrich our inquiry language, which was only the propositional language, to an *epistemic language*, expressing higher-order information, and/or to a *first-order language*. In the former case, this would allow to deal with the process of interrogative inquiry about what other agents know and believe, which plays an important role in multi-agent settings where agents reason and act while taking in account the informational states of the other agents. In the latter case, this would open several issues relative to the logical representation of questions and inferences in the first-order case, and would allow to discuss topics addressed by Hintikka within the framework of interrogative logic, such as the issue of *identifiability* (see Hintikka (1999, p. 64)). Another limitation concerns our restrictive focus on knowledge. This can be overcome by adapting our framework to situations in which the inquirer is seeking information towards other kinds of epistemic attitudes than knowledge. Interesting cases comprise the probabilistic one, in which the agent attributes *probabilities* or *degrees of belief* to formulas, but also different forms of *doxastic* or *justification-based* epistemic attitudes.

How to develop a full-fledged theory of interrogative inquiry from our dynamic logic of interrogative inquiry? From a technical point of view, it seems that all the necessary logical tools are already available to account for the *temporal*, *social*, and *interactive* dimensions of the process of interrogative inquiry. The temporal dimension can be represented using the methodology of van Benthem et al. (2009) which proposes a new system of dynamic-epistemic logic with *protocols*, and which has been applied in van Benthem and Minică (2012) to questioning procedures. The social dimension can be accounted for by extending our dynamic logic of interrogative inquiry to the multi-agent case, i.e., by introducing suitable *group actions* along with operations of *interaction* and *communication* between agents.

Finally, the interactive dimension can be represented by adopting a game-theoretic approach. Recently, Ågotnes et al. (2011) have shown that a dynamic-epistemic account of questions can nicely be incorporated into a game-theoretic framework in order to represent question-answer games. The IMI being formulated by Hintikka in game-theoretic terms, this suggests that a formalization of the IMI is reachable from our dynamic logic of interrogative inquiry, linking back our dynamic-epistemic approach with the original formulation of the IMI.

Acknowledgements This paper has been presented at the Interrogative Model of Inquiry Seminar in Paris (France, September 2011), the Questions, Games, Logic Workshop in Amsterdam (the Netherlands, December 2011) and the Trends in Logic XI Conference in Bochum (Germany, June 2012). I would like to thank the audiences of these events for helpful feedback and comments. I have benefited from discussions of this work with Johan van Benthem, Can Başkent, Emmanuel Genot, Eric Pacuit, Ştefan Minică, Gabriel Sandu, and Fernando Velázquez-Quesada. I am particularly grateful to Fernando Velázquez-Quesada for suggesting many substantial improvements on an earlier version of this paper. Finally, I am thankful to two anonymous reviewers for their comments and suggestions. The author of this paper acknowledges support from a doctoral fellowship of the Research Foundation Flanders (FWO).

Technical Appendix

A Epistemic Logic

We provide here the formal bases of epistemic logic.[25] We first define the language of epistemic logic $\mathscr{E}$ as follows:

Definition 31 (Epistemic language $\mathscr{E}$). Let P be a countable set of atomic propositions. The epistemic language $\mathscr{E}$ is given by

$$\varphi ::= p \mid \neg\varphi \mid \varphi \wedge \varphi \mid K\varphi \quad \text{where } p \in \mathsf{P}.$$

In this language, formulas of the form $K\varphi$ are read as "the agent knows that φ". We will write $\bot$ for $p \wedge \neg p$ and $\top$ for $\neg\bot$. We now define the notion of *epistemic model*:

Definition 32 (Epistemic model). Let P be a countable set of atomic propositions. An epistemic model is a tuple $M = \langle W, \sim, V\rangle$ where:

- W is a non-empty set of worlds,
- $\sim \subseteq W \times W$ is a binary equivalence relation representing the epistemic indistinguishability relation of the agent,[26]

[25]We refer the reader to Fagin et al. (1995), Blackburn et al. (2002), van Ditmarsch et al. (2007) and van Benthem (2011) for general presentations and overviews of epistemic logic.

[26]In all this paper, we make the common assumption that the indistinguishability relation is an *equivalence relation*.

- $V : W \to \mathscr{P}(\mathsf{P})$ is an atomic valuation function indicating the atomic propositions that are true at each world.

We refer to pairs (M, w), where M is an epistemic model and w is a world in M, as *pointed epistemic models*. The intuitive idea behind the use of the epistemic indistinguishability relation is the following: if w denotes the actual world and u is a world such that $u \sim w$, then this means that, given all what the agent knows, she cannot tell between w and u which one is the actual world. Finally, the epistemic language $\mathscr{E}$ is interpreted on epistemic models as follows:

Definition 33 (Semantics for $\mathscr{E}$). Let $M = \langle W, \sim, V\rangle$ be an epistemic model. The semantics for the epistemic language $\mathscr{E}$ is given by

$$\begin{aligned} M, w \models p &\text{ iff } p \in V(w) \\ M, w \models \neg\varphi &\text{ iff not } M, w \models \varphi \\ M, w \models \varphi \wedge \psi &\text{ iff } M, w \models \varphi \text{ and } M, w \models \psi \\ M, w \models K\varphi &\text{ iff for all } u \text{ such that } u \sim w \text{ we have } M, u \models \varphi. \end{aligned}$$

The set of valid formulas of $\mathscr{E}$ on the class of epistemic models can be axiomatized using the following axiomatic system EL:

Definition 34 (Logic EL). The logic EL is given by the following axiomatic system:

1. all classical propositional tautologies
2. $K(\varphi \to \psi) \to (K\varphi \to K\psi)$
3. $K\varphi \to \varphi$
4. $K\varphi \to KK\varphi$
5. $\neg K\varphi \to K\neg K\varphi$
6. from φ and $\varphi \to \psi$, infer ψ
7. from φ, infer $K\varphi$

Then, we have the following completeness result for EL with respect to the class of epistemic models:

Theorem 6 (Completeness for EL). *EL is strongly complete with respect to the class of epistemic models.*

Proof. See Blackburn et al. (2002). □

B Proofs of Propositions 1, 2 and Lemma 1

Proof (Proposition 1). Assume that $M, w \models R(\bigwedge\Gamma \wedge \neg\gamma) \wedge \mathsf{closed}(\Gamma, \gamma)$. By the structural property for semantic trees, we directly have that $\mathsf{T}(w) \in \mathsf{STrees}(\mathscr{I})_{\Gamma,\gamma}$. Since $n_{\Gamma,\gamma} + 1$ is the maximal number of branches of a semantic tree in $\mathsf{STrees}(\mathscr{I})_{\Gamma,\gamma}$, we have to show that for any $i \in [\![0, n_{\Gamma,\gamma}]\!]$, $\mathscr{B}_i(w)$ is either closed or empty. Let $i \in [\![0, n_{\Gamma,\gamma}]\!]$. Since $M, w \models \mathsf{closed}(\Gamma, \gamma)$, we have

$M, w \models \mathsf{closed}(\mathscr{B}_i)_{\Gamma,\gamma} \vee \mathsf{empty}(\mathscr{B}_i)_{\Gamma,\gamma}$. If $M, w \models \mathsf{closed}(\mathscr{B}_i)_{\Gamma,\gamma}$, this means that $M, w \models Br_i\gamma' \wedge Br_i\neg\gamma'$ for some $\gamma' \in \mathbf{T}(\Gamma, \gamma)$, and we get that $\mathscr{B}_i(w)$ is closed. If $M, w \models \mathsf{empty}(\mathscr{B}_i)_{\Gamma,\gamma}$, this means that no element of $\mathbf{T}(\Gamma, \gamma)$ is in $\mathscr{B}_i(w)$, and we get that $\mathscr{B}_i(w)$ is necessarily empty. We conclude that $\mathsf{T}(w) \in \mathsf{STrees}(\mathscr{I})_{\Gamma,\gamma}$ and $\mathsf{T}(w)$ is closed. Now assume that $\mathsf{T}(w) \in \mathsf{STrees}(\mathscr{I})_{\Gamma,\gamma}$ and $\mathsf{T}(w)$ is closed. We directly have that $M, w \models R(\bigwedge \Gamma \wedge \neg\gamma)$. Then, since $\mathsf{T}(w)$ is closed, we have that for all $i \in [\![0, n_{\Gamma,\gamma}]\!]$, $\mathscr{B}_i(w)$ is either closed or empty, and thereby that $M, w \models \mathsf{closed}(\Gamma, \gamma)$. □

Proof (Proposition 2). Assume that $M, w \models R\gamma$. Let $\chi \in \mathbf{ImpConf}(\gamma)$. We want to show that $M, w \not\models \chi$. Assume towards a contradiction that $M, w \models \chi$. Since $M, w \models R\gamma$, we have by the structural property of semantic trees that $\mathsf{T}(w) = \{\mathscr{R}, \mathscr{B}_i\}_{i\in\mathbb{N}}$ is a semantic tree with root γ. Since $\chi \in \mathbf{ImpConf}(\gamma)$, this means that there exist $\gamma' \in \mathscr{I}$ and $i \in \mathbb{N}$ such that (i) $\gamma' \in \mathscr{B}_i$ and $\neg Br_i\gamma'$ is one of the conjuncts of χ or (ii) $\gamma' \notin \mathscr{B}_i$ and $Br_i\gamma'$ is one of the conjuncts of χ. Since we assumed that $M, w \models \chi$, this means that (i) $\gamma' \in \mathscr{B}_i$ and $M, w \models \neg Br_i\gamma'$ or (ii) $\gamma' \notin \mathscr{B}_i$ and $M, w \models Br_i\gamma'$, which is a contradiction given the semantics of the operators Br_i. We conclude that $M, w \models \neg\chi$, and thereby that $R\gamma \to \neg\chi$ for $\chi \in \mathbf{ImpConf}(\gamma)$ is a valid principle on the class of models **TE**. □

Proof (Lemma 1). Let $\mathscr{T} = \{\mathscr{R}, \mathscr{B}_i\}_{i\in\mathbb{N}} \in \mathscr{P}(\mathscr{I})^{\mathbb{N}}$ s.t. $\mathscr{T}$ is not a semantic tree with root γ. Then, for every semantic tree $\mathscr{T}^* = \{\mathscr{R}^*, \mathscr{B}_0^*, \ldots, \mathscr{B}_n^*\}$ with root γ, there exist $\gamma' \in \mathscr{I}$ and $i \in \mathbb{N}$ such that (i) $\gamma' \in \mathscr{B}_i^*$ and $\gamma' \notin \mathscr{B}_i$, or (ii) $\gamma' \notin \mathscr{B}_i^*$ and $\gamma' \in \mathscr{B}_i$. We construct X as follows: for each semantic tree $\mathscr{T}^* = \{\mathscr{R}^*, \mathscr{B}_0^*, \ldots, \mathscr{B}_n^*\}$ with root γ, (i) if there exists γ' such that $\gamma' \in \mathscr{B}_i^*$ and $\gamma' \notin \mathscr{B}_i$ we let $\neg Br_i\gamma' \in X$, and (ii) if there exists γ' such that $\gamma' \notin \mathscr{B}_i^*$ and $\gamma' \in \mathscr{B}_i$ we let $Br_i\gamma' \in X$. By construction, we have that X is a γ-tree impossible configuration such that (i) if $\neg Br_i\gamma' \in X$ then $\gamma' \notin \mathscr{B}_i$ and (ii) if $Br_i\gamma' \in X$ then $\gamma' \in \mathscr{B}_i$. □

References

Ågotnes, T., van Benthem, J., van Ditmarsch, H., & Minica, S. (2011). Question–answer games. *Journal of Applied Non-Classical Logics, 21*(3–4), 265–288.

Aliseda, A. (2006). *Abductive reasoning: Logical investigations into discovery and explanation* (Synthese library, Vol. 330). Dordrecht: Springer.

Baltag, A., Moss, L., & Solecki, S. (1998). The logic of public announcements, common knowledge, and private suspicions. In I. Gilboa (Ed.), *Proceedings of the 7th conference on theoretical aspects of rationality and knowledge (TARK 98)* (pp. 43–56).

van Benthem, J. (2008). Tell it like it is: Information flow in logic. *Journal of Peking University (Humanities and Social Science Edition), 1*, 80–90.

van Benthem, J. (2011). *Logical dynamics of information and interaction*. Cambridge: Cambridge University Press.

van Benthem, J., & Minică, Ş. (2012). Toward a dynamic logic of questions. *Journal of Philosophical Logic, 41*(4), 633–669.

van Benthem, J., & Velázquez-Quesada, F. (2010). The dynamics of awareness. *Synthese, 177*, 5–27.

van Benthem, J., Gerbrandy, J., Hoshi, T., & Pacuit, E. (2009). Merging frameworks for interaction. *Journal of Philosophical Logic, 38*(5), 491–526.
Blackburn, P., De Rijke, M., & Venema, Y. (2002). *Modal logic*. Cambridge: Cambridge University Press.
Ciardelli, I., & Roelofsen, F. (2015). Inquisitive dynamic epistemic logic. *Synthese, 192*(6), 1643–1687.
Collingwood, R. (1940). *An essay on metaphysics*. Oxford: Clarendon Press.
D'Agostino, M. (1999). Tableau methods for classical propositional logic. In M. D'Agostino, D. Gabbay, R. Haehnle, & J. Posegga (Eds.), *Handbook of tableau methods* (pp. 45–123). Dordrecht: Kluwer Academic Publishers.
van Ditmarsch, H., van der Hoek, W., & Kooi, B. (2007). *Dynamic epistemic logic* (Synthese library, Vol. 337). Berlin/Heidelberg: Springer.
Fagin, R., Halpern, J., Moses, Y., & Vardi, M. (1995). *Reasoning about Knowledge*. Cambridge: MIT Press.
Genot, E. (2009). The game of inquiry: The interrogative approach to inquiry and belief revision theory. *Synthese, 171*(2), 271–289.
Gerbrandy, J., & Groeneveld, W. (1997). Reasoning about information change. *Journal of Logic, Language and Information, 6*(2), 147–169.
Groenendijk, J., & Stokhof, M. (1997). Questions. In J. van Benthem & A. ter Meulen (Eds.), *Handbook of logic and language* (pp. 1055–1124). Amsterdam: Elsevier.
Harrah, D. (1984). The logic of questions. In: D. Gabbay & F. Guenthner (Eds.), *Handbook of philosophical logic* (Vol. 2, pp. 715–764). Dordrecht: Reidel.
Hintikka, J. (1976). The semantics of questions and the questions of semantics: Case studies in the interrelations of logic, semantics, and syntax. *Acta Philosophica Fennica, 28*(4).
Hintikka, J. (1988). What is the logic of experimental inquiry? *Synthese, 74*(2), 173–190.
Hintikka, J. (1999). *Inquiry as inquiry: A logic of scientific discovery* (Jaakko Hintikka selected papers, Vol. 5). Dordrecht: Kluwer Academic Publishers.
Hintikka, J. (2007). *Socratic epistemology: Explorations of knowledge-seeking by questioning*. Cambridge: Cambridge University Press.
Hintikka, J., Halonen, I., & Mutanen, A. (1999). Interrogative logic as a general theory of reasoning. In *Inquiry as inquiry: A logic of scientific discovery* (pp. 47–90). Dordrecht: Kluwer Academic Publishers.
Kelly, K. (1996). *The logic of reliable inquiry*. Oxford: Oxford University Press
Peliš, M., & Majer, O. (2011). Logic of questions and public announcements. In N. Bezhanishvili, S. Löbner, K. Schwabe, & L. Spada (Eds.), *Eighth international Tbilisi symposium on logic, language and computation (2009)* (Lecture notes in computer science, pp. 145–157).
Plaza, J. (1989). Logics of public communications. In M. Emrich, M. Pfeifer, M. Hadzikadic, & Z. Ras (Eds.), *Proceedings of the 4th international symposium on methodologies for intelligent systems* (pp. 201–216).
Smullyan, R. (1968). *First-order logic*. Berlin: Springer.
Velázquez-Quesada, F. (2009). Inference and update. *Synthese (Knowledge, Rationality and Action), 169*(2), 283–300.
Wiśniewski, A. (1995). *The posing of questions: Logical foundations of erotetic inferences*. Dordrecht: Kluwer Academic Publishers.

Verificationism and Classical Realizability

Alberto Naibo, Mattia Petrolo, and Thomas Seiller

Abstract This paper investigates the question of whether Krivine's classical realizability can provide a verificationist interpretation of classical logic. We argue that this kind of realizability can be considered an adequate candidate for this semantic role, provided that the notion of verification involved is no longer based on proofs, but on programs. On this basis, we show that a special reading of classical realizability is compatible with a verificationist theory of meaning, insofar as pure logic is concerned. Crucially, in order to remain faithful to a fundamental verificationist tenet, we show that classical realizability can be understood from a single-agent perspective, thus avoiding the usual game-theoretic interpretation involving at least two players.

Keywords Verificationism • Realizability semantics • Classical logic • Untyped proof theory • Axiomatic theories

1 Introduction

Since the 1970s, Michael Dummett and Dag Prawitz proposed basic desiderata that a general verificationist theory of meaning should satisfy. In a successive number of papers and monographs, they tried to show that classical logic fails to meet such desiderata (see, in particular, Dummett 1973 and Prawitz 1977). The outcome of their analysis is that classical operators fail to convey meaning in a verificationist setting and, a fortiori, that classical logic is philosophically flawed.

On the other hand, since intuitionistic logic meets the meaning-theoretic desiderata, Dummett and Prawitz exploited this theory to advocate a form of logical

A. Naibo (✉) • M. Petrolo
IHPST (UMR 8590), CNRS, ENS, Université Paris 1 Panthéon-Sorbonne, Paris, France
e-mail: alberto.naibo@univ-paris1.fr; mattia.petrolo@univ-paris1.fr

T. Seiller
PPS (UMR 7126), CNRS, Université Paris-Diderot Paris 7, Paris, France
e-mail: seiller@pps.univ-paris-diderot.fr

C. Başkent (ed.), *Perspectives on Interrogative Models of Inquiry*, Logic, Argumentation & Reasoning 8, DOI 10.1007/978-3-319-20762-9_9

revisionism: a correct linguistic practice should not be based on classical forms of reasoning but rather on intuitionistic ones. In the last decades, several solutions have been proposed to avoid Dummett's and Prawitz's conclusion about the untenability of classical logic from an inferentialist and anti-realist perspective (we can mention, for instance, the works of A. Weir, S. Read, I. Rumfitt, G. Restall, T. Sandqvist).

Yet, with the only exception of Bonnay (2007), these solutions did not take into account some recent developments of the computational theory of classical logic and almost none of them focused in particular on classical realizability semantics. The aim of this paper is to contribute to fill this lacuna by investigating a way of assessing the philosophical significance of the so-called Krivine's classical realizability. More precisely, we consider the problem of whether classical realizability can provide a verificationist interpretation of classical logic. In order to do this we will analyse realizability semantics not only with respect to the Dummett-Prawitz's verificationism, but also with respect to Hintikka's one. We argue, in particular, that even if classical realizability seems to be much more closer to Hintikka's verificationism, in fact, a special reading of classical realizability can make it compatible also with the Dummett-Prawitz's perspective. Unfortunately, this special reading is too narrow, and it cannot be extended to proper (classical) mathematical theories, something which is possible instead with the standard reading of Krivine's classical realizability.

The paper is organized as follows. In Sect. 2, the notion of realizability semantics is introduced by analyzing Kleene's realizability for intuitionisitic logic. First, its compatibility with the different verificationist approaches it is investigated. Then, a comparison with Krivine's realizability for classical logic is provided. It is shown, in particular, that even if both of these two frameworks consider realizers as computable entities like programs, the latter adopts a wider and richer perspective, allowing to define not only correct programs, but also wrongful ones. In Sect. 3, we introduce some technical concepts and definitions needed to tackle the philosophical question of the relationships between classical realizability and the verificationist theory of meaning. After a brief survey of the syntax of classical realizability, we show how a two-agents based dialogical interpretation can be considered as a natural framework to model the computational behavior of classical proofs. We then compare it with a similar computational setting called "untyped proof theory". In Sect. 4, we investigate the possibility to use classical realizability as a framework for an anti-realist account of classical logic. Some substantial differences occur between classical realizability and Dummett's verificationism. Nonetheless, we are able to show that Krivine's realizability can be made compatible with a single-agent based perspective, not incompatible, in principle, with a Dummettian perspective. In the final section, we show how classical realizability represents a setting flexible enough to provide a computational account of many mathematical axioms and theories. However, our account of classical logic is jeopardized in this extended mathematical setting. We conclude by pointing out some difficulties encountered by our proposal when proper axioms are added to the underlying classical system.

2 The Idea of Realizability Semantics

2.1 *Kleene's Number Realizability*

Historically, the notion of realizability was introduced by Kleene (1945) in order to give a formal semantics for intuitionistic logic and intuitionistic arithmetic. The main source of inspiration for this type of semantics was the finitist explanation of mathematical statements, and in particular existential ones, as it was given by Hilbert and Bernays (1934, p. 32). According to this explanation, a statement of the form $\exists x A(x)$ is considered to convey an "incomplete communication", waiting for the exhibition of a witness t. Only when a finitist method for obtaining t is given, the communication is completed and the statement $A(t)$ can then be effectively asserted (cf. Kleene 1973). In particular, Kleene's idea was that finitist methods were nothing but effective algorithmic methods, eventually representable in a formal setting by (partial) recursive functions. The semantics obtained in such way was thus a semantics based on essentially intensional objects – i.e. algorithms –, rather than on explicitly extensional ones, as in the case of standard algebraic or relational semantics, like Kripke models for intuitionistic logic. This is particularly clear when we represent (partial) recursive functions by using Kleene's normal form theorem: a recursive function f is represented in a unique way by coding the way in which it computes, that is its computational tree:

$$f(\vec{x}) \simeq U(\mu y.T(e, \vec{x}, y)) \tag{1}$$

where T is the Kleene-predicate expressing that the function f, coded by the Gödel number e, when applied to the list of arguments $\vec{x}$, is computed according to a computational tree, coded by the Gödel number y; the result of the computation, when it exists, is then extracted by the function U, and μ, which is the minimalization operator, guarantees that the computational tree considered is the one having the smallest code.

This way of representing recursive functions allows one to describe them not only with respect to what they do – i.e. with respect to the values that are obtained when the functions are applied to certain arguments – but also with respect to how they compute – i.e. with respect to the steps that are accomplished in order to obtain the expected values. Moreover, recursive functions can enumerated, so that for each natural number n there exists a recursive function f, so that (1) can be rephrased in the following way:

$$\{n\}(\vec{x}) \simeq U(\mu y.T(n, \vec{x}, y)).$$

Kleene's realizability consists in associating a formula of intuitionistic logic or arithmetic – proper axioms included – to a natural number n codifying (by a Gödel numbering) a recursive function f which guarantees that A holds. It is for this reason that Kleene's realizability is also known under the name of "number realizability".

The fact that $n \in \mathbb{N}$ realizes, or forces, a formula A is noted by $n \Vdash A$, and inductively defined in the following way (see Sørensen and Urzyczyn (2006), p. 243 and Troelstra and van Dalen (1988), p. 196, with slight modifications):

- $n \Vdash t = s$ iff t and s rewrite to the same numeral $\overline{n}$[1];
- $n \Vdash A \wedge B$ iff $n = 2^q \cdot 3^r$, where $q \Vdash A$ and $r \Vdash B$;
- $n \Vdash A \vee B$ iff $n = 3^q$ and $q \Vdash A$, or $n = 2 \cdot 3^q$ and $q \Vdash B$;
- $n \Vdash A \to B$ iff for each m, such that $m \Vdash A$, $\{n\}(m)$ is defined and $\{n\}(m) \Vdash B$;
- $n \Vdash \exists x A(x)$ iff $n = 2^m \cdot 3^r$, where $r \Vdash A(\overline{m})$;
- $n \Vdash \forall x A(x)$ iff for all m, $\{n\}(m)$ is defined and $\{n\}(m) \Vdash A(\overline{m})$.[2]

Notice that $2^q \cdot 3^r$ is an injective pairing function and that without loss of generality we can consider the formula $A(x)$ of the two last clauses to contain only x free. Moreover, according to these realizability clauses the set of realizers is consistent, since $0 = 1$ cannot be realized. And since by definition $\bot \equiv 0 = 1$, the following clause holds:

- $n \Vdash \bot$ for no n.

2.2 *Realizers as Verifiers*

What is peculiar to realizers is that they reflect, at the level of functional operations, the syntactic structure of the realized formulas: there thus exists specific realizers for each formula. In this sense, Kleene's realizability seems to offer a finer-grained semantics with respect to usual algebraic or relational ones, where it is the whole structure that renders true or false the whole set of formulas. In particular, when theorems are considered, algebraic and relational semantics assign them the same semantic value[3] – i.e. the top element of an algebra or the set of all possible worlds of a Kripke frame – with the risk of trivializing, or at least impoverishing, the way in which logical and mathematical theories are understood.[4]

In Kleene's realizability, on the contrary, the semantic value of a formula A corresponds to the set of its realizers – i.e. $|A| = \{t \in \mathbb{N} \mid t \Vdash A\}$ – which provide

---

[1]A numeral $\overline{n}$ stands for a term of the language of arithmetic of the form

$$\underbrace{s(\ldots s}_{n \text{ times}}(0)\ldots).$$

In other words, numerals are terms denoting natural numbers, written in a canonical form.

[2]This means that the numbers realizing universal formulas correspond to total recursive functions.

[3]The semantic value of a formula A is that feature allowing one to determine the semantic notions associated to A, like meaning and truth (cf. Dummett 1991, pp. 24, 30–31).

[4]It is worth noting that the difference we sketched between Kleene's realizability semantics and the algebraic or relational semantics can be taken as a particular instance of the difference between

'witnesses for the constructive truth of existential quantifiers and disjunctions, and in implications [carry] this type of information from premise to conclusion by means of partial recursive operators. In short, realizing numbers "hereditarily" encode information about the realization of existential quantifiers and disjunction' (Troelstra 1998, p. 408). This means, in particular, that the disjunction and the existential properties (for intuitionistic arithmetic) are satisfied (see Sørensen and Urzyczyn 2006, p. 243). Kleene's realizability could then be thought as a formal way of capturing the intuitionistic notion of truth, as corresponding to the possession of a construction, and thus respecting the BHK interpretation. Since this is obtained by interpreting intuitionistic arithmetic over a fragment of arithmetic itself, then Kleene's realizability could be see as a formal and rigorous characterization of the BHK interpretation, namely by using the technique of *inner models*.[5]

The idea that Kleene's realizability can be seen as a definition of the intuitionistic notion of truth, in the same way as Tarski's notion of satisfiability is seen as a definition of the classical notion of truth, seems to be corroborated by the fact that Kleene's realizability allows us to exclude classical principles. For example, by a simple application of the excluded middle, the formula

$$\forall x(\exists y T(x,x,y) \vee \neg\exists y T(x,x,y)) \tag{2}$$

is shown to be provable, and thus valid, in classical arithmetic. On the contrary, according to Kleene's realizability, the validity of (2) corresponds to the existence of a total recursive function deciding $\exists y T(x,x,y)$, which correspond to the possibility of deciding the halting problem. But this is known to be impossible. Thus, there are no realizers for (2). And since there are no realizers for $\bot$ too, by applying a classical reading of the metalanguage expressions in which the realizability clauses are formulated, we can then conclude that the negation of (2) holds.[6]

However, since realizers correspond to recursive functions, they not only seem to serve in order to establish intuitionistic truths, but they also seem to convey an effective method, or procedure, in order to *verify* these truths. Kleene's realizers can then be seen as *verifiers*, and thus, to know the semantic value of a formula corresponds to know how to verify it. In this way, Kleene's realizability can be considered as a framework allowing one to respect a verificationist account of the semantics of linguistic expressions, similar to the one proposed by J. Hintikka (1996, § 10).

construction-oriented semantics and conditional-oriented semantics studied by Fine (2014, § 1). According to Fine, the first has to be considered as an exact semantics, while the latter an inexact one. The reason is that, in the first case, the semantical entities are wholly, or exactly, relevant for establishing the truth of a given statement. On the contrary, in the second case, the semantical entities are relevant for establishing the truth of a statement only in a loose and inexact way, which is made particularly evident by the fact that in this kind of semantics the monotonicity of the forcing relation holds (see Fine 2014, p. 551).

[5]We due this observation to Göran Sundholm.

[6]The idea is that, according to the standard practice in intuitionistic logic, we consider $\neg A$ as defined by $A \rightarrow \bot$.

2.2.1 A Comparison with Hintikka's and Dummett's Verificationism

According to Hintikka, in the case of first-order logic, the truth values of a formula are defined with respect to a given domain of objects by the existence of winning strategies for two players games; where one player (the Verifier) tries to verify the formula, while the other one (the Falsifier) tries to falsify it. Differently from usual algebraic or relational semantics, this definition does not simply look at truth as coming out from some kind of structural and 'abstract relationship between sentences and facts', but it also gives an operational definition of it (Hintikka 1996, p. 22). In particular, the idea is that linguistic games are constituent of the use of the notion of truth, and since the rules of a game are, in principle, learnable and teachable, the definition of truth which is given is based on an activity of justification of a certain sentence with respect to a certain set (or domain) of objects (cf. Bonnay 2004, p. 107; Boyer and Sandu 2012, p. 822–823). However, the simple existence of a winning strategy does not assure that such a notion of truth can be accessible to human agents. The reason is that, in the case of first-order logic, winning strategies for the Verifier correspond to Skolem functions,[7] and these functions do not necessarily correspond to constructive strategies. More precisely, if one does not want to look only for a definition of truth, but also for its knowability, it is necessary to guarantee the epistemic accessibility to the set of truths. As proposed by Hintikka, this can be achieved by restricting the set of winning strategies to those that can be effectively played by some idealized human agent, namely those that correspond to recursive functions (see Hintikka 1996, p. 214–215).[8] It would be therefore natural to consider Kleene's realizers as methods of verifications, in Hintikka's sense, guaranteeing – at least in principle – an access to the truth value of a formula. As Hintikka himself says, 'the technical interpretation of my [constructivistic] interpretation [of logic and mathematics] does not stray very far from Gödel's *Dialectica* interpretation of first-order elementary arithmetic or from Kleene's realizability interpretation' (Hintikka 1996, p. 235).

Still, Hintikka's verificationism is not the only form of verificationism existing. Intuitionistic principles and theorems are often justified by making appeal to another form of verificationism, i.e. Dummett's verificationism. This proposal results to be more radical that Hintikka's one, since any appeal to a given domain of objects is rejected, and the verification procedures which are allowed are only those acting

[7]Notice that the strategies adopted by the Falsifier correspond, instead, to Kreisel's counterexamples (Boyer and Sandu 2012, p. 823). In this sense, if we focus on the winning strategies for the Falsifier – instead of the winning strategies for the Verifier – Hintikka's framework can be adapted for justifying a form of falsificationism.

[8]It is worth noting that an idealized human agent is not an agent totally freed from any kind of contingent constraints: on the contrary, she possess the very same epistemic capacities that any other concrete human beings possess, the only difference being that her capacities are perfect. More precisely, like every concrete human being, she can deal with only a finite amount of resources and information, and her actions can be performed only in a finite amount of time and space; however, unlike concrete human beings, her finite capacities are not subject to any fixed bound.

at a linguistic-inferential level. More precisely, the idea is that a verification for a formula A consists in an effective method for obtaining a *canonical proof* of A, that is a proof terminating with an introduction rule for the principal connective of A. This method, in general, is composed of two steps: (i) the exhibition of a (possibly) non-canonical proof of A, and (ii) the application of the normalization algorithm to this proof, in order to obtain a (new) proof satisfying the so-called introduction form property (see Dummett 1973, p. 240; Tieszen 1992, p. 72).[9]

The crucial difference of Dummett's verificationism with respect to Hintikka's verificationism is that, by grounding the process of verification on the notion of proof, a verifier cannot transcend human epistemic capacities, since a proof is, by definition, something which is connected to our linguistic capacities. In other words, the idea is that we are always in a position to recognize a proof when we see one (Kreisel 1962, p. 202), since when a set of linguistic expressions (i.e. signs) is given, it is possible, by means of mechanical, syntactical, calculation on these expressions alone, to decide whether or not the given set of expressions is a proof of a certain sentence (Sundholm 1994, p. 144).[10] This guarantees in particular the satisfaction of

---

[9]A non-canonical proof is called by Dummett a *demonstration*; its relation with a canonical proof is explained in the following manner:

> We [...] require a distinction between a proof proper – a canonical proof – and the sort of argument which will normally appear in a mathematical article or textbook, an argument which we may call a 'demonstration'. A demonstration is just as cogent a ground for the assertion of its conclusion as is a canonical proof, and is related to it in this way: a demonstration of a proposition provides an effective means for finding a canonical proof. (Dummett 1973, p. 240)

According to Dummett, the notion of canonical proof is the semantic key concept of the notion of meaning. More precisely, to know the meaning of a sentence A corresponds to know the conditions for its (direct) assertion, which corresponds, in turn, to know what counts as a canonical proof of A. Thus, grounding the notion of truth on that of canonical proof is a way to assigning priority to the notion of meaning with respect to the notion of truth. Furthermore, as Dummett remarks, the conditions for the truth of a sentence and those for its correct assertion do not, in principle, collapse: possessing an effective method for obtaining a canonical proof does not necessarily mean to be able to *concretely* execute this method and, eventually, get access to this proof (cf. Dummett 1998, p. 122–123). The reason is that human agents could be subject to contingent limitations – e.g. space or time limitations – which do not allow them to terminate the execution of the procedure (e.g. in the case of the normalization, this procedure corresponds to an algorithm of exponential size complexity, which is unfeasible for concrete human agents with limitation of space). Therefore, it is only when idealized human agents are considered that the collapse between the two notions could obtain.

[10]It has been argued that the decidability of the notion of proof is in fact an excessively strong assumption. For example, Sundholm (1986, p. 493) argues that the proof relation is only a semi-decidable notion, since 'we recognize a proof when we see one, but when we don't see one that does not necessarily mean that there is no proof there.' However, prominent representatives of this form of verificationism, especially Dummett himself, have firmly advocated the decidability of the notion of proof. A quite exhaustive list of places in which Dummett supports this idea can be found in Sundholm (1983, p. 155).

Dummett's *manifestability requirement*: when a sentence is true, we should always be in a position to manifest our recognition of its truth.

A question which naturally arises is to understand if Kleene's realizability is compatible with Dummett's form of verificationism, as well as whether it is compatible with Hintikka's one. But answering this question corresponds, in fact, to answer another question, that is, to understand whether the intuitionistic notion of truth specified by Kleene's realizability is complete with respect to the intuitionistic notion of proof. The answer to this question is negative, since there exist natural numbers realizing formulas which are not provable in intuitionistic logic or arithmetic. In particular, it can be shown that for every closed formula A, either A or $\neg A$ is realizable (see Sørensen and Urzyczyn 2006, pp. 244–245). This result is, in fact, nothing but a generalization of the way in which we showed the negation of (2) to be realizable: either there is a realizer for A or, if there is not, since $\bot$ is never realized, then any arbitrary number can realize $\neg A$. The very same negation of (2) is an example of a sentence which is realizable, but not provable.

But there is also a second aspect which prevents Kleene's realizability from being compatible with Dummett's verificationism. Differently from the case of proofs, it is not possible to decide whether a given number n realizes or not a certain formula A (see Dummett 1977, p. 320; Sørensen and Urzyczyn 2006, p. 244–245). For example, consider the formula $\forall x(x = x)$. This formula is realized by every Gödel number corresponding to a total recursive function. But the set of total recursive function is not enumerable by a total recursive function, and a fortiori not decidable. Hence, Kleene's realizability cannot satisfy Dummett's manifestability requirement, since a formula A could be realized by a certain realizer t and we would not recognize it as such.[11]

2.3 From Intuitionistic to Classical Realizability

The previous discussion pointed out the following situation: even if Kleene's realizability has been conceived as a semantics for intuitionistic logic and arithmetic, it contains in fact several classical features as, for instance, the classical reading of its defining clauses – and especially the interpretation of $\bot$ as the absence of any realizer, which induces meta-level reasonings using classical logic (cf. von Plato 2013, p. 103) – or the fact of relying on the notion of recursive function, which is

[11]It is worth noting that some authors, like van Atten (2014, § 4.5.2), considers that an essential aspect of the BHK interpretation is that the concepts 'that figure in meaning explanations [...] have to do with our cognitive capacities'. In particular, the idea is that the concept of construction which figures in the BHK interpretation should be conceived such that we recognize a construction when we see one. Accepting this reading of the BHK interpretation – which means indeed to assume that Dummett's verification is a declination of it – would then mean to accept that Kleene's realizability is not a formal version of the BHK interpretation, as claimed before.

defined with respect to a classical logic background.[12] One can find confirmation of this aspect in the fact that Kleene's realizability allows one to judge as true some principles that are not intuitionistically acceptable, like Markov's principle, i.e.

$$\forall x(P(x) \vee \neg P(x)) \rightarrow (\neg \forall x \neg P(x) \rightarrow \exists x P(x))$$

where P is a predicate on natural numbers, or a limited version of the excluded middle, i.e.

$$A \vee \neg A$$

where A is a closed formula (see Dummett 1977, § 6.2).[13] However, the presence of these classical features is not yet sufficient for a direct and straightforward use of Kleene's realizability as a semantics for classical logic: as we have already seen, with such a semantics it is not possible to realize a classical principle like (2).[14]

Nevertheless, it would be possible to get a realizability semantics for classical logic by using Kleene's realizability (or some little modification of it) in association with a special kind of parametrized negative translation – similar to Friedman's one (see Friedman 1978) – as showed by Oliva and Streicher (2008). However, what we are interested in here is a more direct way of expressing a realizability for classical logic. We will focus our attention on what is called Krivine's classical realizability (see Krivine 2009), and we will give it a conceptual analysis, by trying to understand, in particular, its connections with the verificationist approaches sketched before.

At a first sight, Krivine's realizability can be considered to share two fundamental features with Kleene's realizability: (i) it makes appeal to a computational-based notion of realizer, and (ii) this notion is revealed to be broader than that of proof.

---

[12]Think of the fact that it is possible to define a recursive function by making appeal to the principle of the excluded middle, as for example

$$f(x) =_{df} \begin{cases} 1 & \text{if the Goldbach conjecture is true} \\ 0 & \text{if the Goldbach conjecture is false} \end{cases}$$

However, there are also other, and more critical, aspects of the notion of recursive function which are inherently classical. For example, the regularity condition, which is used in order to define a function f from a relation R by minimization, states that $\forall \vec{x} \exists y R(\vec{x}, y)$. Here, the existential quantifier is understood classically, in the sense that there is no algorithmic procedure for extracting the witness, otherwise the definition of algorithmic procedures via the notion of recursive functions would be circular (cf. Heyting 1962, p. 195). For further details about the non-constructive aspects of the definition of recursive functions see Coquand (2014) and Sundholm (2014).

[13]Note that Kreisel (1973, p. 268) seems to have in mind a very similar situation when he asks if the '(logical) language of the current intuitionistic systems [have been] obtained by *uncritical* transfer from languages which were, tacitly, understood classically'.

[14]This means, in particular, that Kleene's realizability does not allow one to realize the principle of excluded middle for open formulas.

Nevertheless, Krivine's realizability cannot be taken as a simple extension of Kleene's realizability. The reason is that the way in which (i) and (ii) are conceived is radically different from Kleene's realizability.

As it concerns point (i), the notion of computation considered by Krivine is a broader notion than that considered by Kleene. In particular, an algorithm is no longer identified with a recursive functions on natural numbers. In Kleene's realizability we have that the computational aspects are mainly focused on the inputs and outputs of a function. This is particularly clear in the case of the implication and the universal quantifier: given a certain input, if there is no output, the condition is not satisfied, and thus the formula not realized. According to this interpretation, a function is then conceived essentially in a set-theoretical way: it is reducible to a set of pairs of natural numbers. In this sense, the domain and the codomain of a computable function are already fixed from the beginning – in both cases they correspond to the set of natural numbers – and thus a computable function has to be considered as a typed entity. On the contrary, in Krivine's classical realizability, algorithms are considered to be entities having a deeper intensional nature. Their behavior is not established in advance by making appeal to a ready-made notion of type, but it is manifested only when the algorithm is executed – or better, tested – within a given *context* (possibly composed by other algorithms). It is only after that its behavior has been manifested that it will be possible to assign a certain type to the algorithm. Moreover, this type will not be assigned in an absolute and unchangeable way, since this assignment depends from the context in which the algorithm is tested.

As it concerns point (ii), in Krivine's realizability the number of realizers exceeds the number of proofs. However, differently from what happens in Kleene's realizability, this does not mean that there exist formulas which are realized but not valid in the theory under consideration.[15] It means, instead, that the set of realizers of a formula does not contain only proofs, but also other kind of objects. These objects correspond, in particular, to what can be called *tentative proofs*, that is (deductive) *arguments* whose inferential steps are not totally justified, and thus not necessarily logically correct.[16] The presence of this kind of objects is mainly concerned by the attempt of avoiding computationally trivial interpretations of negative formulas.

As we have seen, in Kleene's realizability the formula $\bot$ is never realized. The consequence is that negative formulas $\neg A$ are either never realized, or they are realized by every (partial) recursive function. In both cases, their computational content is lost, since it is completely trivialized, namely it would not be possible

---

[15]This does not mean that Krivine's realizability always guarantees the theory to be complete with respect to the notion of (classical) proof. This depends indeed from the language in which the (classical) theory is presented. If it is a first-order theory, then completeness holds, but if it is a second-order theory, this could no more be the case (as it depends from the way in which the predicate variables are interpreted in the model). Our presentation of Krivine's realizability rests on a second-order theory (see Sect. 3). The possible lack of completeness is then due to the fact that a second-order language is adopted, and not to the way in which the notion of realizability is conceived.

[16]Indeed, as Prawitz (2006, p. 511) remarks, 'an invalid proof is not really a proof'.

to distinguish two negative formulas on the basis of their computational content. In order to avoid this situation, it has to be possible to define a set of realizers also for $\perp$. But since $\perp$ correspond to a(n always) false formula, and verifying a false formula is contradictory, the idea is then to liberalize the notion of realizers, by defining them not only in terms of verifiers, but also in terms of falsifiers. In this sense, Krivine's realizability seems to be much closer to Hintikka's verificationism than Kleene's realizability, since according to Hintikka, the verification-games are defined with respect to two players, the Verifier and the Falsifier (even if the conceptual priority is eventually assigned to the Verifier, since what counts is the definition of the truth of a formula, and this relies on the definition of the winning strategies associated to that formula). In Sects. 4.3 and 4.4 we will take a step further and we will try to understand if, from the point of view of Krivine's realizability, this two players perspective could become compatible also with Dummett's verificationism.

3 Krivine's Classical Realizability

3.1 Definitions

The change of perspective induced by Krivine's realizability with respect to the computational account of realizers confers to this framework a greater flexibility than Kleene's realizability. In particular, Krivine's realizability can be applied to the case of classical logic – and even extended to proper mathematical theories, like arithmetic and set theory (see Sect. 5) – by exploiting the fact that to every axiom can be assigned a different term-constant codifying a certain programming operation. For example, if we take Peirce's law

$$((A \to B) \to A) \to A$$

to be the axiom distinguishing classical logic from intuitionistic logic, it is possible to associate it with a program instruction corresponding to the `call-with-current-continuation` control operator of the programming language SCHEME, as shown by Griffin (1990). Similarly, the axiom of countable choice is associated to a program instruction akin to the `quote` instruction of the programming language LISP (Krivine 2003). We will come back later to these examples (see Sects. 3.2 and 5).

The fundamental notion of computation on which Krivine's account rests on three key ingredients: *terms*, *stacks*, and *processes*. From a syntactical point of view, terms are composed by purely λ-terms enriched by two sorts of constants:

(i) *instructions*, noted with κ, and ranging over a non-empty set $\mathcal{K}$, containing at least the constant `cc` which corresponds to the control operator `call-with-current-continuation`.
(ii) *continuations*, noted with k_σ, and where σ ranges over the set of stacks.

Stacks are *lists* of closed terms, the last element of which is a stack constant α; we here suppose that the set of possible stack constants is a singleton $\{\diamond\}$, where $\diamond$ somehow stands for the empty stack. Notice however that some models considered by Krivine, among which the *threads model* (Krivine 2012), use several distinct (and even an infinite number of) stack constants. Terms and stacks are defined by mutual induction according to the following Backus-Naur grammar:

Terms	t, u	$::=$	$x \mid \lambda x.t \mid (t)u \mid \kappa \mid k_\sigma$	$(\kappa \in \mathscr{K})$
Stacks	σ	$::=$	$\diamond \mid t \cdot \sigma$	(t closed)

The system obtained in this way is usually called λ_c (see Krivine 1994, 2003, 2009).

It is worth noting that Krivine's classical realizability has been mainly conceived for theories formulated in second-order logic. For this reason, among the set of terms the operators of pair construction, projection, injection, and case analysis do not appear: at the second-order level they become definable (see Sørensen and Urzyczyn 2006, pp. 280–281). As already mentioned, terms correspond to programs for verifying given sentences, as in the case of Kleene's realizability. From the morphological point of view, they can be divided into two categories: those that contain continuations and those that do not. A term containing no continuation constants is called a *proof-like* term. Intuitively, such a term corresponds to a (logically correct) proof, and thus it can be considered as a verifier in Dummett's sense. We will return to this point in Sects. 3.3.2 and 3.3.

Stacks, on the contrary, correspond to the evaluation contexts of programs, as they are the environments within which programs "react" and exhibit a specific behavior. Finally, processes are obtained by letting (closed) terms and stacks interact. Thus, contexts can be seen as *tests* for programs. Given a (closed) term t and a stack σ, a process is noted by $t \star \sigma$. Computation is then defined by exploiting an evaluation relation on processes, noted with $\leadsto$, and defined in the following rewrite rules:

$$\begin{array}{lcllcll} \lambda x.t & \star & u \cdot \sigma & \leadsto & t[x := u] & \star & \sigma & \text{(pop)} \\ (t)u & \star & \sigma & \leadsto & t & \star & u \cdot \sigma & \text{(push)} \\ \mathtt{cc} & \star & t \cdot \sigma & \leadsto & t & \star & k_\sigma \cdot \sigma & \text{(grab)} \\ k_{\sigma'} & \star & t \cdot \sigma & \leadsto & t & \star & \sigma' & \text{(restore)} \end{array}$$

An examination of these clauses shows that in order to calculate the result of an evaluation it is not needed to know how the context σ is made, with the only exception of the grab rule. In this case, it is not the form or the structure of the term[17] that determines the computational action which has to be executed, but the

[17]Notice that under the Curry-Howard correspondence for intuitionistic logic a term representing a program corresponds to a proof written in intuitionistic natural deduction. This means that the form of the term reflects the form of the proof, namely the order of application of the inference rules.

form of the context. This means, in particular, that the computational process does not immediately reduce to the computation of a value when an argument is given to a term but it passes through the interaction between the term and the context in which it is asked to be evaluated. We will try to clarify this point in the next section by studying the cc instruction, which is a constant and thus has no proper internal structure: its computational behavior will then depend only from the context in which it is evaluated or tested.

3.2 Dialogues

The way in which realizability semantics operates, and more precisely the way in which processes and their evaluations have to be understood, can be explained in term of dialogues – or better, disputes – between two agents: the *prover* – i.e. the term –, which has to produce a construction of a certain sentence A, and the *skeptic* – i.e. the stack – which doubts of the existence of this construction and thus tries to challenge the prover with respect to A. Consider the following example, involving Peirce law and inspired by Sørensen and Urzyczyn (2006, pp. 144–145).

1. The prover asserts $((A \to B) \to A) \to A$, which corresponds to affirming that a construction cc of $((A \to B) \to A) \to A$ holds thanks to the application of a 0-ary rule.
2. The skeptic does not agree with this assertion, and tries to challenge it by proposing to the prover the following problem: to exhibit a construction of A, given a construction of $(A \to B) \to A$. In order to do this, she provides a term t realizing $(A \to B) \to A$, asks the prover to provide a term a realizing A – using cc and t –, and prepares herself to challenge the fact that a realizes A with a *test* a' for A.

This situation corresponds to considering a process $\mathrm{cc} \star t \cdot a' \cdot \diamond$, where $a' \cdot \diamond$ is the *context* of the challenge, that is the set of presuppositions from which the skeptic moves in order to challenge the prover.[18]

3. In order to continue the dispute, the prover makes use of the presuppositions of the skeptic and claims $A \to B$ (for a more detailed justification of this step see p. 185). This claim corresponds to the introduction of a continuation constant $k_{a' \cdot \diamond}$, coming out from the result of the evaluation of the process $\mathrm{cc} \star t \cdot a' \cdot \diamond$ via the grab rule, which gives $t \star k_{a' \cdot \diamond} \cdot a' \cdot \diamond$.

[18]We will try to clarify later what do we mean here for 'presuppositions' (see Sect. 4.4). For the time being, it is sufficient to remark that since a context is a list of closed terms, it cannot be a set of hypothesis, as hypotheses correspond to free variables. Moreover, while hypotheses do not presuppose any epistemic attitude towards their truth or falseness, presuppositions are *believed* to be true.

If t does not use its argument:

$$\begin{aligned} \texttt{cc} \star t \cdot a' \cdot \diamond &\rightsquigarrow t \star k_{a'\cdot\diamond} \cdot a' \cdot \diamond \text{ (grab)} \\ &\rightsquigarrow \dots \\ &\rightsquigarrow a \star a' \cdot \diamond \end{aligned}$$

If t uses its argument:

$$\begin{aligned} \texttt{cc} \star t \cdot a' \cdot \diamond &\rightsquigarrow t \star k_{a'\cdot\diamond} \cdot a' \cdot \diamond \text{ (grab)} \\ &\rightsquigarrow \dots \\ &\rightsquigarrow k_{a'\cdot\diamond} \star a \cdot \sigma' \\ &\rightsquigarrow a \star a' \cdot \diamond \qquad \text{(restore)} \end{aligned}$$

Fig. 1 The term cc is a realizer of Peirce's law

From the point of view of processes, this amounts to saying that it can be given as an argument to the term t, that is, one could consider the application $(t)k_{a'\cdot\diamond}$, which via the push rule reduces to $t \star k_{a'\cdot\diamond} \cdot a' \cdot \diamond$. But this brings us in a situation where we do not know for sure what will happen. Indeed, the way the process $t \star k_{a'\cdot\sigma} \cdot a' \cdot \diamond$ will reduce depends on how the term t is constructed.

Without going into the details, we can notice that t is a realizer of $(A \to B) \to A$. As we will see in Sect. 3.3.1, this means that any process of the form $t \star u \cdot a' \cdot \diamond$, with u a realizer of $A \to B$ and a' a test for A, will win the dispute. In other terms, when given a realizer of $A \to B$ as an argument, the term t reduces to a realizer of A. This can be done in two ways (see Fig. 1). First, t could be a term that does not use its given argument, e.g. t "throws away" the argument, that is t is of the form $\lambda x.u$, where x does not appear in u.[19] In that case, the skeptic provides, in the end, a realizer a of A, and the dialogue continues directly at step 5. The second possibility is that t actually uses its argument to compute its output. The dialogue then continues as follows.

4. At some point during the reduction process, one reaches a step of the form $k_{a'\cdot\diamond} \star a \cdot \sigma'$, where a is a realizer of A. The prover claims that $k_{a'\cdot\diamond}$ is indeed a realizer of $A \to B$, but the skeptic considers its use to be unjustified. She then challenges the prover to provide, given a construction a of A, a construction of B.
5. Since the skeptic gives to the prover a construction a of A, the prover comes back to the first challenge, and uses exactly this construction a in order to satisfy it. In case the computation went through step 4. above, this corresponds to the evaluation of $k_{a'\cdot\diamond} \star a \cdot \sigma'$ into $a \star a' \cdot \diamond$ by the restore rule. In case the term t

[19] Notice that the condition that x does not appear in u is not necessary for t not to use its argument. In other words, t could not use the argument in the computation, even if x appears in u. For instance, consider the term $t \equiv \lambda x.(\lambda y.a)x$, where x and y do not appear in a. Then t is of the form $\lambda x.u$, where x appears in u, but we have the following reduction sequence: $\lambda x.(\lambda y.a)x \star k_{a'\cdot\diamond} \cdot a' \cdot \diamond \rightsquigarrow (\lambda y.a)k_{a'\cdot\diamond} \star a' \cdot \diamond \rightsquigarrow \lambda x.a \star k_{a'\cdot\diamond} \cdot a' \cdot \diamond \rightsquigarrow a \star a' \cdot \diamond$.

provided by the skeptic did not use its argument, the computation reaches $a \star a' \cdot \diamond$ without using the restore rule, since $t[x := k_{a' \cdot \diamond}]$ reduces to a term a realizing A.

The prover has thus been able to meet the challenge of the skeptic because, by appealing to the presuppositions held by the skeptic, she has been able to transform an attack of the latter into its own defense. And since in order to do this the prover used only information coming from the skeptic (namely, a and a'), the skeptic cannot but accept them. It is in this sense that we can say that the prover possesses a winning strategy.

However, this possibility of switching the role of a move in a dispute is not the only aspect which characterizes the dialogical account of classical logic. There is in fact another aspect which is linked to the use of contexts, and which essentially distinguishes intuitionistic dialogues from classical ones. When we look at intuitionistic dialogues, we can notice that the prover always replies to the challenge that the skeptic advanced in the immediately previous step. The defense of the prover consists then in setting up a function which returns a value for every argument proposed by the skeptic (see for more details Sørensen and Urzyczyn 2006, § 4.6). When we look at classical dialogues, we can notice, instead, that the prover can move back to a previous challenge and reply to it, by making reference to the context in which this challenge was previously made, thanks to the restore rule.

3.3 *Classical Realizability and Untyped Proof Theory*

We expose here the realizability interpretation of classical logic. This follows a well-known technique consisting in typing terms a posteriori, i.e. assigning types to terms according to their interactive behavior, that is, what they effectively compute. For instance, the lambda term $\lambda x.x$ could be typed by $A \to A$, for any formula A. This induces *subtyping*, which means that a given term can be assigned to several types at the same time.

3.3.1 Realizability Interpretation

Let us indicate with Λ the set of terms, and with Σ the set of stacks.

Once the processes and their reductions defined, they are used to interpret formulas. More precisely, we define the realizability relation $t \Vdash A$, where t is a term and A a formula. The definition proceeds by induction, however differently from the definition given in the case of Kleene's realizability, this definition requires two semantic values and not just one. In particular, one defines for each formula A, what can be called its *falsity value* $\|A\| \subset \Sigma$ – corresponding to its set of falsifiers – and its *truth value* $|A| \subset \Lambda$ – corresponding to its set of verifiers. In order to define those sets, one needs to fix once and for all a so-called *pole* which is a subset $\perp\!\!\!\perp \subset \Lambda \star \Sigma$ of processes which is closed under anti-evaluation: if $t \star \sigma \rightsquigarrow u \star \tau$ and $u \star \tau \in \perp\!\!\!\perp$, then $t \star \sigma \in \perp\!\!\!\perp$. This last condition is quite natural since it is meant to ensure that if a process $t \star \sigma$ reduces to an element of $\perp\!\!\!\perp$, the process $t \star \sigma$ is itself an element of $\perp\!\!\!\perp$. We develop further the intuitions behind the pole in the second part of this section. So, once this pole fixed, one defines:

- the set $T^{\perp\!\!\!\perp}$, where T is a subset of Λ, as $\{\sigma \in \Sigma \mid \forall t \in T, t \star \sigma \in \perp\!\!\!\perp\}$;
- the set ${}^{\perp\!\!\!\perp}S$, where S is a subset of Σ, as $\{t \in \Lambda \mid \forall \sigma \in S, t \star \sigma \in \perp\!\!\!\perp\}$.

For convenience, the set of formulas is extended with a predicate symbol $\dot{F}$ for all function $F : \mathbb{N}^k \to \mathscr{P}(\Sigma)$ mapping a k-tuple to a set of stacks. If we want to realize the axioms of Peano arithmetic, we can consider first-order closed terms to be interpreted on natural numbers, i.e. we have a map $[\![\cdot]\!]$ from first-order closed terms to natural numbers. For further details about these definitions we refer to Guillermo and Miquel (2014). The truth value $|A|$ of a formula is defined from the falsity value $\|A\|$ of A by $|A| = {}^{\perp\!\!\!\perp}\|A\|$. The falsity value of a formula is defined by induction (which uses the truth value in the case of the implication).

$$
\begin{aligned}
\|\dot{F}(e_1, \ldots, e_n)\| &= F([\![e_1]\!], \ldots, [\![e_n]\!]) \\
\|A \to B\| &= |A| \cdot \|B\| = \{t \cdot \sigma \mid t \in |A|, \sigma \in \|B\|\} \\
\|\forall x\, A\| &= \bigcup_{n \in \mathbb{N}} \|A[x := n]\| \\
\|\forall X\, A\| &= \bigcup_{F : \mathbb{N}^n \to \mathscr{P}(\Sigma)} \|A[X := \dot{F}]\|
\end{aligned}
$$

The relation "t realizes A" is then defined by $t \Vdash A \Leftrightarrow t \in |A|$.

Example 1. In order to give better intuitions, let us illustrate this definition for the case of implication. Suppose that one wants to show that a given term t realizes a formula $A \to B$, i.e. one wants to prove that $t \Vdash A \to B$. This amounts to providing a proof that $t \in |A \to B|$, i.e. $t \in {}^{\perp\!\!\!\perp}\|A \to B\|$. So, one wants to show that, for any element $\sigma \in \|A \to B\|$, the process $t \star \sigma$ is an element of $\perp\!\!\!\perp$. Using the above definition, it is in fact possible to know more about σ, namely that σ is of the form $u \cdot \sigma'$, where $u \Vdash A$ and $\sigma' \in \|B\|$. This means that we are trying to prove that $t \star u \cdot \sigma' \in \perp\!\!\!\perp$. Since $\perp\!\!\!\perp$ is closed under anti-evaluation, this implies that $(t)u \star \sigma' \in \perp\!\!\!\perp$, since the latter reduces to $t \star u \cdot \sigma'$ by a push rule. Since this can be deduced for all $\sigma' \in \|B\|$, this means that $(t)u \Vdash B$, i.e. $(t)u$ is a realizer of B. In conclusion, a realizer t of $A \to B$ is a term such that for every realizer u of A, the application $(t)u$ is a realizer of B.

The definition of the realizability interpretation through falsity values reinforces the interpretation of evaluation contexts as falsifiers, that is as *counterexamples* that when opposed to the corresponding verifiers they produce a deadlock, i.e. something corresponding to a sort of antinomic situation.[20] Moreover, it has to be noticed that in analogy with the untyped setting – exposed below, the notion of termination is not

[20]Strictly speaking, these antinomic situations do not imply the incoherence of the system itself. The reason is that, as we already mentioned, verifiers, as well as falsifiers, are only posits. In this

an absolute and unchangeable one, but it depends on which processes configurations have been chosen to represent the terminating states, or better, the terminable ones. In other words, the pole $\perp\!\!\!\perp$ is chosen as an *arbitrary* set of process closed under anti-evaluation.

3.3.2 Classical Realizability as an Untyped Proof Theory

In Naibo et al. (2015) the notion of *untyped proof theory* is introduced in order to describe a general framework for dealing with an abstract mathematical (and in particular, geometrical) notion of proof from which it is possible to generate a class of deductive systems suitable both for logical and proper mathematical theories. More precisely, an untyped proof theory represents a very abstract model of computation, based only on two fundamental notions, that of execution and that of termination. In this sense, the idea is to describe a logical or mathematical theory from a computational point of view, in a similar vein as it is done in the theory of constructions of Kreisel (1962, 1965) and Goodman (1970, 1973a,b).[21]

We first recall the general definition of such a framework and then explain to what extent it relates to Krivine's realizability. An *untyped proof theory* is given by:

- A set of untyped paraproofs Π;
- A notion of execution $Ex : \Pi \cdot \Pi \rightarrow \Pi$;
- A notion of termination given by a set of untyped proofs Ω.

This definition accounts for a number of so-called *dynamical models* of linear logic such as Geometry of Interaction (Girard 1989), Ludics (Girard 2001), and

sense, it is not astonishing to conceive two logically incompatible situations together: the resulting conflict between these two situations would be only a conflict in principle, not an actual one. On the contrary, a genuine incoherence is obtained when two contrary evidences are present, namely when it is possible to exhibit two proofs of two opposite propositions, respectively (see Miquel 2009a, p. 81). This way of understanding incoherence is the same professed by Hilbert: incoherence is definable only at the level of 'concrete objects' (Hilbert 1926, p. 376), i.e. at the level of finitary arithmetic, and not at the level of logic.

[21]Notice that while the notion of execution seems to be (in a form or another) universally accepted as a fundamental ingredient of the notion of computation, the notion of termination needs some explications. In some more specific and "concrete" models of computation, like the one represented by partial recursive functions, termination is not a necessary notion (think precisely of the partiality condition). Following Kreisel (1972), this represents an analysis of *mechanical* effective computability, in the sense that the execution has to be performed by mechanical following a finite list of instruction. However, nothing is said about who has to follow this list of instruction. If it is a human-agent that has to follow it, then the number of steps that she can perform must be finite, since finiteness is a property defining human-agent (see note 8). This means that each execution has to terminate. The notion of termination seems then to be linked to the analysis of what Kreisel calls *human* effective computability. Beside this computational aspect, termination plays a second key role in the present context. From a meaning theoretic point of view, termination ensures us that we are not transcending the capacities of the human agent, thus allowing us to respect the pivotal desideratum of an anti-realist theory of meaning.

Interaction Graphs (Seiller 2014). From the notions of termination and execution, one derives a notion of *orthogonality* over the set of untyped paraproofs, i.e. it is possible to define $\perp\!\!\!\perp \subset \Pi \times \Pi$ as the set $\{a \cdot b \mid a, b \in \Pi, Ex(a \cdot b) \in \Omega\}$. From this notion of orthogonality, then one defines the interpretation of formulas in a similar fashion as in the realizability case.[22]

The classical realizability setting is very close to the untyped proof theory framework, except for the loss of symmetry. Where realizability considers two disjoint sets of terms and stacks, untyped proof theory considers a single set of paraproofs. This can be explained by the fact that untyped proof theory is meant for interpreting linear logic formulas, while classical realizability is meant for interpreting classical logic. Linearity allows for the consideration of *one-element stacks* exclusively, that is, those being naturally identified with the term they contain. Modulo this difference, everything works in the same way. In particular, the notion of execution in classical realizability is simply the evaluation of processes. While, as it concerns the notion of termination, even if in classical realizability it is not considered explicitly,[23] the pole of classical realizability corresponds to the induced orthogonality in untyped proof theory. In this sense, classical realizability can be understood as an instance of untyped proof theory.

Moreover, classical realizability and untyped proof theory share the possibility of representing incomplete or logically incorrect (deductive) arguments as well as their computational counterparts, that is, wrongful programs.[24] As explained in Naibo et al. (2015), the approach undertaken by untyped proof theory differs from the usual techniques adopted in standard proof theory, as it considers a set of objects – the *paraproofs* – which is much larger than the set of proofs. More precisely, among the set of paraproofs, only a limited subset can be mapped to logically correct and closed derivations,[25] while the others represent aborted or logically incorrect derivations.

[22]Notice, however, that one defines the interpretation of linear logic formulas, and not classical logic formulas, as it will be clarified below.

[23]Although the pole is sometimes defined from a set of processes which could be understood as a notion of termination (see Guillermo and Miquel 2014). For instance, one can take an arbitrary set of processes Ω and then define a pole $\perp\!\!\!\perp_{\Omega}$ by simply considering the closure of Ω with respect to anti-reduction.

[24]We use the terminology of "wrongful programs" as opposed to "proved programs". Indeed, programs corresponding to proofs in a formal system are *proved* in the sense that they do exactly what they are expected to. More precisely, the corresponding proof can be understood as a certificate that ensures the program is well-behaved (i.e. produces the right type of output when given the right type of input), and terminates. With this idea in mind, a wrongful program is a program which is proved using a incorrect arguments: it is therefore provided with an *unreliable* certificate of well-behaviour and termination.

[25]Notice that in this sense a proof is considered as a closed (logically) valid derivation (or argument), respecting the definition given in Prawitz (2006, p. 511).

In other words, this means that the set of logically correct and closed derivations – i.e. the set of proofs – can be interpreted as a specific subset of the set of paraproofs, which are shown to share a specific common property. The set of *winning paraproofs* is then defined as the set of those paraproofs satisfying this property. Although all interpretations of proofs are winning paraproofs, it is not clear in general if a winning paraproof is the interpretation of a proof. In the specific framework of Ludics (Girard 2001), the winning paraproofs are defined as those that do not use a specific non-logical axiom rule named *daimon*, which allows to derive any sequent of the form $\vdash A$ where A is a positive formula. A similar situation appears in classical realizability, since not every term corresponds to a proof. More precisely, the only terms which can be associated to proofs are those that do not contain any continuation constant, that is the so-called proof-like terms (see p. 174): every proof corresponds to a proof-like term, even if the converse is not true in general (a proof-like term need not be typeable[26]). From a more technical point of view, the proof-like terms are those that correspond to winning strategies in a dispute, like the one we described in Sect. 3.2. Proof-like terms are then the realizability analogues of the winning paraproofs. Pushing further this parallel with untyped proof theory, and especially with Ludics, one can think of the continuation constants as those parts of programs, or deductive arguments, which make them incorrect. In other words, continuation constants play a role analogous to the aforementioned daimon rule.

The fact that terms could contain continuation constants plays a crucial role, as it means that every formula – even those that are not provable – can be associated to a non-empty set of realizers. In particular, $\bot$ – which in a second-order framework is defined by $\forall X.X$ – can be realized by some terms, not corresponding to proofs, as they contain continuation constants (see, for instance, the term $k_\sigma x$ of the derivation at p. 185). This represents a fundamental aspect differentiating Krivine's realizability from Kleene's one, as it allows one not to trivialize the interpretation of formulas of the form $\neg A$.

Before focusing our analysis on some specific philosophical problems emerging from classical realizability, it is important to point out a major difference between the untyped proof theory approach and classical realizability. Although it is possible to understand classical realizability as an instance of untyped proof theory, there is a *methodological* difference between the two of them. Untyped proof theory somehow works in a top-down fashion: one considers a huge set of paraproofs – i.e. a specific class of mathematical objects – with a homogeneous notion of execution, and then shows what logical/computational principles can be interpreted there. Classical realizability, on the contrary, works in a bottom-up fashion: one extends syntactically the set of paraproofs with in mind a notion of reduction of processes that captures a computational principle, e.g. the `quote` operator (see Sect. 5).

---

[26]For instance, the term $(\lambda x\lambda y.((y)(x)\lambda z.z)(x)\lambda z.\lambda w.z)\lambda z.(z)z$ is not typable in System **F** even though it is strongly normalizable (Giannini and Ronchi Della Rocca 1988).

4 Which Theory of Meaning for Classical Realizability?

As we have seen in Sect. 3.3.1, Krivine's realizability represents an operational semantics for classical logic, allowing one to assign a computational meaning to classical principles. It becomes than natural to ask if it is also possible to use Krivine's realizability in order to define some kind of anti-realist theory of meaning for classical logic, and in particular a theory of meaning based on the computational uses associated to classical principles and clàssical operators, rather than their truth-conditions.

4.1 Analogies with the Finitist Interpretation

Let us first remark that it seems not to be an exaggeration to say that Krivine's proposal respects, in some sense, the spirit of Hilbert's finitist programme, which we have seen to be the starting point of Kleene's realizability interpretation. More precisely, like in Hilbert's account, sentences are meaningful only when they can be associated – or somehow reduced – to concrete objects or to finitist operations defined over these objects. In particular, in the realizability setting, standard Hilbert's strokes – i.e. |, ||, |||, etc. – are replaced by terms and contexts, and since terms and contexts are syntactical objects – that is nothing else but finite configurations of signs – they are also objects existing in time and space (see Martin-Löf 1970, p. 9). These objects can thus be considered as concrete as Hilbert's strokes are.[27]

In order to show that Krivine's realizability can also recover the notion of finitist operation, the usual identification of this notion with that of primitive recursive function – as proposed by Tait (1981) – has to be abandoned, and it has to be replaced with Kreisel's idea according to which the class of finite operations corresponds to the class of provably recursive functions in arithmetic (Kreisel 1960; see also Zach 2015, § 2.3).

The class of provably recursive functions is exactly the class of functions that Kreisel characterized in establishing his *no-counterexample interpretation* (Kreisel 1951, 1952). Now, the no-counterexample interpretation, as explicitly stated by Krivine (2003, p. 260) and, as we implicitly sketched in Sects. 3.2 and 3.3, is the method inspiring Krivine's analysis of the computational content of logical and arithmetical theorems: when a sentence is provable, it is shown that is possible to extract an effective procedure capable of falsifying every possible counterexample for that sentence (see Bonnay 2002, for more details). However, this does not mean

[27] Actually, as C. Parsons remarked, Hilbert's strokes, as well as syntactical objects in general, are *quasi-concrete* objects: they are not simple tokens, but a particular kind of types, the 'intrinsic [property of which is] to have instantiations in the concrete' (Parsons 2008, p. 242).

that Krivine's realizability could be eventually neither reduced to be a simple variant of Kreisel's no-counterexample, nor to be a simple re-interpretation the finitist programme. As we already mentioned, Krivine's realizers are not "ready-typed" functions but untyped programs, the evaluation of which needs the definition of a context. Moreover, Krivine's realizability does not necessarily ask for the extraction of a witness from an existential statement (Rieg 2014, p. 9). This is because the finitist operations are not here carried out at the level of individuals denoted by first-order (closed) terms, but rather at the level of programs for (classically) provable sentences. In other words, the witness which is looked for is not the one for statements of the form $\exists x A(x)$, but the one for judgments of the form $\vdash_{\mathtt{C}} A$, for a certain sentence A and where $\mathtt{C}$ is a derivation system for classical logic. It is for this reason that in what follows we restrict our analysis to the case of propositional logic.

4.2 Differences with Dummett's Verificationism

Since the natural witness for a judgement of the form $\vdash_{\mathtt{C}} A$ is a proof of A – or a proof-term codifying a proof of A –, it would then be natural to look at Dummett's verificationism as the closest theory of meaning with respect to Krivine's realizability semantics. However, it is quite immediate to notice that there is some important differences dividing these two theories.

As we already remarked, the class of terms in classical realizability do not correspond to the class of proofs, being it much bigger. Restricting the attention to the subclass of proof-like terms is still not sufficient for dealing only with proofs, since, as we said in Sect. 3.3, there is not a perfect correspondence between these two notions. Moreover, in order to assign a type A to a certain proof-like term – and thus making it a realizer – it is necessary to make appeal to a set of contexts. In other words, this means that in classical realizability the understanding of a sentence A is not based on a single semantic notion – that of a proof of A (or better, that of a canonical proof of A) – as it is the case for Dummett's verificationism, but it requires to make appeal to two semantic notions at the same time: (i) programs – corresponding in a loose way to proof (when we restrict ourselves to consider only proof-like terms) – and (ii) contexts. As we have seen, these two notions are complementary, so that a special kind of *bivalence* is introduced at the semantic level: every well-formed object belonging to the realizability level corresponds either to a program or to a context. Following Dummett (1963), it is exactly the acceptance of a bivalence principle which commits someone to accept a realist approach with respect to semantical notions.

The question then arises if it is possible to avoid such a built-in form of bivalence in classical realizability in order to make it compatible with a verificationist and anti-realist approach. One first step in this direction is represented by the shift from the two-agents dialogical perspective presented in Sect. 3.2 to a single-agent perspective. By providing an account of classical realizability in terms of a single agent, one could hope to avoid, at least in principle, bivalence.

4.3 From a Dialogical to a Single-Agent Perspective

As we already mentioned in Sect. 4.1, differently from recursive functions, programs are not reducible to some particular kind of step-by-step set-constructions on natural numbers, but they aim at expressing every kind of actions effectively performable on syntactical objects in general, even on those that would not be considered in principle as well-typed. It is this general and abstract character that allows one to assign a computational content even to those formulas that do not correspond to theorems or axioms, and thus to show it is possible to assign to these formula a specific semantic value. More precisely, the semantic values are set of terms which contain continuation constants. This means that the semantic value of a formula – and in particular its truth value – is obtained under the hypothesis that some counterexample for another formula is given. Let us clarify this point through an example.

According to the usual classical semantics, a formula $A \to B$ can be made true not only when a proof of it is given, but also when a counterexample of A is given. As we have seen in Sect. 3.2, counterexamples can be represented by stacks. Moreover, as we have seen in Sect. 3.1, the information present in a stack σ can be codified by a continuation constant k_σ, and since a continuation constant is a term, then it is plausible to think this term as typeable with $\neg A$. Formally speaking, if $\sigma \in \|A\|$, then k_σ is a realizer of $\neg A$: for any element $\pi \in \|\neg A\|$, by definition $\pi \equiv t \cdot \rho$, with $t \in |A|$, then the process $k_\sigma \star t \cdot \rho$ reduces to $t \star \sigma$ which belongs to $\perp\!\!\!\perp$. In this way, modulo a certain degree of approximation, we can think of $A \to B$ as obtained through the following derivation in a natural deduction setting where formulas are decorated in a Curry-Howard fashion[28]:

$$\dfrac{\dfrac{\dfrac{\dfrac{k_\sigma : \neg A \qquad [x : A]^{(1.)}}{(k_\sigma)x : \bot}\,\to \text{elim}}{(k_\sigma)x : \forall X.X}\,df}{(k_\sigma)x : B}\,\forall^2 \text{ elim}}{\lambda x.(k_\sigma)x : A \to B}\,\to \text{intro (1.)}$$

[28]The deduction system adopted here is described in details in Miquel (2009a, p. 85). The idea is that by working in second-order logic we obtain a *polymorphic* type system, that is a system where terms could be associated to more than one type. Since in this paper we adopted the convention to present terms in Curry style, this means that the information concerning types is not present in the terms, and thus polymorphism is not explicitly manifested inside terms – by means of some abstraction operator –, but remains implicit (see Hindley and Seldin 2008, p. 119–120). It is for this reason that the rule $\forall^2$ elim is not associated to any new operation on terms.

The approximations that we have made in this derivation are mainly two. The first one is to consider that the falsity value of the formula A is not empty. The second one is the result of a mismatch between the point of view of realizability and the point of view of natural deduction. In Krivine's framework, untyped objects are considered, and their interaction – like the application of one to the other – is operated at the level of closed terms.[29] In natural deduction, instead, typed objects are considered, and it is possible to operate also on open terms, i.e. on terms containing free variables. This implies that the typing relation ":" used in the above derivation contains the realizability relation, but it is not equivalent to it. More precisely, the idea is that not every deduction step can be read as expressing a realizability relation between a term and a formula. For example, $x : A$ does not express a realizability relation, since x is not a closed term. The premiss and the conclusion of the derivation, however, can be read as expressing realizability relations. Since $\lambda x(k_\sigma)x$ is the η-expansion of k_σ, and η-equivalent terms can be identified from the computational point of view, then we can consider to be equivalent to work with $\neg A$ instead of $A \to B$.

Notice also that our type assignment to k_σ is not obtained by exploiting the instruction $\mathtt{cc}$, but it is directly extracted from the intuitive reading of the role played by a context σ, i.e. that of a falsifier. However, we can recover Krivine's reading of k_σ once a proof of A is effectively given, i.e. when x is substituted by a closed term u. Looking then from the structural point of view, it should be noticed that $k_\sigma : \neg A$ cannot be considered as a dischargeable hypothesis, since k_σ is by definition a closed term and not a variable. But it cannot be considered a closed premiss either, since it has not been justified by a proof, but it comes from the "reification" of a context. In a certain sense, the role played by $k_\sigma : \neg A$ is that of a *pretension*, namely the pretension to accept that it is the case that $\neg A$, i.e. to work *as if* $\neg A$ has been proved.

In the dialogical setting, we can interpret the assumption $k_\sigma : \neg A$ as reflecting the prover's attitude to think that the skeptic wants to *refute* her, i.e. to think that the skeptic believes $\neg A$. In turn, this attitude can be seen as the prover's understanding of the "context of the game": from the fact that the skeptic systematically challenges her claims, the prover evaluates that the skeptic does not only doubts about her assertions, but wants also to refute them. However, by interpreting $\neg A$ as a pretension, we open the way to pass from a dialogical, multi-agent position to a single-agent-based perspective. This shift is necessary if one wants to stay as close as possible to a Dummettian theory of meaning. Indeed, the fundamental divergence distinguishing Dummett's and Krivine's settings that we discussed in Sect. 4.2 remains unchanged even if one switches from the computation reading of realizability to its dialogical reading: the distinction between the Verifier – i.e. the prover – and the Falsifier – i.e. the skeptic, provided that we consider negative hypotheses – reintroduces exactly the same form of bivalence that one finds between programs and contexts.

[29] As we mentioned at p. 174, processes usually operate on closed terms.

4.4 Negative Hypotheses as Postulates

The shift operated by working *as if* $\neg A$ has been proved corresponds to consider that $k_\sigma : \neg A$ plays the role of a *postulate*, in an Aristotelian sense, i.e. as 'something [which is] not in accordance with the opinion' of the person to whom the discourse is addressed (Aristotle, *Posterior Analytics*, 76b32–34; Barnes 1993, pp. 16, 141–142). From this perspective, the reading of negated assumptions decorated by a continuation constants becomes clear: they are *presuppositions*, which are believed to be true, i.e. special kind of hypotheses to the truth of which an agent commits herself.

One should carefully distinguish this kind of hypotheses from the usual ones, that is, like those used in standard natural deduction. Assuming a sentence to be true can have indeed two different senses: a *potential* and an *actual* one. This distinction is made explicit by Martin-Löf (1991). In the potential sense, assuming that 'A is true' corresponds to assume that the assertion of A is *justifiable*, i.e. that *in principle* there could be found an evidence in favor of it – even if *in fact* it could occur that this evidence is not available, nor it will ever be available. By making such of an assumption we are thus keeping open every kind of possibility: both the existence as well as the non-existence of an evidence in favor of A. On the contrary, in the actual sense, assuming that 'A is true' corresponds to assume that the assertion of A has already been *justified*, i.e. that there is an evidence in favor of it. By making such of an assumption we are thus *pretending* that an evidence in favor of A effectively exists – even if it is not the case, in the sense that we cannot prove this existence claim.

As we just said, the first kind of hypothesis corresponds to standard hypothesis in natural deduction, which are used for the formation of conditional statements. In order to prove a sentence of the form $A \to B$, we do not necessarily need to possess a proof of A. For example, we can prove $(A \wedge \neg A) \to \bot$, even if $A \wedge \neg A$ is not provable at all (cf. Sundholm 1994, p. 163–164). Following the standard notation adopted in the Curry-Howard correspondence between proofs and programs, we will decorate this kind of assumptions using term-variables of the form x, y, z, etc. The proof of $(A \wedge \neg A) \to \bot$ will be thus decorated in the following way:

$$\dfrac{\dfrac{\dfrac{[x : A \wedge \neg A]^{(1.)}}{p_2(x) : \neg A}\wedge\,\text{elim}_2 \qquad \dfrac{[x : A \wedge \neg A]^{(1.)}}{p_1(x) : A}\wedge\,\text{elim}_1}{(p_2(x))p_1(x) : \bot}\to\text{elim}}{\lambda x.(p_2(x))p_1(x) : (A \wedge \neg A) \to \bot}\to\text{intro (1.)}$$

where p_1 and p_2 are the first and second projection, respectively.[30]

The second kind of hypothesis corresponds, instead, to those hypotheses used for establishing (proper) admissibility results. In order to establish the validity of an

[30]Making appeal to projections is for simplicity and shortness of notation. In fact, as we said at p. 174, these operators can by defined in the second-order setting in which Krivine's realizability is conceived.

inference rule of the form $\frac{A}{B}$, it is asked to assume that A has been proved, and show that under this assumption B can also be proved. This corresponds to take the sequent $\Vdash A$ as an hypothesis, and show that $\Vdash B$ can be concluded. But doing this seems to generate two sorts of complementary problems. On the one hand, if we want to discharge this second kind of hypothesis, we have to discharge sequents, which means that we are dealing with some kind of higher-order rules similar to those used by Schroeder-Heister (1984). On the other hand, the conceptual distinction between two kinds of hypothesis risks to be flattened by the following result:

Proposition 1. *Let* $\mathscr{B} = \{\Vdash A_1, \ldots, \Vdash A_n\}$, *where the* $\Vdash A_i$ *stand in the position of hypothesis. Then,* $\vdash_{NJ+\mathscr{B}} \Gamma \Vdash C$ *if and only if* $\vdash_{NJ} \Gamma, A_1, \ldots, A_n \Vdash C$.[31]

This result concerns the derivability level, while it says nothing about the proof-structure level. But, as we have seen in the case of the definition of canonical proofs, proof-structure is an essential ingredient of Dummett's verificationism: the key-semantical entities are not proofs in general, but proofs having a particular form, concerning the order of application of inference rules.

We are thus in a situation, in which, on the one hand, we would like to keep track of the distinction between the two kinds of hypothesis we have introduced – so to keep track also of the structural difference between the proofs using one kind of hypothesis or the other – and, on the other, to respect the result stated in the previous proposition – and thus treat the second kind of hypothesis as hypothesis acting on formulas and not on sequents. In order to do this, we can take the second kind of hypothesis as formulas decorated by a different set of variables than the first kind of hypothesis. In particular, we can decorate the second kind of hypothesis using the variables a, b, c, etc., and operating their dischargement using an abstraction operator different from standard λ-abstraction (used for the first kind of hypothesis). The behavior of this operator can be explained by reflecting on the conditions that Dummett's theory of meaning has to satisfy in order to certify his soundness.

4.4.1 A Verificationist Account of Classical Logic

Dummett's theory of meaning rests on a what is called a *fundamental assumption*: the assertion of a sentence A, having $\dagger$ as principal connective, should always be performable in a direct way, that is, by means of a $\dagger$-introduction rule (see Dummett 1991, p. 254). In the case of intuitionistic logic, this assumption is respected by considering assertions performed under zero assumptions, which means that only the assertions of theorems are considered. This seems a to be indeed a too

[31] Notice that we consider to work here with a natural deduction presented in a sequent calculus style. The proof of the proposition can be found in Negri and von Plato (2001, pp. 134–135). In general, in order to prove the 'only if' direction, the idea is to replace every $\Vdash A_i$ sequent used in the proof of $\Gamma \Vdash C$ with an identity sequent $A_i \Vdash A_i$. While in order to prove the 'if' direction, the idea is to apply a cut rule on the A_i, having $\Vdash A_i$ and $\Gamma, A_1, \ldots, A_n \Vdash C$ as premisses.

narrow interpretation of the fundamental assumption. Satisfying the fundamental assumption when only empty sets of assumptions are considered seems to be just a *minimal* test that the verificationist theory of meaning has to pass in order to be considered as a sound theory. But what about a maximal test? How should it look?

It seems to us that by making appeal to the second kind of hypothesis analyzed in the previous section this maximal test can be defined, and it would take the form of a *robustness test*:

> *There should exist at least a proposition A that can be directly asserted under the worst possible (and non-trivial) assumption, i.e. under the assumption that $\neg A$ is true, in the sense that an evidence for the refutation of A is supposed to effectively exist (and $\neg A$ has not been introduced by a weakening rule).*

The formulation of this test suggests that it is possible to restrict our attention to the use of negative hypotheses, i.e. what we called postulates. Formally speaking, this means that given derivation of the form:

$$\begin{array}{c} a : \neg A \\ \vdots \\ t : A \end{array}$$

it should be possible to rearrange the order of the rules so to conclude using an introduction rule of the principal connective of A.

The problem is that by using again the hypothesis $a : \neg A$, it would be possible to conclude $(a)t : \bot$, which means that under the assumption of the effective possession of a proof of $\neg A$, an inconsistency can be proved. In order to avoid that the addition of the second kind of hypothesis leads to inconsistency, it would be sufficient to deactivate $a : \neg A$ immediately after having derived $t : A$ – so that the hypothesis cannot be used again –, and then continue to assert A. This corresponds to use the following inference rule:

$$\dfrac{\begin{array}{c} [a : \neg A]^{(n.)} \\ \vdots \\ t : A \end{array}}{\nu a.t : A}\ CM\ (n.)$$

where ν is an abstraction operator acting exclusively on the second kind of hypothesis.

This rule corresponds to the principle of *consequentia mirabilis*, i.e.

$$((A \to \bot) \to A) \to A$$

which with respect to intuitionistic logic is equivalent to the Peirce's law (see Ariola et al. 2007, p. 407). This means, in particular, that when *CM* is added to the system of intuitionistic natural deduction (NJ), one obtains a system which allows to recover full classical logic.

A fundamental feature of such a classical system is that it satisfies a form of *quasi-canonicity* of proofs. More precisely, thanks to a result due to Seldin (1989), it is possible to show that if A is a theorem of classical logic, then there exists a proof of it using only one occurrence of the *CM* rule, namely the last one. This means that the conclusion of the penultimate step of the derivation is also A, and that this occurrence of A is intuitionistically derived under the only assumption $\neg A$. But since $\neg A$ is an Harrop formula, then this derivation enjoys the introduction form property, and thus this immediate sub-derivation of A terminates with an introduction rule of the principal connective of A.

The classical system obtain via *CM* does not fully fit in the proofs-as-programs paradigm: providing a direct computational interpretation of *CM* is not a trivial matter. However, a parallel with Kreisel's no-counterexample interpretation can shed light on the implicit computational features of the system. In particular, this should be sufficient in order to guaranteeing that *CM* can recover those computational features of classical logic captured by Krivine's realizability.

The Kreisel's no-counterexample account

(1) Consider $A \equiv \exists x \forall y A_0(x, y)$ and $\neg A \equiv \forall x \exists y \neg A_0(x, y)$, where A is a theorem.
(2) A counterexample to A would consists in a function f such that

$$\forall x \neg A_0(x, f(x)) \qquad (*)$$

(3) Appealing to the consistency of the system guarantees that there exists a functional Φ satisfying the Herbrand normal form of A, i.e.

$$\forall f A_0(\Phi(f), f(\Phi(f)))$$

(4) The functional Φ represents a counterexample to (*), i.e. a counterexample to the existence of the function f.
(5) The computability of the procedure is assured by proving Φ to be recursive. In this particular example, since A is a Σ_1^0 formula, then Φ is even primitive recursive (see Parsons 1972).

The *CM* account

(1′) Consider A and $\neg A$.
(2′) A counterexample to A would consists in a proof of $\neg A$, which means to take

$$u : \neg A$$

(3′) The existence of a derivation $\mathscr{D}$ from $\neg A$ to A, and the subsequent application the rule *CM*, guarantees the consistency of the system, as it allows to transform any alleged proof of $\neg A$ into a proof of A, i.e.

$$\nu a.(t)a : A$$

where ν is an abstraction operator acting on variables used to indicate postulates.

(4′) The proof-term t represents a counterexample to the existence of any possible closed proof-term replacing a.

(5′) The computability of the procedure is assured by the fact that $\mathscr{D}$ uses only intuitionistic means.

Even if the classical system based on the rule *CM* is obtained from an analysis of Krivine's system λ_c, it involves nevertheless some significant differences with the latter. First, it allows one to transform into a rule of inference what in Krivine's is treated like an axiom, that is, the classical principle expressed by the Peirce's law. This means, at the level of terms, to transform the constant $\mathtt{cc}$ into a complex term making use of the abstraction operator ν. This transformation, in turn, has been made possible by distinguishing between two kinds of hypothesis, which allows in particular to avoid the use of contexts. The fundamental consequence is that the sneaking of bivalence is blocked: one does no more need to make appeal to a dialogical setting, as the only fundamental semantic concept is the one of proof, as requested by the Dummettian verificationism.

We conclude this section by noting that the ν operator acts similarly to the μ of $\lambda\mu$-calculus (Parigot 1992), with the major difference that in $\lambda\mu$-calculus the μ operator is paired with a second rule allowing the formation of contexts and the evaluation of a term in such a context. In the typed setting, these can be seen as an introduction and an elimination rule for classical negation. On the other hand, in the classical setting we sketched, there is no appeal to contexts: the meaning of logical constants is fixed by the intuitionistic rules and *CM* plays the role of a *structural* rule, in the sense that it acts on the structure of derivations – i.e. at a "global" level – and it allows one to control the discharge of postulates.

5 The Computational Meaning of Axioms

In the previous section, by operating an extension of the notion of hypothesis used in natural deduction systems, we have been able to offer an understanding of the *logical* part of Krivine's realizability in terms of proof-analysis. In other words, by the introduction of a derivation system based on two kinds of hypothesis, we have given a presentation of classical logic which is compatible both with Krivine's realizability and Dummett's verificationism.

However, as we have already anticipated, Krivine's realizability can also be used to give an interpretation – in the sense of assigning a semantical value – to the axioms of proper mathematical theories. But differently from Kleene's realizability, it does not only allow one to interpret the axioms of arithmetic. It covers also the axioms of set theory.

As we already seen in the case of pure (classical) logic, the interpretation given by Krivine's realizability is a computational one. And the notion of computation is, in turn, based on that of execution. The notion of execution is not a stable one, thought. In particular, by adding a new proper axiom to the system, a new realizability model is obtained, because a new constant instruction is added. And when a new instruction is added also the notion of execution has to be extended.

Consider, for example, the *axiom scheme of countable choice*, according to which every countable family of non-empty sets has a choice function. Written in the language of set theory it takes the form:

$$\forall x \in \mathbb{N}\, \exists y \in S.A(x,y) \rightarrow \exists f \in S^{\mathbb{N}}\, \forall x \in \mathbb{N}.A(x, f(x))$$

When we want to add it to second-order arithmetic $\mathbf{PA}^2$, we can simply write:

$$(\mathbf{ACC}) \quad \forall x \exists Y A(x,Y) \rightarrow \exists Z \forall x A(x, Z(x))$$

where Y is a k-ary second-order variable, Z a $k+1$-ary second-order variable, and $A(x,Y)$ is any arbitrary formula not containing Z free.

The system $\mathbf{PA}^2 + \mathbf{ACC}$ is a theory adequate enough to formalize analysis. In order to realize **ACC**, and thus construct a realizability model for this theory, a new instruction χ has to be introduced, behaving in the following way (see Krivine 2003, p. 271):

$$\chi \quad \star \quad t \cdot \pi \rightsquigarrow t \quad \star \quad \underline{n}_t \cdot \pi$$

where $\underline{n}_t$ is the Church numeral[32] corresponding to the natural number n_t, which is the number that has been associated to the term t by a (not necessarily recursive) enumeration of the set of closed terms. When this enumeration it is a recursive one, then χ can be implemented by means of the `quote` instruction of LISP.[33]

---

[32] A Church numeral is a representation in pure λ-calculus of natural numbers, such that a given natural number n corresponds to the λ-term

$$\lambda f.\lambda x.\underbrace{(f)\dots(f)}_{n \text{ times}}x$$

For more details see Sørensen and Urzyczyn (2006, p. 20).

[33] Notice that χ does not directly realize **ACC**. What can be proved instead is that there exists a function $F : \mathbb{N}^{k+2} \rightarrow \wp(\Sigma)$, with $\wp(\Sigma)$ the power set of the set of stacks Σ, such that:

$$\chi \Vdash \forall x(\forall y(Nat(y) \rightarrow A(x, F(x,y))) \rightarrow \forall Y(A(x,Y)))$$

The introduction of χ induces a modification on program execution, since a new evaluation clause has to be considered, and new contexts of evaluation can be created by exploiting the function enumerating closed terms. But in order to have a full characterization of the execution, it has to be checked whether the new evaluation clause remains compatible with previously defined program transformations, in particular with β-reduction (which corresponds to the reduction defined by the pop and push rules). Actually, this is not the case for the χ operator (see Krivine 2003, p. 271). This means that χ leads up to differentiate terms that otherwise would have been computationally identified. Hence, the identity criterion for computational entities not only rests on their behavior – rather than on some pre-fixed features, like their nature or form –, but it also strictly depends from the situations in which this behavior is manifested. More precisely, when new instructions are introduced, and the context of computation changes, the behavior of terms could change as well.

From a philosophical point of view, this phenomenon seems to support a sort of *anti-essentialist* point of view, according to which an entity is recognized to belong to a certain category of objects not because it possess a fixed set of defining characteristic properties, but because we can use it for performing certain kind of operations. From the technical point of view, we know instead that the Curry-Howard correspondence establishes a precise connection between the notion of β-reduction and that of proof-normalization. The incompatibility of the β-reduction with certain kinds of instructions suggests then that the proof-normalization does not play any central role within realizability framework. But since the proof-normalization is at the core of the possibility of obtaining canonical proofs (see p. 169), this seems to represent a conclusive evidence in favor of the idea that Krivine's realizability is conceptually distinct from Dummett's verificationism.[34]

However, this is not a completely astonishing situation. From the verificationist point of view, assigning a semantic value to proper axioms is a discouraging task, because assigning a set of canonical proofs to proper axioms is a sort of a counter sense, since by definition proper axioms are sentences which are accepted (as true) without any specific proofs to be exhibited. On the contrary, in Krivine's account, the meaning of a proper mathematical axiom is not given on the basis of its inferential behavior, but on the basis of its computational behavior. The latter not being defined

where $Nat(y) \equiv \forall X(X(0) \wedge \forall x(X(x) \rightarrow X(s(x))) \rightarrow X(y))$. It is then easy to show that the term $\lambda z(z)\chi$ realizes what can be called the *intuitionistic countable choice axiom*:

$$\textbf{(IACC)} \quad \exists U \forall x(\forall y(Nat(y) \rightarrow A(x, U(x, y))) \rightarrow \forall Y A(x, Y))$$

where Y is a k-ary second-order variable, U a $k+2$-ary second-order variable, and $A(x, Y)$ is any arbitrary formula not containing U free. In order to realize **ACC** it is sufficient to show that **ACC** can be obtained from **IACC** by means of (i) logical equivalences, (ii) the least number principle, and (iii) the principle of extensionality for functions (see Miquel 2009b, §§ 8.1, 8.2.). It is by performing these deductive steps that an essential appeal to classical logic is made.

[34]A similar kind of blindness with respect to proof-structure is advocated by Kreisel (1951, pp. 155–156, note 1) when he compares his unwinding program with Brouwer's constructivism.

in absolute terms, but with reference to a given set of contexts, that is, to those situations which oppose to the axiom and try to falsify it. The idea is thus to identify those entities which realize the axiom in spite of all possible attempts made to refute it. And even if by definition those cannot be proofs, they remains nonetheless accessible to human agent, since they correspond to operations consisting in an algorithmic manipulation of a given set of syntactical objects, where the latter represent the context of evaluation.

Certainly, it could be objected that it would be possible to transform the mathematical axioms into some kind of inference rules, as we have done for the Peirce law in the previous section. The problem is that in order to render this transformation faithful with respect to Krivine's realizability we have to show that the so-obtained inference rules possess a computational content, and this is not a trivial question. For example, when axioms are transformed into inference rules following the method proposed by Negri and von Plato (2001, § 6; 2011), this seems not to be possible. On the contrary, when axioms are transformed into rewrite rules (acting on the formulas involved in the logical inference rules), as proposed by Dowek and Kirchner (2003), it seems to be possible to preserve the computational content (see Dowek and Werner 2005; Dowek and Miquel 2007). However, rewrite rules are not inference rules, and thus it is not clear to which extent this approach is compatible with Dummett's verificationist.[35] We must then conclude that we lack a general method for assigning a verification interpretation to Krivine's realizability, when it is applied to mathematical theories going beyond pure logic.

6 Conclusion

We have exposed how the compatibility of Krivine's classical realizability with Dummett's verificationism can be obtained only when it is possible to give an inferential treatment of Krivine's computational clauses. This seems to be the case for pure classical logic, as shown in Sect. 4, but not for proper mathematical theories. Krivine's approach allows indeed to give a computational meaning to proper mathematical axioms by assigning them a specific program instruction, while Dummett's verificationism seems not to be a suitable framework for dealing with proper axioms, since axioms are traditionally considered as sentences which are accepted without asking for a proof of them.

However, it should be noticed that the sensibility of the execution operation to the addition of new program instructions seems to prevent classical realizability from being a *uniform* framework for the treatment of axioms. This represents a major difference with respect to the untyped framework presented in Sect. 3.3.2, where the presence of two peculiar ingredients contribute to guarantee the possibility of working with a general and unique notion of execution. On the one hand, the appeal

[35]For a detailed discussion of these questions see Naibo (2013, in part. chap. 9).

to the *daimon* rule (see p. 181) allows one to define a general notion of axiom, subsuming all kinds of axioms, being them proper axioms or logical ones. On the other had, no real distinction is made between terms and sacks: from the point of view of untyped proof theory, both of these entities correspond to paraproofs, and are thus treated in an homogeneous way.

It would be then interesting to compare these two frameworks in detail, in order to understand whether they belong to different philosophical projects or not. In Naibo et al. (2015) it is claimed, indeed, that the untyped theory framework is not compatible with a verificationist approach, and this claim is based on the treatment of the notion of proper axiom. It would be interesting to understand if the same arguments can be applied also to the case of Krivine's realizability.

Acknowledgements We would like to thank Marco Panza for the interest he manifested in our work and Luiz Carlos Pereira for the valuable discussions about the verificationist aspects of classical logic. This work has been partially funded by the French-German ANR-DFG project *BeyondLogic* (ANR-14-FRAL-0002) and by the CAPES-COFECUB project *Preuve, démonstrations et représentation* (Sh813–14).

References

Ariola, Z., Herbelin, H., & Sabry, A. (2007). A proof-theoretic foundation of abortive continuations. *Higher-Order and Symbolic Computation, 20*, 403–429.

van Atten, M. (2014). The development of intuitionistic logic. In E. N. Zalta (Ed.), *The Stanford encyclopedia of philosophy*. http://plato.stanford.edu/archives/spr2014/entries/intuitionistic-logic-development/.

Barnes, J. (1993). Commentary to Aristotle. In *Posterior analytics* (pp. 81–271). Oxford: Clarendon.

Bonnay, D. (2002). *Le contenu computationnel des preuves:* No-counterexemple interpretation *et spécification des théorèmes de l'arithmétique*. Master thesis, Université Paris 7 Paris Diderot.

Bonnay, D. (2004). Preuves et jeux sémantiques. *Philosophia Scientiæ, 8*, 105–123.

Bonnay, D. (2007). Règles et signification: le point de vue de la logique classique. In J. B. Joinet (Ed.), *Logique, dynamique et cognition* (pp. 213–231). Paris: Publications de la Sorbonne.

Boyer, J., & Sandu, G. (2012). Between proof and truth. *Synthese, 187*, 821–832.

Coquand, T. (2014). Recursive functions and constructive mathematics. In M. Bourdeau & J. Dubucs (Eds.), *Constructivity and computability in historical and philosophical perspective* (pp. 159–167). Berlin: Springer.

Dowek, G., & Miquel, A. (2007). Cut elimination for Zermelo set theory (manuscript).

Dowek, G., & Werner, B. (2005). Arithmetic as a theory modulo. In J. Giesel (Ed.), *Term rewriting and applications* (Lecture notes in computer science, Vol. 3467, pp. 423–437). Berlin: Springer.

Dowek, G., Hardin, T., & Kirchner, C. (2003). Theorem proving modulo. *Journal of Automated Reasoning, 31*, 33–72.

Dummett, M. (1963/1978). Realism. In M. Dummett (Ed.), *Truth and other enigmas* (pp. 145–165). London: Duckworth.

Dummett, M. (1973/1978). The philosophical basis of intuitionistic logic. In M. Dummett (Ed.), *Truth and other enigmas* (pp. 215–247). London: Duckworth.

Dummett, M. (1977). *Elements of intuitionism*. Oxford: Clarendon.

Dummett, M. (1991). *The logical basis of metaphysics*. London: Duckworth.

Dummett, M. (1998). Truth from the constructive standpoint. *Theoria, 64*, 122–138.

Fine, K. (2014). Truth-maker semantics for intuitionistic logic. *Journal of Philosophical Logic, 43*, 549–577.

Friedman, H. (1978). Classically and intuitionistically provably recursive functions. In G. H. Müller & D. Scott (Eds.), *Higher set theory* (pp. 21–27). Berlin: Springer.

Giannini, P., & Ronchi Della Rocca, S. (1988). Characterization of typings in polymorphic type discipline. In *Logic in computer science* (pp. 61–70). Los Alamitos: IEEE Computer Society Press.

Girard, J.-Y. (1989). Geometry of interaction I: Interpretation of system F. In R. Ferro, C. Bonotto, S. Valentini, & A. Zanardo (Eds.), *Logic colloquium '88* (pp. 221–260). Amsterdam: North-Holland.

Girard, J.-Y. (2001). Locus solum: From the rules of logic to the logic of rules. *Mathematical Structures in Computer Science, 11*, 301–506.

Goodman, N. (1970). A theory of constructions equivalent to arithmetic. In A. Kino, J. Myhill, & R. E. Vesley (Eds.), *Intuitionism and proof theory* (pp. 101–120). Amsterdam: North-Holland.

Goodman, N. (1973a). The faithfulness of the interpretation of arithmetic in the theory of constructions. *The Journal of Symbolic Logic, 38*, 453–459.

Goodman, N. (1973b). The arithmetic theory of constructions. In A. R. D. Mahtias, & H. Rogers (Eds.), *Cambridge summer school in mathematical logic* (pp. 274–298). Berlin: Springer.

Guillermo, M., & Miquel, A. (2014). Specifying Peirce's law in classical realizability. *Mathematical Structures in Computer Science*. Online first. doi:http://dx.doi.org/10.1017/S0960129514000450.

Griffin, T. (1990). A formulae-as-types notion of control. In *Proceedings of the 17th ACM symposium on principles of programming languages*, San Francisco (pp. 47–58). ACM.

Heyting, A. (1962). After thirty years. In E. Nagel, P. Suppes, & A. Tarski (Eds.), *Logic, methodology and philosophy of science. Proceedings of the 1960 international congress* (pp. 194–197). Stanford: Stanford University Press.

Hilbert, D. (1926). Über das Unendliche. [On the infinite] English trans. E. Putnam & G. J. Massey. In P. Benacerraf & H. Putnam (Eds.), *Philosophy of mathematics: Selected writings* (2nd ed., pp. 183–201). Cambridge: Cambridge University Press, 1983.

Hilbert, D., & Bernays, P. (1934). *Grundlagen der Mathematik I*. Berlin: Springer.

Hindley, J. R., & Seldin, J. P. (2008). *Lambda-calculus and combinators: An introduction*. Cambridge: Cambridge University Press.

Hintikka, J. (1996). *The principles of mathematics revisited*. Cambridge: Cambridge University Press.

Kleene, S. (1945). On the interpretation of intuitionistic number theory. *Journal of Symbolic Logic, 10*, 109–124.

Kleene, S. (1973). Realizability: A retrospective survey. In A. R. D. Mathias & H. Rogers (Eds.), *Cambridge summer school in mathematical logic* (pp. 95–112). Berlin: Springer.

Kreisel, G. (1951). On the interpretation of non-finitist proofs. Part I. *The Journal of Symbolic Logic, 16*(4), 241–267.

Kreisel, G. (1952). On the interpretation of non-finitist proofs: Part II. Interpretation of number theory. *The Journal of Symbolic Logic, 17*(1), 43–58.

Kreisel, G. (1960). Ordinal logics and the characterization of informal notions of proof. In J. A. Todd (Ed.), *Proceedings of the international congress of mathematicians*, Edinburgh, 14–21 Aug 1958 (pp. 289–299). Cambridge: Cambridge University Press.

Kreisel, G. (1962). Foundations of intuitionistic logic. In T. Nagel, P. Suppes, & A. Tarski (Eds.), *Logic, methodology and philosophy of science* (pp. 98–210). Stanford: Stanford University Press.

Kreisel, G. (1965). Mathematical logic. In T. Saaty (Ed.), *Lectures on modern mathematics* (Vol. 3, pp. 95–195). New York: Wiley.

Kreisel, G. (1972). Which number theoretic problems can be solved in recursive progressions on Π^1_1-paths through *O*? *The Journal of Symbolic Logic, 37*, 311–334.

Kreisel, G. (1973). Perspectives in the philosophy of pure mathematics. In P. Suppes, L. Henkin, A. Joja, & G. C. Moisil (Eds.), *Logic, methodology and philosophy of science IV: Proceedings of the fourth international congress for logic, methodology and philosophy of science*, Bucharest, 1971 (pp. 255–277). Amsterdam: North-Holland.

Krivine, J.-L. (1994). Classical logic, storage operators and second-order lambda calculus. *Annals of Pure and Applied Logic, 68*, 53–78.

Krivine, J.-L. (2003). Dependent choice, 'quote' and the clock. *Theoretical Computer Science, 308*, 259–276.

Krivine, J.-L. (2009). Realizability in classical logic. *Panoramas et Synthèses, 27*, 197–229.

Krivine, J.-L. (2012). Realizability algebras II: New models of ZF + DC. *Logical Methods in Computer Science, 8*, 1–28.

Martin-Löf, P. (1970). *Notes on constructive mathematics*. Stockholm: Almqvist & Wiksell.

Martin-Löf, P. (1991). A path from logic to metaphysics. In G. Corsi & G. Sambin (Eds.), *Atti del Congresso "Nuovi problemi della logica e della filosofia della scienza"* (Vol. 2, pp. 141–149). Bologna: CLUEB.

Miquel, A. (2009a). *De la formalisation des preuves à l'extraction de programmes*. Habilitation thesis, Université Paris 7 Paris Diderot.

Miquel, A. (2009b). Classical realizability with forcing and the axiom of countable choice (manuscript).

Naibo, A. (2013). *Le statut dynamique des axiomes. Des preuves aux modèles*. PhD thesis, Université Paris 1 Panthéon-Sorbonne.

Naibo, A., Petrolo, M., & Seiller, T. (2015, in press). On the computational meaning of axioms. In A. Napomuceno, O. Pombo, & J. Redmond (Eds.), *Epistemology, knowledge and the impact of interaction*. Berlin: Springer.

Negri, S., & von Plato, J. (2001). *Structural proof theory*. Cambridge: Cambridge University Press.

Negri, S., & von Plato, J. (2011). *Proof analysis: A contribution to Hilbert's last problem*. Cambridge: Cambridge University Press.

Oliva, P., & Streicher, T. (2008). On Krivine's realizability interpretation of classical second-order arithmetic. *Fundamenta Informaticæ, 84*, 207–220.

Parigot, M. (1992). $\lambda\mu$-calculus: An algorithmic interpretation of classical natural deduction. *Logic Programming and Automated Deduction, 624*, 190–201.

Parsons, C. (1972). On *n*-quantifier induction. *The Journal of Symbolic Logic, 37*, 466–482.

Parsons, C. (2008). *Mathematical thought and its objects*. Cambridge: Cambridge University Press.

von Plato, J. (2013). *Elements of logical reasoning*. Cambridge: Cambridge University Press.

Prawitz, D. (1977). Meaning and proofs: On the conflict between classical and intuitionistic logic. *Theoria 43*, 2–40.

Prawitz, D. (2006). Meaning approached via proofs. *Synthese, 148*, 507–524.

Rieg, L. (2014). *On forcing and classical realizability*. PhD thesis, École Normale Supérieure de Lyon.

Schroeder-Heister, P. (1984). A natural extension of natural deduction. *Journal of Symbolic Logic, 49*, 1284–1300.

Seiller, T. (2014). Interaction graphs: Graphings. arXiv:1405.6331.

Seldin, J. (1989). Normalization and excluded middle I. *Studia Logica, 48*, 193–217.

Sørensen, M. H., & Urzyczyn, P. (2006). *Lectures on the Curry-Howard isomorphism*. Amsterdam: Elsevier.

Sundholm, G. (1983). Constructions, proofs and the meaning of logical constants. *Journal of Philosophical Logic, 12*, 151–172.

Sundholm, G. (1986). Proof theory and meaning. In D. Gabbay & F. Guenthner (Eds.), *Handbook of philosophical logic* (Vol. 3, pp. 471–506). Dordrecht: Reidel.

Sundholm, G. (1994). Vestiges of realism. In B. McGuinness & G. Oliveri (Eds.), *The philosophy of Michael Dummett* (pp. 137–165). Dordrecht: Kluwer.

Sundholm, G. (2014). Constructive recursive functions, Church's thesis, and Brouwer's theory of the creating subject: Afterthoughts on a Parisian joint session. In M. Bourdeau & J. Dubucs (Eds.), *Constructivity and computability in historical and philosophical perspective* (pp. 1–35). Berlin: Springer.

Tait, W. W. (1981). Finitism. *The Journal of Philosophy, 78*, 524–546.
Tieszen, R. (1992). What is a proof? In M. Detlefsen (Ed.), *Proof, logic and formalization* (pp. 57–76). London: Routledge.
Troelstra, A. S. (1998). Realizability. In S. R. Buss (Ed.), *Handbook of proof theory* (pp. 407–473). Amsterdam: Elsevier.
Troelstra, A. S., & van Dalen, D. (1988). *Constructivism in mathematics* (Vol. 1). Amsterdam: North-Holland.
Zach, R. (2015). Hilbert's program. In E. N. Zalta (Ed.), *The Stanford encyclopedia of philosophy*. http://plato.stanford.edu/archives/spr2015/entries/hilbert-program/.

www.ingramcontent.com/pod-product-compliance
Lightning Source LLC
Chambersburg PA
CBHW071444230926
51846CB00001B/342
* 9 7 8 3 3 1 9 3 8 7 2 9 1 *